PENGUIN BOOKS
THE PATH OF THE BUDDHA

Renuka Singh has a doctorate in Sociology from Jawaharlal Nehru University, New Delhi. For the last twenty-five years, she has been working in the field of gender studies and has also worked with several non-governmental organizations, and at the Women's Studies Centre, Delhi University. She has been a Research Fellow at the Centre for Cross-Cultural Research on Women at Oxford University and UGC Senior Scientist at JNU. Currently, she is an Associate Professor at the Centre for the Study of Social Systems, Jawaharlal Nehru University, and also the Director of Tushita Mahayana Meditation Centre, New Delhi.

Renuka Singh is the author of *The Womb of Mind* (1990), *Women Reborn* (1997) and has co-authored *Growing up in Rural India* (1989). She has compiled and edited *The Path to Tranquillity* (1998), *The Transformed Mind* (1999) and *The Little Book of Buddhism* (2000). These books have been published in several languages.

The Path of the Buddha

Writings on Contemporary Buddhism

EDITED BY RENUKA SINGH

PENGUIN BOOKS

An imprint of Penguin Random House

PENGUIN BOOKS

USA | Canada | UK | Ireland | Australia
New Zealand | India | South Africa | China | Singapore

Penguin Books is part of the Penguin Random House group of companies
whose addresses can be found at global.penguinrandomhouse.com

Published by Penguin Random House India Pvt. Ltd
4th Floor, Capital Tower 1, MG Road,
Gurugram 122 002, Haryana, India

Penguin
Random House
India

First published by Penguin Books India 2004

ISBN 9780143030379

Typeset in Sabon by Mantra Virtual Services, New Delhi
Printed at Repro India Limited

Contents

ACKNOWLEDGEMENTS vii

INTRODUCTION ix

OVERCOMING NEGATIVE
EMOTIONS 1

A LAY-PRACTITIONER 16

BUDDHAS IN HIBERNATION 26

A MONASTIC ON THE
MOVE 45

SEEKING THE VIEW 55

PATH TO
TRANSFORMATION 72

THE BUDDHIST WAY OF
LIFE 87

THE HUMAN MIND 93

WORKING WITH
EMOTIONS 111

THE REFORMIST'S ROLE 124

MAITREYA PROJECT 134

ENGAGED BUDDHISM 143

IN HARMONY WITH
NATURE 157

BUDDHIST SUGGESTIONS FOR A
JUST SOCIETY 164

BIRTH OF A BUDDHIST
PUBLISHING COMPANY 172

BUDDHIST OIKOUMENE 189

SOME THOUGHTS ON FUTURE
OF BUDDHISM 201

DETAILS ABOUT THE
CONTRIBUTORS 214

Acknowledgements

This book is an outcome of the cooperation and efforts of many individuals and institutions and I am grateful to all of them. I am indebted to the contributors for highlighting some aspect of Buddhism through their experience of the ethical, radical, holy or sacred. It is also interesting to see how they have directed their lives to the perception of this wonder. I have been enriched with my association with all these colleagues and friends.

In particular, I thank my spiritual masters, His Holiness the Dalai Lama and Venerable Lama Zopa Rinpoche, for their constant support and inspiration. For their patience and help, I am obliged to my colleagues and staff at the Centre for the Study of Social Systems, Jawaharlal Nehru University, New Delhi.

Though the idea of this book was conceived in India, it materialized only in Italy. My friends, Gloria and Sergio Scapagnini, in Rome provided a peaceful haven for me to do research on this book. The beautiful villa of my friends, Francesca and Luciano Stella, near the Gulf of Naples, with Mount Vesuvio on the right and the island of Capri on the left, proved to be very conducive to my writing work. I thank them for their hospitality and presence.

I deeply appreciate the invaluable help rendered by my friend Dr Jackie Tarter in the completion of this work and for her insights into the status of Buddhism in the West.

I would like to express my thanks to my editors, V.K. Karthika and Kalpana Joshi, at Penguin for their hard work in giving a final shape to the manuscript and to my doctoral students, Meera Mohanty and Sarah Jayal Sawkmie, for helping me with the proof-reading. Also, thanks are due to my publisher, David Davidar, for his encouragement, vision and conviction.

No list of acknowledgements would be complete for me without a thank you to my mother, Diljeet Kaur, and my sister, Ashma Singh, who are no more but their integrity, simplicity and loving kindness continue to inform my life. Last but not the least, I am forever grateful to all my family members—Pritam Singh and the Pauls—for their unstinting good-humoured support.

This book is also about lives in turmoil resulting in such an open yet committed journey. I dedicate this spiritual challenge of our time to all those who wish to somehow respond to it.

RENUKA SINGH

Introduction
Renuka Singh

Despite our technological advancements and endeavours to control the forces of nature, most of us are trapped in the misery of human existence. We find ourselves, experientially or intellectually, distant, empty, alienated, anxious, lonely and estranged from the world. We feel uncertain of our basic values. This human predicament is reflected well in the terrifying imagery of Kafka, Kierkegaardian anxiety, Marxian alienation and Heidegger's analysis of inauthenticity.

Insights from the Buddhist path can provide the means to alter our predicament. Buddhism has existed for roughly over 2,500 years, has taken many forms and has weathered several vicissitudes of time and circumstances. However, the intent of Buddhist teaching has not changed; it is to enable earnest seekers to end their suffering. Buddhist teachings and Shakyamuni Buddha's life have inspired people throughout the ages to embark upon the journey to their own enlightenment.

In our modern, technologically sophisticated, violence and pollution-ridden globalized world, what role is Buddhism playing? What does it signify in the lives of people? Is it faith, philosophy or practice? In today's world, how do individuals or masses come in contact with Buddhism and its subsequent change of heart? Each chapter in this book deals with these questions, and each is self-sufficient. The chapters can be read in any order, but they form a whole greater than the constituent parts, a tapestry woven from inner callings and obligations.

The book's contributors come from different walks of life and were invited to address the essential aspects of Buddhism relevant to their paths of spiritual progress or to the development of a more compassionate community. Barring a couple of chapters that are based on a lecture, the rest have been written especially for this collection. Through the personal narratives, the contributors reveal the degree of their involvement with Buddhism. Their perspectives provide different emphases and altered tonings. While not intended to give a comprehensive account, the chapters do provide a look at emerging images of contemporary Buddhism.

My approach to the study of Buddhism has been that of Existential Sociology. It can be defined as the study of human experience in the world in all its forms. The fundamental, though not exclusive, method of Existential Sociology is direct personal experience and more formal research practice. The aim is to understand the wellsprings of our actions and their consequences. Such an understanding will, hopefully, guide us to solve our daily problems, at both individual and societal levels. Thus, human experience remains the basic realm of our concern. I was in the fourth grade when I first read the story of Gautama Buddha. It resonated very deeply in me, and he was the only historical character with whom I could identify completely. Perhaps, the seeds of my interest in Buddhism were sown then. Later, the idea of suffering as a source of knowledge and creativity fascinated me, and I revelled in the notion that one had to earn one's happiness through suffering. Finally, it was while I was in my late twenties that I abandoned this Dostoyevskian sort of glorification of suffering as I realized that people lose their humanity when their pain and agony cannot be contained.

I had been raised in a progressive Sikh family and attended a radical university, and in fact it was my scientific cast and openness of mind that led me to Buddhism's direct approach to understanding the nature of mind. 'No amount of study will help,' said His Holiness the Dalai Lama when I met him in 1986. 'You have to practice!' That marked my introduction to the practice of meditation, and my involvement with Buddhism has deepened over these years. Buddha's life constantly reminds me of the culture of peace, that violence will not put an end to violence, and that only love will bring an end to hatred.

Recounting the life of Shakyamuni Buddha is significant to the development of Buddhist truths. Prince Siddartha Gautama of the Shakya tribe was born in northern India (now Lumbini in Nepal) in the sixth century BC. He lived a life of opulence throughout his youth. One day he went out of the eastern gate in the walls around Kapilavastu, his father's capital city, and encountered an old man. Another day, he passed through the western gate and saw a funeral procession. The next day, he went out from the southern gate and met a sick man. When, on the fourth day, he went out by the northern gate, he saw an ascetic. Motivated by the wish to understand how and why such suffering existed, he wished to find a way to deal with the sorrows of human existence. Being innately sensitive and perceptive, Shakyamuni devoted himself to the discovery of the true nature of all existence. At twenty-nine, he came to terms with his spiritual dilemmas and renounced the world.

For six years, Gautama studied under many great ascetics and immersed himself in rigorous spiritual practices. Such austerities did not provide enlightenment. He then tried to follow the middle path between extremes of self-mortification and over-indulgence. Ultimately, he achieved enlightenment after a period of intense meditation as he sat beneath the Bodhi tree in Bodhgaya. Even though other Buddhas had existed before him, Gautama Buddha was the first to affirm the Buddhist truth in the course of history, and is considered to be the founder of Buddhism.

The Middle Path is the Eightfold path, which is divided into three groups: wisdom, morality and concentration. Under wisdom is the Right View and Right Thoughts. Morality pertains to Right Speech, Right Action and Right Livelihood, and concentration deals with Right Effort, Right Mindfulness and Right Concentration. The aim of Buddhist meditation is to purify the mind and, finally, lead to the attainment of wisdom and enlightenment. Samatha meditation helps in developing one-pointedness of mind and concentration while Vipassana enables us to attain intuitive insight into the nature of reality and leads to the realization of enlightenment. Buddhist teachings also reveal that all living things exist in total interrelationship, and nothing in the universe remains static. Interdependence or the Law of Cause and Effect is the fundamental precept of Buddhism. Theories of consciousness, karma and rebirth are also derived from this understanding. Hence, one can overcome one's suffering when all negative karma and worldly attachments have been eliminated. Impermanence and the unsatisfactory nature of all conditioned phenomena, selflessness and nirvana as tranquility have been taught to help people understand the true nature of reality and free them from Samsara, the wheel of suffering.

As some scholars maintain, Buddhism cannot be seen as a religion but rather as a pan-human phenomenon that is unbinding. It is a way completely open to interpretation and deals not with gods or the divine but with the transformation of human beings. One is expected not to accept the Buddha's teachings without careful examination in the light of one's experience. Also, in the following section, the fluctuating fortunes of Buddhism throw light on its current status and future.

The four main periods of development in the history of Buddhism are: preclassical, classical, medieval and modern.[1] The preclassical refers to the period during the lifetime of Buddha when his teachings and practice were consolidated. So, between 500 BC and first century AD, the Theravada or Hinayana school developed, and Pali scriptures were available to the seekers for study. In the classical period, Mahayana Buddhism, which had emerged around the third century BC, spread into China, Korea and Japan. In the medieval era, from seventh century AD onwards, Vajrayana, sometimes called the Mantrayana, took shape with a strong core of magical and sacramental rites. It disappeared from India and spread into Nepal and Tibet. Finally, in the last 200 years, Buddhism proliferated all over Asia and made inroads throughout the world.

Buddhism has thus experienced periods of prosperity and decay, followed by revival and disappearance. Its rise can be attributed to several factors. By challenging the orthodox systems of Indian thought, it had much to offer in terms of promoting egalitarianism as it rejected the caste system, ritualism and theism. It was ethical and non-violent in nature, and eventually allowed the women to enter the Sangha.

Royal patronage played a crucial role in spreading Buddha's message. Buddha's followers propagated his teachings systematically, but schisms developed a century after his passing away. King Ashoka, the third monarch in the Mauryan dynasty, became a Buddhist and Buddhist edicts were carved on stones and pillars all over the country. Many reliquary monuments (stupas) or memorials were built that are still being excavated in India, Pakistan and Afghanistan. However, when the Mauryan dynasty fell, Buddhism declined.

Under the patronage of Kanishka, the third monarch of the Kushanas, Mahayana Buddhism flourished again, and the famous Gandhara style of Buddhist art came into being. So, during the first millennium, Hinayana spread into the southern countries, whereas Mahayana spread into the northern parts. In Hinayana, liberation means freedom from emotional upsets which are seen as the main cause of man's involvement in Samsara. Here the saintly figure is the Arhant who has 'slain the foe'. The goal of Mahayana is the attainment of Buddhahood for the sake of all sentient beings so as to enable them to find their path and goal. The Hinayana school was represented by the Vaibhasika and Sautrantika systems of Buddhist philosophy, whereas the Madhyamika and Yogacara represented the Mahayana school.[2] Fa Hsien (AD 400), a Chinese Buddhist pilgrim, documented this information, while the other pilgrim, Hsuan Tsang, two centuries later, mentioned the differences between these two schools. Thus, these main schools of Buddhism could be distinguished from each other by the motivation of the practitioner.

Buddha's teachings, now also know as Dharma, were introduced in Tibet during the fourth century AD. In the seventh century AD, the king of Tibet married two Buddhist princesses and became a Buddhist. He sent one of his ministers, Thonmi Sambhota, to India to create a written script so that the Buddhist texts could be translated from Sanskrit into Tibetan. Between the eighth and the eleventh centuries, many Indian scholars like Shantirakshita, Padmasambhava and Atisha (later known as Dipamkara Srijana) were invited to disseminate the Buddha Dharma in Tibet, also called the Land of the Snows. Buddhism in India came under threat as the invaders razed the monasteries to the ground, killing monks and burning texts. Scholars believe that the Tantrayana had degenerated, which also caused Buddhism to disappear from India. Today, His Holiness the Dalai Lama (living in exile in India) has brought back to us the unbroken lineage that could be traced back to the Buddha. The practitioners of both Sutrayana and Tantrayana differ in their motivation. They both want to work for the enlightenment of others, but differ in the speed with which they want to attain their objective. So, all the Buddhist traditions, Hinayana, Mahayana and Tantrayana or Vajrayana, that originated in India have been preserved by the Tibetans and have now been safely exported and reintroduced in India.

Indians, irrespective of their class/caste praxis, in general, do not experience a socio-cultural uprootedness. They appear to be religious, philosophical and deeply entrenched in their daily cultural practices. The assimilating tendency of the Hindu paradigm needs to be kept in mind as well. It is well known that Buddha is seen as an avatar or an incarnation of Vishnu. After Buddhism's development in India, it spread easily to neighbouring countries. Today, it has penetrated even the remote countries of the world.

Although Buddhism has been called a museum piece primarily preserved at Nalanda, Kushinagar, Ajanta, Ellora, Sarnath, Sanchi and Bodhgaya, one cannot overlook the fact that Buddhism's middle-path and culture of wisdom have been reflected in the lives of ordinary Indians and that Buddhism is coming alive again in India. I would like to describe the different undercurrents of revitalization of Buddhism that are visible in India today. Apparently, plenty of activity is transpiring on several levels. For instance, Fiske has pointed out four different aspects of this process: the Maha Bodhi Society, the growing interest among intellectuals in philosophic Buddhism, the new centres of Tibetan Buddhism, and the Dalits or Neo-Buddhists.[3]

The Maha Bodhi Society: This society was founded by Anagarika Dharmapala (David Hewavitarane) in 1891 in Colombo, Sri Lanka; primarily to restore the ancient site at Bodhgaya and establish a monastery for monks from all Buddhist countries. In its foundation phase up to the 1920s, Col Olcott, director and chief adviser, did much for this society. A journal was published that aimed not to propagate Buddhism but to supply information in order to procure shrines. Its adherents in the early days included Madame Blavatsky, Mrs Annie Besant, Sir Edwin Arnold, Mr Justice Woodruffe and Paul Carus.

In the 1920s and '30s, a period of scholarship began. Former members of the Arya Samaj, Anand Kausalayama of the Punjab, Jagdish Kashyap of Bihar, and Rahul Sankrityayan of Uttar Pradesh, joined this society. They collected, edited and translated the Pali texts. After Independence, its name was changed to the Maha Bodhi Society of India. As to who controls the society now remains a disputed fact, but it has branches all over India.

The Intellectuals: The study of Indian philosophy requires a consideration of Buddhist logic and metaphysics. Centres of Buddhist studies have been established at universities in Benaras, Kashmir, Chennai, Punjab, Delhi, Kolkata, Travancore and

Mumbai. Many new Buddhist institutes also thrive in India. Obviously, Buddhism holds a great appeal for intellectuals, especially its rationalistic and ethical dimension. Yet, very few intellectuals give up Hinduism and become practising Buddhists, probably because they see a close connection between the two.

Indian literature has borrowed extensively from Buddhism; Tagore's works especially are replete with Buddhist imagery and themes. Also, Gandhiji, for instance, adopted the non-violent method of Buddhism to gain India's Independence. The *Dhammapada*, it seems, was one of Nehru's favourite books. India's policy of non-alignment has obviously been grounded in Buddhist philosophy.

Tibetan Buddhism: During the last century, Tibetan Buddhism received severe blows, was devastated, and was literally on the verge of extinction. Tibetan Buddhism is primarily a cultural and religious phenomenon and has occasionally emerged as a political force. The main objective of the exiled Tibetans is to keep their religion alive in India. For the 1,00,000 Tibetans-in-exile, the main challenge has been to secure their livelihood. Besides the support extended by Indians, much help has been forthcoming from different parts of the world.

The four schools of Tibetan Buddhism are: Nyingmapa, Kargyupa, Sakyapa and Gelugpa. Tibetans, of all sects, are scattered and settled in the hilly areas of north India as well as in Karnataka. His Holiness the Dalai Lama is the spiritual and temporal leader of Tibet. Other senior lamas do not lead an insular life in India. They are highly respected for their knowledge, attainments and courage. Institutions like the Tibet House, the Indo-Tibetan Cultural Society, and various Buddhist meditation and retreat centres too are trying to preserve the Tibetan culture.

Tibetans are receiving modern education, encouraged by His Holiness, and many of them are studying in Europe and the US. At times, this has alienated them from their own traditions. The Tibetans believe that without a qualified master, one cannot progress in the religious life. The use of a single literary language has strengthened their cultural identity, and has become the scriptural and liturgical means of expression. Now the better known works of Kanjur or (Buddha) word, and Tanjur, or translated treatises, are available in the national libraries of Western Europe and the US. Recently, Japan has been expanding its collections of Buddhists works as well.

Tibetan monks are represented in the Maha Bodhi Society temples, are teaching or studying in universities, and are working with the largest group of Indian Buddhists, the followers of Dr Ambedkar. Certainly, Neo-Buddhists have gained legitimacy and support from the Tibetan Buddhists, and it is rather difficult to ignore the latter group as a religious and cultural force in India.

The Neo-Buddhists: The subaltern groups in India were mobilized by Dr B.R. Ambedkar who launched a struggle for their social emancipation. He worked for decades to reconstruct Buddhism as an emancipatory religious ideology. The conversion movement in 1956 brought at least three and a half million of the former untouchable castes into Buddhism. Ever since, this phenomenon has not ceased to expand. Back in the 1920s, the Izhavas in Kerala reached out to the Buddha Dharma for their upliftment, and around the turn of the century, Tamils reinvented Buddhist traditions and established the South Indian Buddhist Association. For the subaltern groups, a Buddhist world view does not simply express their emancipatory present but links them with their historical past and holds out hope for a better future. Thus, many of those oppressed for centuries have found in Buddhism a means for their psychological liberation and advancement.

In addition to the growth of Buddhism in India in the twentieth century, it has made astounding advances in the West. Many Westerners have shown keen interest in Buddhism which is also called the religion of reason. Its non-theistic form, code of conduct and ethics, attitude of non-attachment in a materialistic world, non-violence, promotion of the peace movement, and advocacy of vegetarianism hold a great appeal for Westerners.

In the initial stage, T.W. Rhys David's translations of the Pali canon gave access to the original sources of Buddhism. Sir Olcott and the Theosophical Society helped the Sinhalese Buddhists to reassert their religion in the wake of Christian proselytizing. The first president of the Buddhist Society of Britain and Ireland, Christmas Humphreys, a lawyer, introduced Buddhism through the Theosophical Society in London. Sir Edwin Arnold's portrait in verse of the life of Gautama Buddha, 'The Light of Asia', awakened a lively interest in Buddhism.

Among the great scholars who disclosed Buddhist scriptures to the West, Friedrich Max Müller deserves much credit. In the *Sacred Books of the East*, he undertook a scholarly and reliable publication of the textual sources of the Indian religions. In 1879, the first book series called, 'The Sacred Books of the Buddhists', appeared.

Buddhism was introduced into the US in the last quarter of the nineteenth century when Japanese and Chinese families began to emigrate to California. Hawaii became an important stronghold of Buddhism. In 1893, when the World's Parliament of Religions met in Chicago, Anagarika Dharmapala was invited to speak about Theravada Buddhism. Inspired by his speeches, C.T. Strauss from New York, who had studied comparative religion, converted to Buddhism. He initiated a Buddhist movement among Americans.

At the same conference, a Zen master, Soen Shaku, impressed Paul Carus, a highly influential publisher. D.T. Suzuki, pupil of Soen Shaku, was introduced to Carus, and wrote prolifically on Zen, which was well received on both sides of the Atlantic. The flower power generation came under its influence but in the form of a counter culture. 'Beat Zen', encouraged by the writings of Alan Watts, and works by writers such as Allen Ginsberg, Jack Kerouac and Gary Snyder, depicted a community of dropouts, who believed in their own anarchist notions of spontaneity and tapping of one's Buddha-nature. Alan Watts' work helped to popularize Zen, particularly from the 1960s onwards.

The Zen boom in the American therapeutic circles is related to its concern with breaking out of the rational domain. It tries to liberate people from the prison of conceptual thinking and instantly unites them with the transcendent reality.

Many institutes, temples and societies sprang up after Buddhism gained favour among the American intellectuals. Some of these are: the American Buddhist Academy, the First Zen Institute of America, the Society of Buddhist Friends, the American Buddhist Association, the Cambridge Institute, and Foundation for the Preservation of the Mahayana Tradition. In addition, chairs for Buddhist studies at universities of the highest academic ranking exist at the universities of California, Chicago, Princeton, Yale, Harvard and Hawaii. Scientists have initiated dialogues with Buddhist teachers, in particular with His Holiness the Dalai Lama. 'Mind and Life' conferences are being held at regular intervals and several books that explore the relationship between science and spirituality have been published.

In the 1970s, Tibetan Buddhism reached a new height as it emerged as a religious alternative in the West. The Chinese invasion of Tibet in 1959 caused His Holiness to flee his country and settle in India, while numerous other Tibetan monks and lamas sought refuge in the US and Europe. Although schisms have developed among some schools of Tibetan Buddhism, and they are riven with sectarianism, nevertheless, it enjoys popularity and deep commitment from its followers.

Additionally, other forms of Buddhism like Soka Gakkai or a form of Nichiren Buddhism—Japanese—and Vietnamese version of Thich Nhat Hanh are making headway in the religious consciousness of Westerners. Also, Osho, an eclectic philosopher, drew peoples' attention to his community in Oregon, USA, and Pune, and left a mark on their lives. The Western Buddhist order, established by Sangharakshita, who was born in London as Dennis Lingwood in 1925, maintains an open attitude towards the different schools of Buddhism. The practitioners belonging to this order are making changes and adaptations to make Buddhism seem more appropriate to the indigenous culture.

European thought has also reflected its Buddhist leanings. Although Herder, Kant and Hegel studied Indian philosophy and religion, the strongest influence of Buddhism on German ideas was through the philosophy of Arthur Schopenhauer. Max Weber, Max Scheler, Tucci and Derrida have through their work revealed their preoccupation and predisposition towards Buddhism.

Benz maintains that Buddhism has had an impact on modern psychology, psychotherapy and psychiatry. The discovery of the unconscious by Freud, Jung and Adler has opened up new areas to explore and understand creativity, the psyche and mental disturbances. Thus, ego is caught in the clutches of its own contradictions and becomes an apparent sufferer of the problem. Here, one must realize that it is not the ego that has a problem, but that ego is the problem. Buddhist visualization and meditation techniques have helped therapists in facilitating the healing process. Benz feels that Buddhism has also served as an impetus in developing Christian meditation. Jesuit fathers, in particular H.M. Enomiya Lasselle, have delivered many lectures to international audiences.[4]

Factors like the globalization of modern media and cyber-space connections, numerous exhibits of Buddhist art, cultural festivals, Hollywood films and film stars, sportsmen, publication of books and magazines, and circulation of Buddhist knowledge in educational circles have all helped expand the base of Buddhism. Also, inspired by appeals to human rights, cultural preservation and spiritual awakening, innumerable individuals and organizations are taking care of Buddhist refugees and their political cause.

Even though worldwide there has been a rapid growth of interest in Buddhism in the last quarter of the twentieth century, His Holiness the Dalai Lama doesn't see any special significance in this phenomenon, especially the tendency towards sectarianism amongst new practitioners in the West. His Holiness sees this as a disturbing development. Religion, he asserts, should never become a source of conflict. Unfortunately, it can create divisions within the human community.[5]

Today, Buddhism has spread in a rather thin manner and for it to have any future, one requires a solid foundation of the Buddhist realizations. As Ven. Lama Zopa Rinpoche says, 'When we talk about the propagation of Buddhism, we have to remember that there are two types of teaching—the words and the realizations. Of these, it is the latter that makes the difference. It is easy for the words to continue for centuries—all we need is a few good libraries. But without the living experience of the meanings of the words that comes through purification, creation of merit and effective meditation, the words are dry and tasteless and cannot be a vehicle for Buddhism to continue into the distant future. For this to happen, we need serious meditators spending years, if not their entire lives, in retreat under the supervision of experienced masters. Is this happening today?'

1. G.D. Chryssides, *Exploring New Religions*, Casell, London, 1999, p. 92.
2. Ninian Smart, *Religions of Asia*, Prentice Hall, N.J. 1993.
3. A.M. Fiske, 'Buddhism in India Today' in *Buddhism in Modern World*, Ed. H. Dumoulin & J.C. Maraldo, Collier Books, N.Y. 1976.
4. E. Benz, *Buddhism in the Western World*, Ibid.
5. Dalai Lama, *Freedom in Exile*, Abacus, London, 1992, pp. 223–24.

Overcoming Negative Emotions
His Holiness the Dalai Lama

Change or progress or transformation of the mind is in a way easy, in a way difficult. But one thing is quite certain: I believe that if you constantly endeavour to make the effort and have the conviction, you can transform your mind. You might think that you have made little progress but there is sufficient reason to persevere with your efforts because you are changing all the time, albeit very slowly. Buddhadharma, as also some ancient Hindu traditions, believe in re-birth, life after life. So any progress we make in the spiritual field in this life will impact positively on our next life. And so our attempt will continue . . .

Buddha Shakyamuni tells us that a practitioner should think in terms of eons, not just days and hours. From a Buddhist viewpoint, life has no beginning. What we do have is the desire to overcome suffering. But desire alone is not enough to achieve the goal. What we need is the correct method to help us achieve this aim. Only with unceasing effort can there be an end to suffering. Buddha himself demonstrated this very clearly.

I wish to begin by sharing some of my experiences at the Kumbha Mela. Actually, this was not my first visit to the event; I went there in 1966 too. It was a very short stay that did not give me an opportunity to talk privately with some of the leaders who were present there. But this time, in addition to my public commitments, I did get to meet and have relaxed discussions with the Shankaracharya and some other spiritual heads.

During my 1966 visit, I received some letters from a Buddhist group expressing their displeasure about my visit to the Kumbha Mela, which they perceived as a Hindu festival. This time too some of my friends expressed their reservations about my trip. I think everybody knows of my interest and commitment to the promotion of human values, the promotion of religious harmony. These will remain my chief concerns till I die.

For more than fifteen years, whenever I have had an opportunity to undertake pilgrimages to the holy places of different religious traditions, I have gone with great enthusiasm. I got to see Jerusalem and Lourdes. In India too, I make it a point to visit holy places, be they mosques, temples or churches; it is my way of paying my respect to those religions. It was for this reason that I went to the Kumbha Mela this year—to pay my respect to the ancient Hindu tradition. I have now been in this country for forty-one years and have always felt it important to show my regard for other traditions and make an effort to learn about them. I include those traditions which are alien to India, like Christianity, Islam, Judaism, as well as those traditions which were born and grew within this country, like Hinduism, Jainism, Buddhism, Sikhism, and so on. I think these traditions have a very special, close relationship with each other.

Even at the time of the Buddha there were endless debates over Buddhist and non-Buddhist traditions. Nagarjuna, Aryadeva, Buddha Palita, Chandrakirti, Dharmakirti and later Shantirakshita, Kamalashila and other great Buddhist masters wrote extensively on ancient Hinduism. This type of argument is, I feel, very useful, very beautiful. At the same time, within Buddhism itself, there is a lot of lively debate on the whole issue of acknowledging the importance of other religions. To me, having two contradictory views that help one argue the merit of each is extremely vital to the development of a sharp mind. These arguments are not political bickering. They are, on the contrary, very positive developments. I firmly believe that without these arguments, Buddhist logic or Buddhist thinking may become stunted. However, there are those who are short-sighted or narrow-minded and sometimes take the ongoing debate in the wrong way. This misinterpretation causes divisions and leads to fighting and conflict. I sincerely feel it is really important to make an attempt to welcome opposing views and to learn from them.

Buddha himself, during the early period of his life as a Siddha, learned much from Hinduism. He experimented with whatever he had imbibed and only then attained enlightenment. In doing this, he rejected many of the old Hindu ideas and views but he also accepted many traditions like shila, samadhi and Vipassana. Where Buddhism and non-Buddhism differ is in the concept of Anatma and Atma. Anatma is my business; Atma is their business. No problem!

I believe in Anatma and my belief gives me so much. It colours my views, my feelings. But to the Hindus, Atma theory makes the most sense. I accept those kinds of divisions. I genuinely feel that if I am to have a closer relation with other traditions, I must make the effort to develop a better understanding of the views expressed by them.

This was why I attended the Kumbha Mela. After two days there, I felt great satisfaction. I truly admire the Hindu religious leaders I met there. They have very open minds. When I met one of the Shankaracharyas, he firmly held my hand and recited, *Buddham Sharnam Gacchami*—it was beautiful. He spoke about how the Buddha stood for compassion, maha-karuna and non-violence. All the leaders felt it was important that we come closer for the greater good of mankind. I feel this could be a new beginning.

To my great distress, some Buddhists in this country, especially Neo-Buddhists, have a rather negative attitude towards Hindus. I keep explaining that harbouring negative feelings is not the Buddhist way. At the same time, I will have to say that the time has come to do away with the caste system and other outdated customs that have been a part of Hinduism. We should openly state it: these customs are out of date. I wish we could work actively to eliminate all kinds of negativism. If we decide that instead of criticizing others, we will try to understand them and improve our relationship with them, the politicians and other mischievous elements who manipulate people on the basis of religious differences will eventually be isolated.

So, that's the story of my sojourn to the Kumbha Mela. Actually, I was told that it would be a very dirty and dusty place. I went prepared, though I was quite resigned to catching the flu or something. Fortunately, no flu, in spite of the fact that it was not the most hygienic of places! There's something else I want to share with our Buddhist friends, particularly the Tibetan Buddhists. More than 25 million human beings gathered at the Kumbha Mela, and they were all vegetarian. Not one animal was sacrificed, and I thought it was wonderful; I hesitate to mention this but I have to acknowledge that if 10,000 Tibetans were to gather in a place, I think the butchers would be very busy.

For the past several years, a number of monastic institutions have been making an attempt to promote vegetarianism in the monasteries. We must intensify our efforts when we have bigger gatherings. Now, to get to the topic of 'Overcoming Negative Emotions'.

We all know that without emotions our lives become colourless. Feeling emotion is always very good, but it is important to make distinctions between the kinds of emotions one feels. There are certain feelings that make one feel good for the moment but those same emotions can prove destructive in the long run. On the other hand, there are times when one feels discomfort while experiencing certain feelings, but it could well turn out that these emotions prove beneficial in the long run. It is important to be able to distinguish between what kind of emotions are useful and what kind negative, and therefore to be discarded. I believe that all living beings, including plants, have the right to survive. It is equally true for me that those beings that experience pain and pleasure have the right not only to survive but also to survive happily. That's our basic right. Sentient beings, those who have the capacity to feel, who have cognition, all have the desire to overcome suffering, to overcome pain, to achieve happiness and pleasure. But there are two levels of experiences that bring pleasure or pain. One is mainly sensorial. One derives satisfaction even when one sees something good or beautiful. Sounds that are melodious can make us feel happy. This experience is shared by the entire animal kingdom. We all feel satisfaction, joy and physical pain.

To human beings, the sensorial level is no doubt very important. Material comforts are necessary to us because they bring us sensory pleasure. We enjoy the sight of a beautiful garden, the sounds of beautiful music, pleasant aromas, food that tastes good, and also seek sexual pleasure. All these we have in common with the animals.

However, if we continue to remain at the level of the senses, we will not be complete human beings. This is because of this thing called intelligence. It is a fact that we possess a greater degree of intelligence than any other living creature. We can think, not just of the past and the present, but are able to think of the future—not just this lifetime, but through many lifetimes and generations. Human beings have the capacity to keep memories that belong to a long, long past; we have written and recorded thousands of years of experiences. But this very intelligence that seems such an enviable quality also gives us additional sources of worry. We have too many expectations and along with these come doubt, fear and suspicion. This is what distinguishes us from simpler animals.

It then goes without saying that unhappy feelings result from human intelligence. This kind of unhappiness cannot be suppressed or pacified by mere material comfort. There are rich people who have every kind of material comfort imaginable and no cause for worry but they cannot seem to escape from unhappiness. Physical comfort cannot guarantee mental comfort. On the other hand, if one is truly in a happy state of mind, it is not too difficult to subdue the desire for material satisfaction. I will go so far as to say that in some cases passing through physical hurdles can bring one greater mental peace.

This is because when you are mentally prepared for hardship, you are ready to face any amount of physical discomfort. The mental level of experience is superior to the sensorial level. That is why material progress or development is essential, but material gain alone cannot satisfy, cannot fulfil, all human requirements. We human beings need more. The destroyer of our mental comfort is what we call negative emotion.

Feeling emotions like extreme compassion, caring and genuine concern bring little disturbance to the mind. Emotions like these can only be deliberately developed and arise through training, through reasoning. They do not come instantly. On the other hand, feelings of anger and jealousy come instantly because there may be a superficial reason for their appearance. They are more often than not destructive whereas karuna or compassion, and a sense of caring are, in the long run, very beneficial, useful and helpful, not just to the person who feels them but also to the society at large. The distinction between negative and positive emotions is entirely based on the fact that by nature we all want happiness and do not want suffering. Therefore, anything— external as well as internal—which ultimately brings us happiness is positive. Anything that causes pain, both to oneself and others, is negative. Buddhist thinking is based on the fact that we all crave happiness. We have a basic right to happiness. Therefore, our aim should be to seek out those things that can produce deep satisfaction, joy and delight, all of which are positive emotions. Negative emotions are to be rejected because they destroy the happiness we work so hard to seek.

I would like to share with you the three levels through which to counteract negative emotions. The first level follows secular ethics and does not touch upon any religious belief. It is simply to try to use our intelligence to analyse what happens in a given situation. Begin by identifying the long-term and short-term benefits or consequences of negative emotions. When we become aware of what consequence our feelings may have in the long term, we will deliberately attempt to restrain our negative emotions. Look at the possible consequences of ill-will or hatred. As soon as we begin to detest someone, peace of mind vanishes. We lose sleep. We begin to eat poorly and our digestive system suffers. The final consequence is the ruination of physical health. Therefore, strong negative emotions are really very, very destructive to both peace of mind and good health. When you have such negative feeling towards others, you also begin to think that other people also have the same kind of attitude towards you. As a result, you feel suspicion, nervousness and discomfort whenever you meet someone.

Suspicion is not something I consider to be an inherent part of human nature, because we human beings are social animals. Whether we like it or not we have to live in the human community; we can't survive in isolation. We put ourselves in a very difficult situation when we deal negatively with those people upon whom we are very much dependent. So it is that a big city might seem like a vast human community, but that is actually where many individuals feel very lonely. Often times, people do not trust and respect others.

One is bound to come across mischievous people but treating everyone you meet as a brother or sister will make them respond accordingly. After all, we all experience the same things. Just as I feel anger, the man in front of me also feels anger. I sometimes feel jealousy, and so it is with him too. We are not fundamentally different; treat others the way you treat yourself. There's nothing to hide . . . everything is in the open, straightforward. In this way, I think it is possible for trust and friendship to develop.

So, it is obvious that much of the unhappiness we experience in life is due to errors of human intelligence; we don't analyse situations correctly, so we experience negative emotions. To overcome negative emotions, we have to become aware of their long-term and short-term consequences. We also have to examine the reality of the situation. Reality is composed of interdependent parts. Things happen for many reasons. That is reality. But more often than not, that is not the way we perceive it; if an incident takes place that makes us unhappy, we lay the blame somewhere or the other. Then we develop anger. Instead, if we were to think, look hard at reality, we might realize that everything that happens has more than one reason behind it, and that our own attitude has a lot to do with any situation that develops . . . Similarly, when good things happen, then too there are many causes, many factors that are involved. Having understood this much, it is now time to make a distinction between good and bad. If someone takes advantage of us, it *is* wrong, it is unjust, and we must try to stop them . . . But our countermeasures must not include negative emotions. Unbelievable as it sounds, it is possible to do such a thing effectively, and what's more, measures taken without negativism are far more effective in resolving your situation than those taken in anger or spite. Thus, it is clear that we control our own lives, and if one were to constantly practise giving good emotions a free rein, we will eventually be convinced that certain emotions are really useless and even harmful. Once we develop this conviction, we begin to distance ourselves from our negative emotions. We no longer welcome them.

This is one level of countering negative emotions where religious affiliation has no role to play. All one needs is a genuine sense of caring and concern for the human community. If your fellow humans are happy and successful, you too will automatically benefit. If humanity suffers, you suffer . . . Once you realize how important it is to have the right attitude, you will bring about a change in your way of thinking. A sense of caring, of commitment, of discipline, of oneness with all of humanity—there is nothing more relevant in today's world. I call this secular ethics, and this is the first level to counter negative emotions.

The second level is one that is taught by all major religious traditions, whether Christian or Muslim or Jewish or Hindu. They all carry the message of love, compassion, forgiveness, tolerance, contentment and discipline. These are countermeasures for negative emotions. When anger is imminent, when you begin to feel hate, think tolerance. Mental dissatisfaction leads to anger and hatred and what you need to counter it is patience. Greed is another emotion that works on various levels. The desire to want something all the time brings much unhappiness to one's personal life; then there are other consequences like destruction of the environment, exploitation of fellow men, widening gap between the rich and the poor. Greed is essentially a self-centred emotion and can only be countered by contentment.

Self-discipline is the key to contentment. It is the only way to resist negative emotions and protect oneself from long-term disaster. All religious traditions talk about compassion and forgiveness. If we accept religion, we should also take religious methods seriously and sincerely and use them in our day-to-day lives. Only then can we develop a meaningful life. For example, we Tibetans might carry a rosary and chant something or the other but it is of no use if the mind is elsewhere. Some of our Christian brothers and sisters might go to church regularly to pray but nothing really changes once they come out and get on with life . . . The real practice is outside, not inside the church. It is outside that we encounter real-life situations that are riddled with anger, jealousy, attachment and so forth. All real practice is to be done outside places of worship.

I recall meeting a Christian minister who bemoaned that people did not seem to be interested in the doctrine of Christianity any more because they felt it had little relevance in daily life. I sincerely think that this is not due to any shortcoming in the Christian message but rather because of wrong emphasis. Religious practice is not just prayer. Religious practice is using the methods I have mentioned to evoke love, compassion, forgiveness. If these methods are taken seriously and put into practise in one's daily life, they become very relevant. For example, when you are about to lose your temper, remember that God will be happy if you practise tolerance. Think of God when you feel greedy; it will help you cultivate contentment. In short, if we sincerely apply the essence of any major religious tradition to our day-to-day lives, it will not take you long to see the importance of the teachings of your religion. Life becomes more meaningful. This is the second level of countermeasure one can take recourse to overcome negative emotions.

The third level is the Buddhist way. If you try to trace the roots of afflictive emotions like anger and so on, you will encounter four kinds of misconceptions. One is the misconception about different types of realities; we tend to see what is impermanent as eternal. That is a source of suffering and mental disturbance. Similarly, we also tend to perceive suffering as happiness. To most of us, contaminated experiences appear to be sources of pleasure, of happiness. Similarly, we think what is impure is pure. To illustrate, we are unable to see the impurity of our psycho-physical body. We tend to see it as something clean and pure and thus develop attachment. Also, we tend to see what is self-less as having an existential self, an independent self. It is basically these kinds of misconceptions that aggravate our minds; all afflictive emotions stem from these mistaken beliefs.

It is to counter these delusions that the Buddha taught the thirty-seven limbs to enlightenment. He spoke about always being mindful on four counts. The first is with reference to the nature of your body. The actual nature of your body is such that it is made up of different types of unclean substances. When you study and reflect closely upon your body, you will be able to see that it is impure and impermanent. If you go into how your body was created, or examine the way it functions, you will realize it is impure, unclean. It was created by semen and ovum from your parents. From the top of your head to the soles of your feet, you will find your body unclean. It produces waste—urine, excretion and so forth—all unclean substances. It is like a machine that is constantly producing garbage; when this machine runs well, everything it expels seems good, but if something goes wrong then, oh, a lot of unusual things happen. Actually, the most expensive and most beautiful things we consume are made dirty by this machine called human body. The body is what causes us further suffering. It is made up of four basic elements—fire, water, air and earth. But all four contradict each other, sending the body into conflict. When we say 'I am happy' or 'I am healthy', we are saying we are healthy in the sense that these conflicting elements are at that moment in time equal in their power. When there is a slight change in the balance, you get disease. The ease is out of balance.

I myself am more than sixty-six years old. Until now, this body has survived because of various reasons. But what use is it for the body merely to survive? However, if our marvellous human intelligence survives and functions normally, we can try to use that intelligence to cultivate infinite altruism and a deeper understanding of reality. That is something wonderful; that is the Buddhist viewpoint. If you reflect along these lines, you will be able to understand clearly how we see this impure body as something pure and clean.

Coming to the second misconception, that of perceiving suffering as happiness. This is obviously not a reference to the ordinary level of consciousness because at a very superficial level, nobody identifies suffering as happiness. My reference is to a more profound level. As I mentioned earlier, there are two types of feelings: feelings of the body and feelings of the mind. Most physical happiness arises because of the lessening of physical unhappiness. If you have been out in the freezing cold for a long while and suddenly find yourself in the sunlight, you feel a sense of satisfaction and happiness. There is no particular satisfaction to be gleaned from that sunlight; it only brings a decrease of suffering from the cold.

To further illustrate this point, if the happiness were long-lasting and genuine, an independent event, then you should be able to stay in that sunlight for a long time and your happiness should increase rather than decrease. But that is not the case. After a while, you will feel hot, and you will need to move into the shade again. The original feeling of happiness and satisfaction that occurred when you moved from the cold into the sunlight will change into suffering if you stay in the sunlight for too long. Similarly, pleasurable physical experiences often have the way of appearing good because they give you momentary satisfaction and enjoyment; deeper analysis will reveal that the feeling of happiness was completely illusory. If it goes on for longer than you want it to, it becomes uncomfortable.

With regard to the mental state of happiness, as long as you are being controlled by afflictive emotions, the mind is not independent, it is not free. If you reflect upon this point, you should be able to see clearly enough that your mind will definitely encounter suffering even if you feel temporarily happy. One who suffers from a chronic ailment may not necessarily feel pain all the time, but neither can you fool yourself that you are healthy; the reality is that you are not free from that chronic disease.

The third misconception is one of seeing what is impermanent as permanent. To think that happiness or indeed life itself will stand still is a common error many of us make. It is a fact that nothing lasts for ever but we persist in believing in the idea of permanency. A king, while building a castle, probably felt that it would stand the test of time, would be there forever. Take the Great Wall. It took many people great hardship to construct that Wall. In the emperor's mind was the thought that his kingdom was permanent. Now there is nothing left except parts of the Wall. Look at Hitler, Stalin, Mao Tse Tung. Each had very strong concepts of MY region, MY ideology, MY power, and they mercilessly killed millions of people to try and make all the things that mattered permanent.

Therefore, it is useful to reflect on impermanence. There are two levels. One is subtle. The other is the impermanence of continuity; if one were to reflect upon the death of a plant, for example, or the cessation of any life form. The end of continuity we can actually see. This is possible because things change from moment to moment. If there were to be no change, it would be easy to observe the end of continuity. By observing and perceiving the disintegration of the continuity of an object or impermanent phenomenon, we conclude that all impermanent phenomenon have a changing nature.

To understand and perceive the nature of impermanence, the nature of disintegration, we should try to understand that every impermanent phenomenon, at the very moment that it comes into existence, does so in the nature of change, in the nature of disintegration. It is far more sensible to reflect upon everything that takes place as change than to think that what you had valued is disintegrated and is no longer in existence.

The fourth misconception is to see what has no self as having a self and therefore, an independent existence. Different Buddhist philosophical schools give different interpretations and explanations as to the meaning of self-lessness. The common Buddhist understanding of the term is that there is no self that is self-sufficient, self-supporting, nothing that inherently exits. If we manage to counter this misconception, I believe we can make a strong attempt to stop grasping, stem feelings of attachment, anger and so forth. The stronger your sense of self as being self-supporting and self-sufficient, the stronger will be your attachment towards your body, towards your house, towards your loved ones and so forth. On the other hand, the greater your understanding of the absence of such a self, the lesser will be your attachment towards material objects.

The Buddha taught us not only about the self-lessness of the human form, but also taught how all phenomena are essentially self-less. This means that not only does a person not have a self-supporting and self-sufficient existence, but also that the objects he enjoys only have the appearance of a permanent existence. We tend to perceive material objects as having an independent existence, but the truth is that there are no such objects, no such enjoyment.

There are various explanations as to why things do not exist as they appear to us. According to the Mind Only (Chittamatra) school of thought, the physical presence of an object is entirely dependent on the nature of an individual's mind. The Madhyamika or Centrist school of thought believes that all such existence is illusory. Our senses combine to make such objects seem real. The more profound and deeper your understanding of the self-lessness of a person and the self-lessness of thought, the more easily you will begin to accept what lies on the other side— that all things are interconnected. Even though mere objects do not have an independent existence, they are interdependent and interconnected.

So in our understanding of the four misconceptions, the first three are antidotes to repudiate these misconceptions. But by understanding the fourth, we will actually succeed in uprooting the seed of the misconception of the self.

To put it in a nutshell, there are different ways to combat negative emotions: the Hinayana way, the Bodhisattva way and the Tantrayana way. They are no doubt different, but their aim is the same: the complete elimination of negative emotions. And that is Nirvana.

In practice, people often look for concrete methods to overcome mental discomfort. However, it is impossible to relieve all anxieties through the means of one method alone: rather like the relationship between a body and its health. A good immune system can immediately counteract infection. But if the disease-fighting ability of the body is itself in a bad shape, even a slight infection is very difficult to conquer. Similarly, if your basic mental attitude has been made healthy and strong through training, through knowledge, through conviction, your healthy mental attitude will be sufficient to counter any tragedy you face, be it the death of a loved one or illness or injustice. Peace of mind is the most important quality one needs to counter unfortunate events positively.

If you are mentally untrained, overcoming problems will be difficult. To train properly, you must have conviction, which comes only with in-depth analysis. In order to analyse thoroughly, you need a lot of material, a lot of information. So it is that the Buddhist way of practice begins with study. Study by listening, by reading, by just absorbing information! Once you gather the information you have collected, you have to analyse it for yourself. Don't just rely on the Buddha's sayings. Do not take his word for it. Rely instead on your own investigations and experiments. This is the only way to develop the courage of conviction. And that is what will eventually make a difference in your mental attitude.

Once you have developed a positive frame of mind, you will find it in yourself to feel genuine compassion and caring. All emotions have to be based on reason and intelligence. That is the Buddhist way. That is the way to overcome negative emotions, to finish them, to stop them.

2

A Lay-Practitioner
Donna Brown

I was born in 1960, and grew up with the wrong idea of everything.

I came from a family who combined spoken respect for old-fashioned morality with a practical approach that anything one could get away with was okay. Traditional views like 'no sex outside marriage' and 'stealing is wrong' were put into words, but a congratulatory wink was aimed at those who escaped the consequences of adultery or buying hot watches from a shady dealer. Getting what one wanted was the goal of life, even if it meant lying or cheating. That my parents did not see this as hypocrisy was only a sign of the times: opportunistic self-interest long ago replaced religion as the guiding force in our culture, leaving a moral vacuum which surely contributed to the cultural upheavals of the 1960s.

As I grew older, I came to disagree with my parents' views, and instead admired the hippies I saw around me. They were less hypocritical, although—in retrospect—probably not less self-centred. But neither my upbringing nor the world around me could give me a real moral compass, and I found myself unsure of how to lead my life. Certainly, I was too self-concerned to devote myself purely to helping others. Not knowing what else to do, I followed the crowd, and sought happiness in relationships, success, friends, possessions, and travel—my generation's version of 'the good life'. I became an ordinary person, neither very good nor very bad. Unfortunately, an ordinary person is almost entirely focused on pursuing one's own happiness, with little thought for others. That was me.

I wanted badly to be a good person, but faced challenges I could not surmount. First, I did not know what goodness was. In my early twenties, I thought leftists were 'good' and sided with them against the seemingly false people on the 'right', until I saw for myself that those on my side also had feet of clay: personal ambitions that steered their agendas, selfish or unethical actions. So I built a career in the government, where I sometimes met genuinely good people. Yet ambition also ruled, and I found a mix of goodness, pride, greed and human weakness instead of what I sought: people who were ethical, kindly and wise. If I had understood what I was looking for, I might have realized I was in the wrong place.

I believed in ethics, and when I realized what was ethical, I did it—but I suffered from not always knowing, or from following the lead of others when I should have known better. Without relying on some—any!—wisdom tradition, I found it impossible to *decide* what was right or wrong. Most people seemed to believe that just grabbing things for themselves was right. I wasn't sure this made sense, but the sheer number of those who believed it made me think I had to be wrong. Sometimes I followed them. Sometimes I hesitated. Rarely, I did the right thing—then wondered if I should regret it when others seemed to profit at my expense.

The second challenge I faced was that even when I could determine what was good, I was not always able to do it. All I had was will power—no method of training my mind. For example, I was an impatient person, and generally felt others annoyed me from stupidity or malice—a false view which I had nothing to counter, and which frequently led me to speak unkindly to others. I was envious when others achieved more than I did, blindly proud of my own accomplishments, and inconsiderate in my speech. I tried to help others, and sometimes succeeded, but I paid more attention to myself than to them. I was good at my job, but pride made me a perfectionist, and I burned myself out in efforts to make everything I touched perfect. There was a big gap between my intentions and reality, and I had no method to assess where I was falling short or to fix the problem.

I also wanted to be wise, but I could never find wisdom. I looked everywhere: university, friends, bosses, politics, feminism, books, theatre . . . I found nothing reliable, and wasted a lot of time believing in this that turned out far less than perfect. I never lost the habit of looking, although I came to doubt that wisdom existed. Sadly, I did not think of religion: a child of my times, I thought religion was superstition, not wisdom.

One thing I remember: in about 1994, at work, some senior people made a decision that I considered unfair to a group of people we were trying to help. I was furious, and exclaimed to my boss, 'One day, I'll go and live in a monastery, where people are *good*!' And I had a picture in my head of a solitary place on a hill, where people told the truth and helped each other. The more I failed at finding wisdom and goodness inside my world, the more I dreamed of a better place beyond it. But I didn't know where.

I was also haunted by the question: 'What for?' I could not see what I was doing anything *for*. I played baseball or read novels or wrote poetry, but when I examined these, I couldn't see where they led: did they make me or anyone else happy? Did they lead anywhere? My career seemed equally unclear: I didn't do things that were harmful, but I couldn't see that I helped humanity much either. What was it for? I worked hard to set up an agency to help women start businesses, a service which was successful—but talked to so many women about going into business, or about running their businesses—and somehow I couldn't see that it brought happiness. I saw so much unhappiness and there was so little I could do.

I've worked in other social projects since then, and seen that it takes enormous effort to help even a few people in a small way. Improving people's lives is a daunting task. And I ended up wondering: is anyone really happier for it? The question was even harder to answer for ordinary pastimes—what for? Every thinking person, at a certain age, has to decide why they are doing what they are doing: is it for their family, their children, their retirement? In Western countries, for 'enjoyment' is a common answer. But enjoyments have such transience and such an inability to cancel out even the ordinary griefs and fears of middle-class life, still less the genuine tragedies that beset humans, that I could not see them as life's goal. By most stands, by my thirties I had everything, but I found 'everything' unfulfilling. I could not see any meaning in it: not in a career, relationships, entertainments, a nice house or car. Worse, I could foresee this 'everything' going on until death, never meaning anything more. What was it for?

So I ran in circles. I wanted something I couldn't find. I tried new things, but each let me down like the last. Caught up in seeking happiness in this or that, increasingly unclear about how to live my life, my mind was a whirl of confusion. What do you do when you have everything but it means nothing?

I dropped everything, and left for Nepal.

Why? The choice was not as abrupt as it sounds. Two things had led to it. First, I had travelled a lot before, including to Nepal and India, where I felt at home. And second, the year before, I had taken up Vipassana meditation. This was the result of venting my dissatisfaction with life one day to a friend, until she finally asked: 'What *do* you want?' 'This!' I responded. And I picked up from the coffee table a postcard I had left there for many days— a postcard from Ladakh, in the Indian Himalayas. It showed a small Tibetan monastery atop a barren hill; behind it rose the massive Himalayas. It was Rangdung Gompa in Zanskar, spectacularly austere in its solitude. '*This* is what I want!' I said. In the lonely gompa I perceived the kind of purity that was missing from my world. That postcard gave me hope—if I couldn't find what I wanted in my own world, there was a chance it existed somewhere else.

My friend's response was to take me to a Vipassana retreat. I did not become a Buddhist at that time: I just learned to watch my mind and gain a bit of mental clarity through detachment from its meandering. Vipassana calmed my mind, although its limited emphasis on teaching did not satisfy my quest for meaning. Nevertheless, it gave me my first taste of Buddhism. I thought that in Asia I would try to learn more.

The day after I arrived in Nepal, an Australian at my guest house told me he was walking up to Kopan monastery that morning—would I join him? Someone else had mentioned Kopan to me as 'a good place', so I happily went. I wouldn't have known the way myself; I knew nothing about it. I had never heard of its founders, Lama Yeshe or Lama Zopa Rinpoche. I had never seen a lama. Even monks were new to me.

Nevertheless, I asked in Kopan's office about courses. I had a year of travelling ahead of me: a little meditation might be a good start. This was October; Kopan offered a one-month course in November. I pictured sitting still for a month, watching my breath. Very calming. Maybe even blissful. I signed up, not knowing that the course contained more teachings and analysis than what I knew as meditation.

In Kopan, I slept in a dorm with seventeen others; there was no place or time to 'watch my breath'. Teachings, teachings, teachings, then guided meditations on specific topics which I wasn't sure I liked. I had never heard of 'precious human rebirth'. I did not feel grateful for my life—what for? Lots of people had better lives than me. On the other hand, I didn't mind 'death'. I thought of death as a well-deserved rest. But, anyway, I didn't have to believe these teachings. In spite of my disenchantment with everything I knew, I still perceived that I was only at Kopan to relax. I was also suspicious of the people in red robes. Were they running a cult? Maybe, they only wanted money. I closely observed our teacher, Ven. Neil Huston, an Australian monk, looking for logical inconsistencies that would give away the show.

One day I was putting on my shoes after a teaching just as

Neil was leaving the temple. As usual, people crowded around him, asking questions, even though he was very overworked. But he listened attentively and tried to answer all the questions. He spoke kindly and didn't brush people off. Out of the blue, the thought struck me: 'He's the first good person I've ever seen.'

All my life I had been looking for someone good. And there he was, standing before me. One good person. I was thunderstruck.

After that, no one stood higher in my eyes. Everything Neil taught gained credibility. If I did not believe *every* word—I still had doubts about the details of the hells—I believed that Neil believed every word, because Neil would not lie. And my faith in him made me make an effort to see how what he taught could all be true, instead of judging what to accept or reject based on my own tastes. Neil taught the Lam Rim (steps of the path), and it was the Lam Rim that slowly made me a Buddhist. But I would never have taken it in without deciding that Neil could be trusted.

When I started taking Neil's words seriously, I found that these were the teachings I had always wanted. Goodness. Wisdom. An explanation of the world that made sense. I had lost hope that what I was looking for existed, but it did. Relief filled me.

One day Neil taught the Buddhist view of the future. Since we live in times that are degenerating, the minds and lives of humans will worsen in the coming centuries. Lifespans will decrease to ten years, while the size of our body will shrink to that of a small child. Eventually, Maitreya Buddha will come and turn things around. 'But it's like that *now*!' I thought, glimpsing how much below our potential we humans live. Cramped by obsessions and mental poverty, we grub like insects in the dust, never looking up—but if we did, we could touch the stars. That was when I started to see the red-robed lamas in a different light, less as suspicious figures and more as guides. It seemed just possible that the wise people I had sought might exist after all.

The truth of rebirth became important, and I believed it because the teachings said it was true—I didn't analyse it for myself until later. Death became something to prepare for, because worse rebirths could come: hells or no hells, who hasn't witnessed the suffering of animals? I didn't know how much bad karma I had amassed, but having done all ten non-virtues, I gladly took refuge in the Three Jewels. I was no longer a spectator at Kopan. And after leading a worldly life in which I had regretfully concluded that happiness must only come from being *not* a good person, it was a great load off my mind to hear that the source of happiness was goodness. My old plan, to be good and wise, could be taken up again. Everything I wanted seemed possible.

I left Kopan with three treasures. First, refuge in the Three Jewels, which, though newly-minted and superficial, remained a commitment that kept me on track; second, pratimoksha vows; and third, the Lam Rim.

My new pratimoksha vows and my minimal understanding of karma—of what was right and what was wrong—were what got me to start cleaning up my life. For example, I had to stop killing insects without concern for the feelings of small creatures, and to stop telling trivial lies to make myself look better. I discovered that not killing anything is the first step in developing compassion, and that honesty improves relations with others and makes life easier. I didn't really steal before I took the vow against it, but the vow slowly helped me to stop trying to 'get' from others and think more of what I could give, as well as to use, and return, borrowed items more carefully, and work at ensuring that I wasn't taking advantage of others. The vow against adultery, which I hesitated before taking, once saved me from what would have been a disastrous mistake. This made it my favourite vow for a time, and taught me that vows are a protection, not a constraint. And though I was never much of a drinker, the vow against alcohol made me do something more constructive with my evenings than baseball and beer. Two or three years later, I was amazed to see how fast vows improved not just my every day life but the clarity of my mind.

Kopan's other precious gift was the Lam Rim. It was incredible luck to be handed the Lam Rim, a jewel beyond compare. In whichever schools of Tibetan Buddhism I've encountered Lam Rim texts, they are unsurpassable mental tools. I had found Vipassana, a practice I never completely abandoned, useful but not sufficient. I needed the teachings and analytical meditation that the Lam Rim provided. The Lam Rim seemed to make clear all the things I had found unclear and explain everything that had baffled me: good and bad, what to do and what not to do, why this or that happens. And it gave me a method to slowly reduce my bad qualities and train my mind in better ones. With the Lim Rim, everything I had searched for was in my hands, like the legendary jewel that grants all wishes.

After I left Kopan, convinced I was a Buddhist, I faced the difficult task of *becoming* a Buddhist. I had to make myself a better person—more generous, ethical, sympathetic and patient; as well as to learn the teachings and practices and use them to purify and develop my mind. At first I was a complete spiritual materialist, looking for enjoyment from Dharma in place of my previous pastimes. Naively, I thought I could become good and wise while having a good time perpetually. Soon, I found out it's much easier to be entranced by the Dharma in the beginning than to put it into practise day after day. It also turned out that practising the Dharma can sometimes be boring or painful. Worse, meeting the Dharma and doing purification does not stop bad things from happening—the weight of past actions is greater than a little elementary Dharma practice. I had to grow up, and realize that human life contains suffering no matter what we do. The Dharma helps us get through bad times without making them worse, keep our head in good times, and build a foundation of ethics, compassion and mental clarity for the future.

One important discovery for me was that Buddhism is logical. I had always clung to logic as the raft in a sea of confusion. I could not have traded in it for illogical beliefs. Fortunately, the Dharma is not about believing what cannot be logically established. Discovering this was another relief—in the beginning, I worried that there would come a point when I would have to believe something that defied reason. But Dharma isn't like that—the more one studies, the more one discovers the depth and solidity of its logical foundation.

Now, five years after Kopan, I know that what I am doing makes sense. I am generally more patient and generous, though very far from perfect. I work at keeping my vows as carefully as possible and I am trying to improve my speech: my goal is to always speak responsibly and never say anything bad about anyone, which is not easy! And now I know what I do things *for*. I know better what it takes to genuinely help others. I know that if you want happiness, you have to work at creating its causes—it is not something that can just be grabbed. And although I don't have wisdom myself yet, at least I know where it can be found. I have a sharper mind in some ways, which may just come from applying myself to learning new things year after year, but I think this also comes from meditating on the Lam Rim.

Sometimes, I think about ordaining as a nun. The vows and robes of an ordained person are said to be the best support for Dharma practice. But the Dharma is at an early stage in Western countries, and while many Dharma centres exist, there are few monasteries or nunneries—none anywhere near my home. I would like a monastic life, but in my own country and near my Lama, who also lives in Canada. In time, I hope to be part of the process of establishing more monasteries and nunneries in the West so that more Western Sangha can develop their believers into meditators, scholars, and teachers.

Right now, though, after a total of four years away from Canada, I am back home working for the government while also trying to do regular Dharma practice. I have a little time for meditation and study during early mornings, evenings and weekends, although it is not as much as I would like. But work can also be a good place to train in patience and kindness, and learn to be less egotistical. There are plenty of opportunities to put others first, to recall that wisdom and compassion mean more than money and status, and to practise not getting angry or blaming others when things go wrong. Work is certainly no obstacle to developing compassion. Although, since I have a good job and the people I work with are quite pleasant, the opportunities for mind transformation are probably fewer than they should be!

I also believe it is false to think that one *must* be ordained to practise Dharma—that only ordained people are committed to Dharma. Tibet, alongside its strong monastic system, had a long tradition of accomplished lay-practitioners, both householders and yogis, male and female. We laypersons, while respecting and appreciating the ordained Sangha, should understand that we can also be 'real' practitioners.

Canada is a good place to practise the Dharma because it is a peaceful and tolerant country. The Dharma isn't as widespread in Canada as it is in some Western countries, but there are Buddhist groups in most cities and a small abbey on the west coast. The Kagyu School too is established in the east. And just as yoga has become popular and mainstream, I think Buddhism will too. I heard recently about some top corporate executives taking up meditation. This shows that people see making money isn't enough; it doesn't take away suffering or answer questions about life. For many people in Western countries, other paths may be the solution. But some will find Buddhism. After spending such a long time in India and Nepal, I came back to Canada with that hope: that the Dharma will be firmly established here. And that, eventually, by coming home, I can help make sure that when people look for it, it is here. That is my plan—to do my part, even though it is small, to ensure that when people in this country look for the Dharma, it will always be here.

3

Buddhas in Hibernation
Kabir Saxena

A Bodhisattva bust from the National Museum adorns one of the bookshelves in my house in a quiet green Delhi suburb. The strong Graeco-Roman features, complete with bushy hair and full moustache, proclaim that it belongs to the Gandhara period. Exuding dignity and determination, the Buddha always seems to me to be conveying a simple yet powerful message: do not fear chaos and confusion. Look inside yourself to find the strength and tenderness you need to survive in this broken world.

Yes, I love that head, chipped nose and all.

The Bodhisattva is my single greatest source of inspiration. I look at him often as I struggle to describe in words that seem so inadequate how deeply his teachings have illumined my life, always offering a practical path to regeneration during times of decay, despair and darkness. The Bodhisattva speaks to me, as statues sometimes do, in a manner that groups like the Taliban can never hope to understand. The giant figures at Bamiyan are no more, sacrificed at the altar of religious fundamentalism, destroyed by people who cannot bear to imagine that mere sculpted stone can indeed awaken our inner glory and compassion.

As countless images of our dying world flicker across TV screens, engraving themselves in our minds as indelibly as they have imprinted themselves in the black-and-white world of newspapers, I feel the urge to pause every now and then to take stock, a compulsive need to examine what effect these images have on my mind and, therefore, on my life. I call upon all my inner reserves of calm in an effort to feel less shattered, and less bewildered, reminding myself of what I am, what all of us are—Buddhas in hibernation.

Initially, I felt the need to go back to my past and investigate my experience as a teenager and an undergraduate. I must confess that my spiritual life has been a veritable labyrinth and I have often found myself at what I presumed were dead ends, though I have managed to extricate myself from potentially disastrous situations. And, eventually, I took that first necessary step towards salvation, and walked straight into an inescapable confrontation with the Buddha's First Noble Truth—the truth of dukkha or suffering. I was an anguished teenager. Loneliness and boredom were my constant companions; grief stricken at the loss of my grandparents to whom I was very close, I was stressed out by a competitive school environment; mutinous with my parents; I craved for a fulfilling relationship with a woman, a relationship for which I was ill prepared; in short, I longed for affection. I realized later that I had a 'psychological hole' in my stomach, and it was this emptiness that finally made me open up to the voice of a hundred spiritual traditions. To borrow the words of Jamyang, the monk in Andrew Harvey's moving book, *A Journey in Ladakh*, my sadness made me open.[1]

I turned to the *Bhagavad Gita*, devoured the writings of Carl Jung, drowned myself in classical music and sought the wisdom of the Buddhist Society at Oxford University. The last, I discovered, contained a motley group of often highly intelligent but neurotic souls flailing around in their emotional roller coasters even as they put up brave faces. Most of their so-called knowledge seemed to me to be largely useless.

I was fortunate enough to catch a spirited performance of Maxim Gorky's *The Lower Depths* by the Royal Academy of Dramatic Arts in London in the early 1970s. There is one scene where the prisoners chorus a refrain:

Every day the sun comes out,
But my prison is dark and dreary.

These words uncannily echo what I felt about my life at that point. This is not to say that there were no moments of happiness or enjoyment, but such times were fleeting, few and far between.

It was, I think, sometime in 1976 that my mother told me that she was dying of cancer and that the doctors had given her just two years to live. She died in July 1977. When she first broke the news to me, it left me feeling strangely cold and numb; my lack of feelings added to my misery in my second year at university. I became withdrawn, more serious, more determined than ever to open up and find the seeker within.

It was around this time that I met Jon Marshall, a jovial social worker, who ran a youth project from Bromley High Street in South London, very close to where I lived. He'd been to Dharamsala in North India, he said, working with the Tibetans and studying the language and Buddhism. He spoke about a college of Buddhism in the Lake District of England and mentioned that they ran courses in Buddhist philosophy and meditation. I memorized the address. I just had to go.

The Easter of April 1977 found me standing at the gates of the Manjushri Institute for Wisdom Culture that had been founded a year or so ago by Lama Thubten Yeshe. The five-day course conducted by Geshe Damcho Yönten, who barely spoke English, and Thubten Pemo, an American nun, who taught us meditation, changed my life forever. The course was based on the Lam Rim tradition of Mahayana Buddhism as enunciated by the illustrious Dipankara Shrījnana or Atisa, an eleventh century Bengali pandit. It was expanded into its present sophisticated and comprehensive form by Je Tsongkhapa (1357-1419)[2], an exceptionally skilful synthesizer of the Buddha's teachings and a great teacher and yogi.

The Lam Rim teachings take the student through contemplations on the precious and rare nature of our present human opportunity, the reality of death and impermanence, the laws of cause and effect (karma), the sufferings of humans, animals and other beings that are caught in a conditioned cycle of death and rebirth (samsara). One also gets an insight into the causes of suffering by exploring the delusions of ignorance, anger and desirous attachment (klesas). A chastened and somewhat subdued student is then led through stages in developing altruism and universal responsibility. The last is something that can only be engendered by great compassion and love. There are teachings on wisdom, the antidote to ignorance,[3] the root of all samsaric suffering (dukkha).

Despite his broken English, the Geshe's[4] kindness shone through. The meditations seemed to prod awake some inner chords in me that had long remained untouched. I was moved in the truest sense of the word and knew that for me there would never be any looking back. At the end of the course, I decided to take refuge in the Buddha, his teachings (dharma) and became part of the spiritual community (sangha). Although I could not understand the short ceremony completely since it was conducted in Tibetan, I knew that I had made a commitment to foster an inner wisdom that would eventually lead me out of the 'dark and dreary prison'.

After graduation, I again went back to Manjushri[5] Institute in August 1979. My mother had passed away two years ago and my contact with Buddhism had helped me to come to terms with her loss. The institute was abuzz with activity and I came to know that Lama Yeshe and Lama Zopa Rinpoche (who was later to become my guru) were visiting. Rinpoche[6] threw us into the deep end from the beginning, expounding upon the importance of recognizing emptiness, making us realize how we do not experience the world and ourselves as they actually exist but rather grasp at illusions, thinking them to be solid, concrete reality. I found this bit hard to comprehend but the Rinpoche's magnetic personality kept me spellbound. There was humour in his style of teaching and I was only one among 200 students who listened to him with rapt attention and dedication.

Lama Yeshe,[7] in contrast, was so cheerful, open and loving towards everybody that it was a delight just to be around him. His outgoing personality was the perfect foil to the almost other-worldly quality that defined Rinpoche, whose lanky build and large penetrating eyes made him look like a being from another universe. During those two weeks of uninterrupted sunshine, so unusual in that part of the world, I soaked in the warmth as much as I did the profound words of my teachers. I grew to admire them immensely and knew, almost intuitively, that my life would be inextricably linked to these two lamas. So it was that I came to be associated with the Foundation for the Preservation of the Mahayana Tradition they had established in Nepal in the early 1970s.

In November 1980 I attended the thirteenth Kopan course at the Kopan monastery that overlooks the Kathmandu valley. The course lasted a month, deepened my understanding of Buddhism, and for the first time I knew what it felt like to have a spiritual home. I gleaned a wealth of knowledge from the course and got a taste of what analytical meditation in a monastic environment can be like. His Holiness the Dalai Lama has maintained that such analysis is essential in developing a meaningful understanding of the concepts of death, impermanence, and other stages of the path (the path reveals the essence of the Buddha's teachings in a step-by-step process).

I discovered that analytical meditation transformed my mind far more effectively than mere reading, listening or talking had ever done.

I wasted most of 1981 in inconsequential activities except for a wonderful seven-day retreat in Delhi. At the end of that week, I was given the opportunity of a lifetime—a private audience with his Holiness the Dalai Lama.

I don't think I have ever been so nervous in my entire life as I was on that fateful day. His Holiness extended me a warm welcome. And then proceeded to dismantle the edifice of spiritual materialism I'd erected by injudiciously taking on far too many tantric commitments in my haste to qualify as a spiritually-arrived Tibetan Buddhist. I was uncomfortable for most of the fifteen minutes I spent in his presence but remember vividly the intense warmth in his eyes, and when he led me to the door at the end of the interview, I was certain there were tears in his eyes. Once outside, Tenzin Chogyal, His Holiness's younger brother, advised me to stay connected with society and not go off into solitary practice. I had just been told as gently as possible that I was yet far from being a mature and intelligent practitioner of the Buddha's dharma. If only I'd been wise enough to take His Holiness' advice firmly to heart.

In August that same year I went back to Manjushri at the suggestion of the Rinpoches. I was a student there till June 1983, at which point Lama Yeshe asked me to return to India and help set up a new centre in Bodhgaya. And that was how the Root Institute for Wisdom Culture came to be established at the holy place of Buddha's awakening. I was there till 1993 and helped run development-oriented projects in neighbouring villages because we felt such programmes were in tune with our brand of 'socially-engaged' Buddhism.

I had begun working full-time for Lama Zopa Rinpoche; Lama Yeshe having passed away in 1984. By now, I had given up all association with the West and given up all thought of ever looking for a salaried job.

❖

I have since been an administrator/teacher at centres[8] in Delhi and Kathmandu. From 1998, I started concentrating solely on teaching basic Buddhist philosophy and meditation to beginners in Dharamsala. The positive feedback we get never ceases to amaze me. For me, this appreciation is proof enough of the power of Dharma.

What is it that moves the hearts and minds of so many beginners? What is it that has inspired me to keep walking the inner path with all its hurdles for twenty-four years? What aspect of Buddhism appeals to me the most? To my mind, they are the half a dozen or so especially skilful teachings that embody not only the tremendous beauty of the Buddhadharma but also the profound wisdom and compassion of its founder, Lord Buddha.

The Buddha realized that he had to provide a spiritual path that was suitable for everyone, irrespective of his or her mental and spiritual capacity. Also, his path needed to be laid out in a progressive fashion so as to enable a person who starts at a relatively basic level to follow it logically and, due to effort, climb the rungs of the spiritual ladder till one reached a comparatively advanced stage of the path that led to nirvana[9] or samyak sambodhi.[10]

So the Buddha by his grace caused three sublime streams of Dharma to flow. The paths are all interlinked, there are no contradictions (if understood in their proper context), and they act as practical guides to subduing and transforming the mind.

The first stream is the Theravada or Hinayana, which, when understood and put into practise, subdues the mind so thoroughly through its teachings on ethical conduct, concentration and wisdom that if followed sincerely, it can help one attain nirvana.

The second stream, Mahayana, opens up the practitioner's vision to such an extent that liberation for oneself alone no longer holds out much appeal and, driven by genuine compassion and a sense of universal responsibility, one strives to attain the state of a fully awakened Buddha. This type of individual will follow the path of the bodhisattva[11] in a manner that is defined by generosity, morality, patience, joy in the effort, concentration and wisdom. The aim is to assuage all suffering. Nothing can illustrate the goal of a Mahayana practitioner better than the words of the great eighth century Bodhisattva Shantideva:

May I myself become the doctor,
nurse and medicine for all
who are sick in this world . . .

My body has been given up to others.
May I be a guide for those who travel . . .
A boat or raft or bridge.
May I be an island for those seeking land,
a lamp for those who need light,
a bed for those desiring rest,
a slave for those requiring a servant.[12]

The Abhidharma refers to the bodhisattva as 'a slave who has not been bought by the world'. He is a servant who does not need to be paid for his willing enslavement. This is the all-encompassing vision of the awakened spiritual warrior as manifest in the Mahayana.

The third stream is the Vajrayana, also called Tantrayana or Mantrayana. This contains the advanced, hitherto secret, teachings of the Buddha and is based on the foundation laid by the previous two levels. The Vajrayana is a guide to rapidly transforming an ordinary person's body speech and mind, into a Buddha through subtle and powerful means that involve considerable psychic mastery.

These three levels of teaching satisfy the requirements of every conceivable spiritual aspirant. Whether one's motive is to achieve happiness in this life, happiness in future lives, attain complete liberation from conditioned death-rebirth (Skt. *samsara*), or the wish to become a Buddha to relieve all suffering—Buddhism not only recognizes all these aspirations but also shows the way to reach these goals by practising one or a combination of these teachings from the three paths. The paths set out by Buddha are not only comprehensive, but are also interrelated and extremely logical. The Buddha asks us not to accept the teachings merely on faith, but to analyse and reason them out for ourselves; to test the Dharma in the same way that a goldsmith would test gold for impurities. There is, therefore, no obligation to accept anything before one has reflected and meditated sufficiently on what is being taught. His Holiness the Dalai Lama has reiterated that such analysis is a crucial component of the path because it directly contributes to the transformation of consciousness. In comparison, the recitation of mantras and other so-called higher practices seem easy and indeed superficial, if they have not been preceded by enough questioning and soul-searching.

Another frequently asked question has to do with the most beneficial way to approach the path. In my opinion, the student must initiate a relationship with himself to experience the actual functioning of his body and mind. It is important to be in touch with the body and know the sensations you are experiencing at any point in time, be they pleasant, unpleasant or neutral. Similarly, one has to constantly be in touch with one's mind and be able to define emotions, thoughts and memories. In short, a student must apply the principle of dynamic awareness and embark on a journey that has been well described as one of 'making friends with oneself'.[13] The raison d'être being that if you can make friends with and understand yourself, if you can generate genuine warmth and love in your heart and mind for yourself, then you will be able to extend all these emotions towards others.

It might be a cliché that loving oneself is the first step towards loving the world, but it happens to be a powerful medicine. It may not impress the academics, but I have to say it works. It works because in my hands, my mind and body become the laboratories where I wield the microscope of awareness to reveal what's going on. In this way, I cut through fantasy, expectation and a false self-image and see myself as I actually am. The teachings of the Buddha are based on the premise that we cannot be free and happy if we live in an illusory world that is actually only an amalgam of the fears, expectations and prejudices thrust upon us by the society we live in.

To achieve this clarity of thought, a student turns to meditation. Apart from helping with the analytical process, meditation also facilitates concentration and is one of the ways to keep distractions at bay. But this is only one of its many components, one that is too often mistakenly thought to be the main element of all meditation.

The very posture of meditation reminds us of our dignity as human beings. The upright bearing signifies a healthy self-confidence. The front is naturally open, defenceless, to indicate that one is not going to hide from himself or others—and is, in fact, more than willing to relate fearlessly with the world. The shoulders are held up straight, no slouch to mar the pose. This is symbolic of the sanity and basic goodness of mankind, and indicates our potential for enlightenment—for waking up completely and unconditionally. In the words of the Buddha, 'be a lamp unto yourself, work out your salvation with diligence'. Buddhist meditation short-circuits one's natural tendency to be superficial and lazy, to not look too deeply for fear of what may lurk beneath our civilized veneer. What it finally reveals is that we are all basically good, we are all potential Buddhas and not just miserable sinners. This realization comes after painstaking effort but what makes it heartening is that it is possible to achieve.

There is no substitute in the Buddhist tradition for sustained meditative discipline. This practice of discovering and connecting with the inner self has remained unbroken since the time of the Buddha. To ignore this aspect of Buddhism and rely completely on books and erudite lecturers, will leave a student unable to connect with the liberating heart of true practice.

In India and Tibet equal emphasis is laid on mind training or thought transformation[14] (Lo jong) since they form another equally important part of the Dharma teachings. These refer not only to methods whereby one can generate feelings of compassion and wisdom in daily life, but also to specific ways of turning even the most adverse of circumstances to one's advantage by taking the path to Buddhahood. These methods teach us not only how to be patient and undismayed by the problems we confront every day, but also how to actually use them to boost our spiritual awareness for speedy awakening. Rather than curse our shortcomings and attack our so-called enemies, a practitioner begins to form a healthy relationship with both, by perceiving them as temporary results of ignorant consciousness and using the situation as an incentive to practise genuine love, both towards oneself and towards others.

Generating sincere compassion depends upon getting in touch with our own 'soft spot',[15] the vulnerable part of us which we usually hide from everybody, including ourselves. It is important to realize that all beings go through the same feelings of sadness, loss, grief and pain, joy and happiness, depression and jealousy, envy and hatred. Investigating these feelings via the medium of meditation can soften a person so that he can feel truly with and for the whole of humanity. I would like to reiterate that it is possible to achieve this result only by practising meditation again and again; there are no short cuts, no magic wands. To a person who has attained the goal of unconditional compassion, even an 'enemy' is really a suffering friend in disguise. The 'enemy' too has his share of dukkha: he too undergoes the trauma of being born, getting sick, becoming old, dying. To quote the great yogin Shabkar (1781-1851):

> Even the enemy who harms you
> has been your parent in previous lives.
> Cultivate patience towards everyone . . .
> However much you may suffer,
> take on yourselves the suffering of others
> and still don't lose heart . . .[16]

Tathagathagarbha or Buddha nature is yet another branch of the teachings of the Buddha that most students find useful because it reveals that, in essence, all of us carry the seed to enlightenment by explaining how temporary mental afflictions have caused us to abandon that part of us that is truly divine. The Tathagathagarbha reassures us that we can redeem what we think is lost forever by selecting appropriate spiritual methods. The Dalai Lama has maintained that, 'The teaching that the Buddha nature is present in all sentient beings, providing the "Substantial cause" for the attainment of Buddhahood, inspires courage.'

In all this, one must recognize the need for a spiritual guide to attain these goals. Just as one needs a teacher when it comes to learning the alphabet or playing the piano, one also requires a mentor to negotiate the tight rope of balanced spirituality. It is not possible for a student to meaningfully take stock of the destruction wrought by ego without a helping hand. Skilful guidance from a qualified person who has the ability to steer us expertly on the ocean of samsara towards the isle of liberation can prove invaluable. The fact that many Tibetan masters are held in great esteem throughout the Himalayan region and the West is not a result of blind adulation based on insecurity. It is a positive acknowledgement of the genuine inner strength and power of these souls, many of whom are Rinpoches (precious ones) who have voluntarily chosen to incarnate as human beings in a world that sorely needs all the kind and wise shepherding it can get:

> The Rinpoche sits in splendour,
> He teaches the dharma to the villagers,
> He teaches his world how to live.[17]

I am often asked whether Buddhism has any relevance in India today. I know of a newly ordained Indian Buddhist who has been exhorted by my guru to study in the traditional method at Sera monastery (once situated near Lhasa, now relocated in Mysore district). Such places are few and are about the only monasteries in India where one can engage in a serious in-depth study of Buddhist scriptures. There has traditionally been 'undisguised hostility to Buddhist studies' in some educational institutions in the country and now, in the backdrop of increasingly militant Hindutva chauvinism, in itself partially a response to the destabilizing effects of Westernization, things are looking even more bleak for alternate spiritual options like Buddhism.

Hinduism is often thought to be a tolerant all-embracing religion. Like a capacious sponge, it has had an ability to soak up and absorb a lot of influences that might have otherwise challenged its core belief in the creator and the permanence of soul, to quote two of the major areas of philosophical divergence between mainstream Hinduism and Buddhism.

However, for religions like Buddhism, this assimilation has come at a price. It has meant that most people who approach Buddhism in India regard it as yet another of the tributaries that eventually finds its way into the river of Sanatana Dharma and cannot see in it anything of value that hasn't already been pronounced by Hindu sages of old. Every time I have attempted to explain the philosophical differences in the two streams, my arguments have been dismissed as being uselessly confrontational. I am told that I am trying to establish differences that do not exist; that I am turning a blind eye to the unity of all the traditions; that Buddha was a Hindu after all.

Hinduism has, at least in the past, been ambivalent towards the Buddha. In the *Vishnu Purana*, for example, the Buddha is portrayed as an avatara, one of the ten incarnations of Vishnu, who manifests as the Buddha in order to teach wrong Dharma to the asuras so that they lose in their struggle against the gods whom they had increasingly begun to overshadow.[18]

In my opinion, the significance of Buddhism will only be understood by modern Indian society when there is greater appreciation of its philosophical brilliance, and when people realize its practical efficacy in restoring balance to their disturbed consciousness. This can only happen if one takes the trouble to study Buddha Dharma under the guidance of authentic teachers, thus disentangling the unique teachings of the Buddha from popular clichéd notions such as 'all is one', 'there are 84,000 rebirths to go through until *moksha*', 'there's no difference between Hindu and Buddhist teachings on karma, the self and the tantric path', 'logical reasoning and debate are mere sophistry' and 'the Buddha forbade the rendering of his own image in statues and the life.' All of which reveal nothing of the profundity of Buddha's teachings or Buddhist practice.

In reality, Buddhists today need to distinguish between the

essential strands of their faith and those belonging to the dominant cultural and religious matrix. It is in this context that Dr Ambedkar realized that in order to take his untouchable comrades beyond personal and socially enforced bondage, he would need to embrace a system that had established itself as clearly different from the orthodox hierarchical casteism endorsed by texts like the *Manusmriti*.

Ambedkar was also clear that 'The enemy you must grapple with is not the people who observe caste, but the Shastras that teach them this religion of caste.'[19] Contrary to Gandhi's opinion, Ambedkar felt strongly that caste had to be totally annihilated, not merely reformed. This was what led to the historic mass conversion where 5 lakh Mahars pledged themselves to Buddhism on 14 October 1956 at Nagpur. We continue to live with the legacy of that day. It has meant, for one thing, that we now have many million 'Buddhists' in India for whom social and political liberation is prioritized over personal enlightenment. And understandably so. Having been exploited and cast out of the respectable rungs of Hindu society for centuries, what the Dalits have longed for, more than anything else, is social freedom.

In *The Buddha and his Dhamma,* published posthumously, Ambedkar presented Buddhism as a kind of rational scientific materialism that stressed the need for an egalitarian society rather than as a doctrine of salvation detached from worldly responsibility. He had little sympathy for the Theravadin Bhikshus' emphasis on austerity and solitary practice since it countered his deeply-held notion that the Sangha, as embodiments of Buddhist moral conduct, should selflessly serve their suffering, exploited brethren. In Ambedkar's version of Buddhism, the Buddha almost comes across as a compassionate social worker, rather than a guide who discloses the path to nirvana. I will not contradict this for the Buddha is all this and more. But the Buddha clearly analysed the causes of social injustice and suffering as originating from the personal and collective past (as in past lives), and not just as a factor resulting from the machinations of a callous and bigoted hierarchical system in the present. This view, however, does not have takers among the Dalit Buddhists—after all, not many of us find it easy to digest that we and we alone are responsible for our current happiness or misery. It is easier to distribute blame. Therefore, if I am poor then somebody else is to blame. If I am an oppressed Dalit then it is the oppressor who is solely responsible for my plight.

This reasoning goes against basic Buddhist teaching on cause and effect, which posits that whatever I experience—good, bad or neutral—is the effect of past actions and that I am now habitually predisposed to experiencing the world a certain way. Of all our past actions, be they mental, physical or verbal, it is the first that reflects most on our present.

To give just one example: if one is a thief or a miser in the present, he may experience poverty sometime in the future. If you are poor and downtrodden in the present, the people exploiting you can only be considered catalysts. The root cause of misery lies in the faulty actions that were performed in the past as a result of delusion and contaminated karma.

This explanation is not palatable to scientific materialists, or to the average person on the street, let alone to the Ambedkar Buddhists. And yet, teachings on karma form the very foundations of basic Buddhist thought. All morality is founded in these teachings.

This is not to say that Buddhism as I have described it rejects the importance of social change and wider social issues like the environment and so on. Just because it is someone's karma to suffer in a certain way, should we ignore their condition because they somehow 'deserve' it? Of course not. All of us can only experience the fruits of happiness by creating the inner causes for it. The act of alleviating the misery of others is meant to show that all of humanity is totally interdependent. We must therefore create awareness in every single individual of the crucial importance of one's intentions in the scheme of things. Every person's actions will serve as critical ingredients for establishing a better world. Compassion leads us to do whatever we can for fellow human beings. But even as we try to help them, we know that essentially each person is responsible for his present and future situation and that even the Buddha 'cannot wash away our sins with water'.

Unfortunately, these profound teachings have been so misused in the past by upper-caste Hindus to perpetuate and legitimize an unequal society that even those who wish to turn to Buddhism find these explanations unacceptable. It is here that the role of a guide becomes even more important. Only a sensitive teacher can bring out the liberating qualities of the religion. We must realize that it is possible to generate an enlightened society without looking to the government for support, without the external 'enemy' having to be destroyed first.

One of the greatest tragedies facing Indian Buddhism today is an almost total lack of appropriate teaching facilities or learned guides that can help create Sanghas. Barring a few Tibetan lamas, some Tibetan-trained Indian monastics and the teachers associated with the Trilokya Buddha Mahasangha based in Pune, there are no well-qualified Buddhists who can take the Dalits under their wing and explain to them that the road to freedom lies within their individual understanding and practice of Buddhism. Merely exhibiting animosity and hostility towards Hinduism and the prevailing caste ideology is not going to further them on the path to salvation.

Middle-class Indians, on the other hand, have had some exposure to the Buddha's teachings through the efforts of His Holiness the Dalai Lama, Karmapa, HE Tai Situ Rinpoche, Lama Thubten Yeshe and Lama Thubten Zopa Rinpoche. But such people are largely wrapped up in family responsibilities and materialism. Whatever spirituality there is tends to be tailored for people in a hurry. To become a pandit in a tenth century Buddhist university might have taken twenty years of study, while developing the mind of a yogi or master would certainly have taken much longer. Now, one can become a 'qualified' Reiki master in a few months and have many ten-day meditation courses on one's spiritual CV without having necessarily experienced any transformation in outlook or lifestyle.

If one were to contrast this scenario with the Tibetan experience in India since 1959, it seems remarkable that from a bedraggled and often sick mass of traumatized humanity that they were in the early 1960s, the Tibetans showed resilience and tenacity enough to rebuild the structures of their society, especially when it came to religious culture. Today, thousands of monks engage in study and debate in monasteries, be they in Dharamsala or Mysore. Many Tibetans pass their Geshe examinations with distinction and take seriously their responsibilities to pass on the Dharma to the younger generation of students. Some have gone abroad to spread the word of the Buddha in the West. The tragedy is that such few Indians have benefited from the experience of these masters. In India, the perception of Tibetans as dirty meat-eating aliens with a weird repertoire of exotic rituals continues to persist.

This attitude trivializes the unbelievably rich Tibetan spiritual heritage even as it dismisses the efforts of the Dalai Lama and his followers who have successfully kept alive the old Indian wisdom traditions of Nagarjuna, Aryadeva, Shantideva, Buddhapalita, Chandrakirti, Dharmakirti, Dignaga, Vasubandhu and Asanga. The philosophical sophistication of these traditions is a far cry from the mindless chauvinism of the modern Indian religious experience.

Global television networks now provide twenty-four hour viewer-friendly religious discourse. So we now have spirituality as spectacle. There are books with titles such as *Seven Steps to Spiritual Success*, *Religion as Business* and *Spiritual Materialism* gone global. The global guru now resides in a website, mere mouse-clicks away.

What is heartening, however, is the fact that genuine Buddhist masters like His Holiness the Dalai Lama can now use these technological advances to spread the message of the Buddha more effectively. Though the Buddha prophesied the disappearance of his teachings in this world—part of a cyclical process where culmination and dissolution precede new life—I take heart from the fact that we have witnessed a remarkable dissemination of his teachings over the last thirty years.

At some point in the future, more and more people will be disillusioned by the vapidity of modern culture and turn inwards to recover once again the universe that lies within. I pray that they excavate this inner kingdom with the techniques taught by Lord Buddha and hope that they discover the treasure buried within their consciousness and initiate steps necessary to create a more harmonious world.

❖

Notes:

1. Andrew Harvey: *A Journey in Ladakh*, p. 65.
2. Tibetan founder of the Ganden Monastery and Gelug school of Tibetan Buddhism.
3. Skt. Avidya: Literally, 'non-seeing,' lack of understanding of the nature of reality.
4. Geshe: A degree awarded after many years of detailed study of the texts and commentaries in the Gelug school.
5. The Buddha of Wisdom, golden yellow in colour, holding a sword in the right hand and perfection of wisdom text in the left.
6. Literally, 'Precious One', an epithet awarded to reincarnate lamas as well as honoured teachers.
7. Yeshe is Tibetan for primordial wisdom. Lama Yeshe (1935-1984) founded the FPMT—Foundation for the Preservation of the Mahayana Tradition—in Nepal in the early 1970s.
8. Tushita Mahayana Meditation Centre in Delhi. Est. 1979. Tushita Meditation Centre, Dharamsala. Est. 1974. Himalayan Buddhist Meditation Centre, formerly Himalayan Yogic Institute, Kathmandu. Est. 1970s.

9.   Self liberation beyond all sufferings for oneself alone.
10. Complete Buddhahood or full enlightenment for the sake of all suffering sentient beings.
11. Enlightenment-bound being who wishes only to attain Buddhahood in order to liberate others from suffering.
12. Chapter III, verses 8, 18, 19 of Shantideva's *Guide to the Bodhisattva's Way of Life*.
13. This and the following paras are from the works of Chogyam Trungpa Rinpoche who fearlessly proclaimed the Teachings in the UK and USA from 1971 to 1987.
14. See *Advice from a Spiritual Friend*, Rabten and Dhargyey, Wisdom, 1984.
15. See in particular Pema Chodron, *Start Where You Are*, Shambhala, 1994, pp. 4-10.
16. *The Life of Shabkar: Autobiography of a Tibetan Yogi*, Trans. by Matthieu Ricard, SUNY Press, 1994, p. 399.
17. Andrew Harvey, op. cit. p. 103.
18. Vishnu Purana (iii: 17) in J.M. Macfie, *Myths and Legends of India*, Rupa, 1993.
19. *Ambedkar: The Annihilation of Caste*, 1936, p. 111. Quoted by Timothy Fitzgerald in his chapter entitled 'Ambedkar, Buddhism and the Concept of Religion' from the book *Dalits in Modern India*, Edited by S.M. Michael, Vistaar Publ., New Delhi, 1999, p. 121.

4

A Monastic on the Move
Robina Courtin

My wish to take ordination as a nun was simultaneous with my desire to become a Buddhist. Buddha's explanations about the mind and karma made utmost sense to me, and from the beginning, it was clear that to renounce the householder's life would be the most effective way to practise the Buddhadharma.

Even as a little girl, I was attracted to the monastic way of life. I first went to mass with my family in Melbourne and knew right away that I wanted to be a priest; it was clear that it would be my vocation. I must have been very young because when it was explained to me why I couldn't be a priest—because I was not a boy—I couldn't grasp the idea at all.

I loved going to mass; I loved Our Lord, Our Lady and the saints. It all felt so natural. I especially loved Saint Therese of Lisieux; she was my hero. This is not to say that I was saintly myself. Far from it. I was a very naughty girl; angry, rebellious, stubborn, always getting into trouble. The nuns at school couldn't see my religious heart at all; all they saw was the 'bad girl'. When I was just twelve, I begged my mother to let me become a nun like Saint Therese, who had become a Carmelite when she was all of fourteen. My mother refused, of course; I cried.

A year later, such devout thoughts far from my mind, I started to think about boys. When I turned fifteen, my religious aspirations took on a social hue, as it were. I always liked to read, to think, to question why the world was the way it was, why there was suffering and how to go about fixing it. I discovered Black American music, jazz in particular. It was a near-religious experience and my heart opened wide to the world.

At nineteen, I gave up God and took up sex, drugs and, eventually, political activism. I'd been studying classical music for years along with my mother, and when I was twenty-three I moved to London to continue my study. It fell by the board pretty quickly, however; it was the 1960s and I was ripe for revolution.

The initial hippie phase quickly morphed into political activism: first it was radical left politics, then the movement against racism, and, finally, feminism. For eight years, I was immersed in my efforts to make the world a better place. In my need to explain the world to myself, I leapt from one ideological/ political platform to the next. I was always moving, moving; looking for answers, for meaning, for clarity and coherence.

I went back to Australia for a couple of years in the early 1970s and got involved in the feminist movement. But the restlessness I had become all too familiar with, reared its head once more and I again began to turn towards spirituality for answers to questions that were plaguing me. I took up martial arts, and I loved it. I tried different types of meditation, attended a few courses. In 1976, I found myself at Chenrezig Institute in Queensland where Lama Yeshe and Lama Zopa Rinpoche were to conduct a course. At that time, I was fully involved in my martial arts training and nothing could've dragged me away. But I broke my foot in a car accident and was forced to stop. I'm forever grateful to the kind man called Bill Bright who knocked me down!

So the Chenrezig Institute it was. I felt that I had finally found my home; *this* was the monasticism I had been looking for. I gave up sex, drugs, cigarettes and alcohol. I stayed there for two months, then returned to Melbourne and began a practice. Lama Yeshe was my guru—although at first I was embarrassed to admit it. It was a bit of a struggle for me to accept that I needed a teacher. I met the Lama again the following year and decided to visit his monastery, Kopan, in Nepal. I took my first vows there in February 1978.

❖

What attracted me to Lord Buddha and his teachings right from the beginning were the coherent, logical explanations of how the mind works, what causes suffering, and how to eliminate it. The precision, clarity and depth of analysis that we take for granted in any scientific investigation are what Buddha says we need to use in the examination of our minds, and that delighted me. It also pleased me that what the Buddha was saying in effect was, don't take my word for it; check it out for yourself. It is considered inappropriate to blindly believe what the Buddha said just because he said it; I needed to discover the truth for myself. The Dalai Lama has always said that, if from investigation and practice, we actually discover that what Buddha says we ought to experience doesn't happen, we must reject the Buddha; he is wrong. In Buddhism, there is no contradiction between mind and religion; they intersect perfectly. Buddha's religion, to put it succinctly, is the composite of his philosophy and psychology and the methods he used to apply them experientially.

Being a nun has never been difficult; I can't imagine not being one. Being Robina is what's difficult: dealing with my out-of-control mind, which is the most essential job for a Buddhist like me. My being a nun makes the job immeasurably easier.

Over the years, I have listened to the Buddha's teachings, contemplated deeply on them and tried with some success to practice what he preached; to me the benefits of being a nun have become very evident. I now have the mental space to work on my mind: I have become familiar with its workings; have begun to understand how to distinguish between the appropriate and the inappropriate; have gradually learned to develop the positive qualities and eliminate the negative.

Our most negative quality as far as I am concerned—the one that cause us suffering and others harm—is attachment. Buddha says we live in a realm of desire and I can see it is true from looking at my life. The ability to desire is so pervasive: it's as if it is the default mode of our mind. Lama Yeshe once said that he could talk to us about attachment 'one whole year,' but unless we built up the requisite resistance through meditation by really looking into our minds, we would never begin to understand it. (In the West, 'attachment' is equal to 'love', the two are virtually interchangeable, whereas for Buddha attachment is necessarily negative, the cause for all suffering, while love is positive and the cause for happiness.)

For Buddha, what we term happiness is actually nothing other than suffering. It is as if we are all junkies who only know how to get our fix of happiness through objects of attachment. Only the degree of addiction varies. But true happiness, according to the Buddha, is when we give up this kind of joy, not seek it. The Buddha's views on what he thinks all human beings are capable of achieving through sheer control of the mind are far more radical than anything expressed by any contemporary school of thought. When the mind is completely rid of all the neuroses arising from negativity, one attains nirvana. Sounds all too simple. Very hard to achieve in practice. Such a concept is unheard of in the West.

It stands to reason then that if one wishes to give up attachment, one of the most effective ways to do it is to remove ourselves from the scene. And given that the strongest object of attachment is always another human being, celibacy seemed to me to be an intelligent choice. It is never enough to give up the object of desire; it seemed to me to be more sensible to give up the whole scenario that went with it.

The funny thing is, it was as if I was destined for this. Everything in my life seemed to have led me in this direction. It was as if I had no choice: the momentum was irrevocable. In retrospect, I wonder why I never wanted to settle down with anyone, never wanted to make a commitment, no matter how much in love I was. I never wanted babies. I always felt that the pleasure of being in a relationship was not worth the pain that went hand in hand: at the back of my mind was always the fear of losing, the feelings of expectation and jealousy. Then there was the attachment to material possessions. I was wary of getting into situations where I would worry over the house, the car, the insurance, the school fees . . .

Developing the potential of good qualities such as love, generosity and compassion—qualities that Lord Buddha believes are an innate part of all human beings—is a long-term thing. We understand this concept when it comes to day-to-day life: we all know an oak tree doesn't grow overnight. But when it comes to happiness as defined by the Buddha, we are unwilling to accept it. We want it *now*, like a child or a junkie we seek the quick fix option. It is very important to understand that developing good qualities is an ongoing process, there is no deadline.

To most Westerners, monasticism is an Asian tradition, irrelevant to their part of the world. But the Buddha explained why the ordained Sangha are crucial: the existence of the Buddhadharma in any one place depends upon the presence there of at least four ordained Sangha practising the full extent of the vinaya, the Buddha's guidelines on moral conduct.

One may well ask why the ordained Sangha is fundamental to the existence of the Buddhadharma, what about the other practising Buddhists in the region? The answer simply is that the essential difference between the lay-practitioners and the ordained Sangha is the level of vows they have taken—in other words, the extent to which they abide by the vinaya.

And why are vows important? While teaching at the Kopan monastery in December 1992, Lama Zopa Rinpoche put forth the choice before us quite simply: one could follow the methods of purification as laid out by the Buddha without holding the vows of morality, but prepare to deal with the distractions of a worldly life, or take the vows of morality and give up the world as we know it and have a clear mind that would definitely help one get ahead on the path more quickly. Vows are believed to have such power that without them, it is rather difficult to progress.

It is important to understand at the very outset that the teachings of the Buddha are meant to be put into practice; often, we mystify religion, and so can't 'hear' it properly. The destruction of delusions and excess emotions is a practical issue, not a moralistic one. The only way to free ourselves from suffering and the causes of suffering—samsara—is to achieve the wisdom that recognizes emptiness; one has to reach deep inside to access a very subtle, non-conceptual level of consciousness; and you can hope to do that only through samadhi, single-point concentration in meditation. And that degree of concentration can only be attained with the practice of morality. And the most sensible, most effective way of practising morality is by keeping the vows of morality, more easily done by being an ordained monk or nun.

We badly need what Buddhism has to offer in the countries I have lived in, especially in the US, where there is so much emotional suffering. Because of our tendency to cling compulsively to a narrow sense of self—a symptom of all samsaric cultures, not just the West—and because of the deeply held belief that our suffering and happiness come from the outside, we have little knowledge of our inner potential and not many ways to develop it.

At the core, Buddhism teaches that our true nature is pure and clear; that who we really are is an amalgam of the good qualities, not the bad ones. To be told this alone is not enough to make one kind, loving and patient; it is difficult to let go of the negative side that we have grasped at so fiercely, for so long. That's the irony of ego. Lama Yeshe calls ego the 'self-pity me,' and the truth of this comes to light with introspection. This is where the practical application of the Buddha's philosophy comes in. It allows us to slowly change our sense of self and thus give up attachment, anger, pride and the rest and begin to have confidence in our good qualities, and therefore unleash our capacity to feel true happiness.

It is easy to think that Buddhism deals primarily with the internal. Everything indeed emanates from the mind as far as Buddha is concerned, and the development of the mind is certainly central to Buddhism. But the final goal is never the individual; ultimately, the religion is all about making the world a better place by reaching out to soothe the sufferings of the rest of humanity. Mahayana says that a bird needs two wings: the wing of wisdom and the wing of compassion. We work on our own minds to nurture the wisdom wing, which, in turn, is the foundation for developing altruism, the compassion wing.

In 1996, when I was the editor of *Mandala*, the international newsmagazine of the Foundation for the Preservation of the Mahayana Tradition, I received a letter from a nineteen-year-old Mexican prisoner in California. He'd read a book by Lama Yeshe and was interested in pursuing the study and practice of Buddhism. We corresponded by mail, I sent him books and eventually visited him and gave him Refuge. Then a friend of his wrote, expressing his interest in Buddhism, then another, and another. By the end of the year, we had a mailing list of forty people in prisons across the US.

We now receive approximately 200 letters every week. We have a network of volunteers in various states who write to or visit prison inmates, teach the Dharma and support their practice. We call ourselves Liberation Prison Project, and in 2000, we started this programme in Australia as well.

Lama Zopa Rinpoche wrote a letter to the young Mexican on his twenty-first birthday. He told him, 'I know you are in prison, but actually it's just the concept: what you label and how you use the place. For another mind it is the same as a hermitage.' Many of the people we communicate with are on death row, have life sentences, and are incarcerated in their windowless cells twenty-three hours a day, often for the rest of their lives.

One might think their lives are unbearable, but they have discovered the truth of what Rinpoche wrote because their prison is nothing compared with the inner prison that holds a vast majority of human beings captive—the prison of attachment, the prison of pride, the prison of anger . . . Their being in prison has served as a wake-up call. It took *this* for them to begin to develop their inner qualities, to truly find freedom.

The irony is that there is so little pleasure in prison, no distractions whatsoever that these convicts are able to develop great discipline in study and practice. And some of them have reported powerful experiences during the course of meditation.

The conditions in these prisons are uniformly appalling. Even in sections where there are only a few inmates, the noise is 'like being in a rock concert,' as one of them said. But unlike those of us who can choose our environment, they cannot ask their neighbours to be quiet.

There was this man who was serving a sentence for killing someone while driving drunk. He developed faith in the Buddha Tara and would get up at 4.30 in the morning for meditation and also take out time for one more session in the evening.

He wrote:

Though the two practice periods are nearly the same in content, they are a world apart in nature. Where the morning period is primarily one of reverence, devotion and dedication, the evening period is more self-discipline and attention to focus. Only because in the evening the other 799 prisoners in the cellblock are wide awake and wound up. The racket is deafening and resembles nothing less than bedlam and chaos. This could be an insurmountable obstacle if I let it be, and for a time it was. But I've kept at it and the obstacle became a stepping stone to closer communion and a sweeter practice.

Because I don't work weekends, I sometimes spend several hours on Friday and/or Saturday nights in Tara meditation and visualization. Last Friday night was especially loud on the tiers for some reason and it was especially hard for me to get centred and focused enough to begin with the visualization. Maybe I was impatient and tried to start prematurely before I was 'in the zone'. Whatever, it was a struggle all the way through. Towards the end after the Jetsun prayer, I was still struggling to hold the image of Tara clearly and block out the racket from the tiers. The harder I tried, the harder it became, and the harder I would try, and I was just about ready to call it a night when it got quiet; real quiet.

Somewhere very far away I knew it was still there and hadn't diminished. Tara became so clear and vivid, so real, unlike anything that I have ever experienced. It was as if I'd been removed entirely from the prison and was very high above it. It was just Tara and me and the whole field of merit as real as I sit here now. I was no longer consciously trying to hold her image. She was there with me on Her own. And all the characters of the field of merit were just as real and vivid.

I feel that I need to qualify this somewhat. It was not a dream. When I do dream, I very seldom have any recall. When I do, it is hazy, vague and without continuity. Nor was this a hallucination. It's been over twenty years, but I'd quite my share of those as well. They always have a surrealistic character that easily defines them.

I would love to report a message or some sort of profound revelation or something of earth-shaking magnitude, but there was none of that. She just sat there and smiled, and never have I felt so close and intimate. As if I were Her and She were me. I felt the deepest sense of peace, security, clarity and ecstasy in every cell, nerve and membrane. It was so intense and so real that the feelings and image are still with me as strong as if it had just happened.

I don't know if this type of experience is common or not. But I have learned from it. I learned that no matter how difficult or how much of an exercise in futility it may seem, *never give up*! The benefit speaks for itself. And from this encounter, Tara is no longer a symbolic archetype that I hope to embody at some point in the future. She has shown me that she is real and attainable and available even to me. This is a milestone for me and like I said, I don't know how, what or why, but everything is changed.

For me, working with such people has been hugely inspiring. Their resilience, confidence and determination in the face of the greatest of odds is awesome. Their dedication proves beyond doubt the truth of what the Buddha preached—believe in your good qualities and become the person you truly are, a Buddha.

5

Seeking the View

Suresh Jindal

My mother was an agnostic Hindu married to a very devout Jain. She never followed any spiritual practices, including prayers and rituals; my father got up at 4 a.m. for his meditations and prayers and never went to work till he had first visited the *sthanak* and listened to the teaching of Jainism from its teachers. But he never forced any of his children to follow his beliefs or practices, other than requesting them to do so at their own volition.

I started my studies at a school run by missionaries. When the Mother Superior asked my father whether I could attend church or not, he left it entirely to me. But I did not want to get up early on a Sunday—the only day in the week when one was not woken up at the usual ungodly early morning hours, that generations of boarding school brats have been subjected to.

My interest in spirituality awakened during the 'flower children' scene of the 1960s at California where I was an engineering student. Along with political radicalism, fashionable atheism and agnosticism, we tripped on Alan Watts and D.T. Suzuki, Krishnamurthy and the Maharishi. I took initiation in TM from the Maharishi, and started reading books on Hindu scriptures, hung around with the Hare Krishna devotees, screaming at redneck Neanderthals who were harassing them.

Back in India, where I joined the Bollywood crowd, I started going to Ganeshpuri, and became a devotee of the great

Mahasiddha Swami Muktananda. Baba bestowed great compassion and kindness on me.

After Baba's nirvana, I could not make a karmic connection with Gurumai—his successor. For a long time, I floundered in a spiritual vacuum for I am one of those who need an embodied guru.

Over the years, I had listened to the teachings of His Holiness the Dalai Lama at Delhi. Since I already had a guru, and was engrossed in my worldly ambitions, I could neither find the time nor did I feel the need to pursue them further.

I was asked to be the Co-Producer of *Buddha* by the original promoters of the film. (Not the one subsequently made by Bertolucci, *The Little Buddha*.) I made a pilgrimage to all the Buddhist places to make an in-house documentary. I reached Dharamsala during the Losar teachings of 1989.

When one's karmic causes have ripened to meet the gurus, a simple phrase, perhaps repeated by the guru a thousand times before, is a key that clears the haziness that has prevented one from seeing the vastness and glory of the guru. On that clear, crisp spring day, a single phrase uttered by His Holiness, '*We all know we are going to die, but when we will die, we don't know. So why postpone practising Dharma?*' created in me the urgency to learn as much as I could about the Dharma.

My friends connected me to Lama Zopa Rinpoche, whose interest in my spiritual practices allowed me the freedom to attend the Kopan course and do a couple of retreats. I could also take time out to attend nearly all the teachings that His Holiness gave in India in the last four years.

The Buddha teaches that there is no Creator-God and that all sentient beings have an equal potentiality for Buddhahood. Sentient beings have different karmas and mental dispositions, but are *all* the same in that they want happiness and liberation from suffering. The choice of a religious inquiry is purely a function and the preference of the seeker's mental disposition and spiritual needs.

Some scientists and mathematicians believe that there is an

objective, independent, solid, permanent and graspable reality existing *our there*. The Buddha teaches that all phenomena and persons are empty of this inherent existence. Reifying it is ignorance and the root cause of suffering in Samsara. The reality *out there* is a dream, a mirage, a bubble, and is like the image of a moon on a still lake,

> Like a star, a mirage, a lamp,
> Illusions, drops of dew, bubbles,
> Dreams, lightning and clouds:
> *Look at all conditioned phenomena as such.*[1]

Darwinism believes in 'survival of the fittest' and 'nature red in tooth and claw'. Hence, according to Darwin, aggression, violence and competition are our intrinsic and legitimate nature. The Buddha teaches that compassion (*karuna*) and loving-kindness (*maitri*) are the real nature of all sentient beings. There is no 'Fall from the Garden of Eden' because of which Man is born inherently evil. All negative acts are due to afflictions of ignorance, covetousness and hatred, and are the true causes of suffering. Because everything is impermanent and ever changing, it is within the potential of every being to get to the roots of our afflictive emotions and attain liberation from all suffering.

Neuro-psychiatrists search for neurons, synapses, proteins, amino-acids, electric fields in the brain that can be manipulated to switch our suffering from ON to OFF and vice versa. In the 'scientific method', they are trained to believe that there is a fundamental particle, energy or wave pattern in the form of cells, electrical pulses, and organic bodies that determine the behaviour of all matter in the universe, including the bodies of all sentient beings. Once we can understand, harness and manipulate that energy, we can create euphoric, mental and emotional affliction-free human beings and create a Paradise and a Utopia on earth. By stimulating different parts of the cortex, you can measure varied responses of pain and euphoria, but in the Buddhist view, 'mind' is much more than the brain alone.

The brain is the mere instrumentality of the mind, which is subtler and can access higher levels of awareness beyond the physical. The mind has various functions like thought, emotions, ego, sensation and memory. What we experience is the mind and not the brain. The mind not only reflects the physical reality of the sense but can also transcend it, and infer the reality beyond it. Research has allowed scientists to map the brain and its functions with great curative powers for mental dysfunctions, but it cannot determine what causes and conditions create emotional and mental afflictions. Science has no means to measure or explain consciousness. Or what causes mental states, like hate or affection, to trigger off certain kinds of neural activity.

Buddhism does not have a ceremony like a Bar Mitzvah, reading the Kalima, a sacred thread ceremony, a *shuddhi* ritual, or a baptism. One becomes a Buddhist by realizing that this is the path that is best suited to one's mental disposition and conviction through logic and reasoning. Then you take refuge in the Three Jewels—the Buddha, the Dharma and the Sangha.

When we want to learn physics, we must seek:

- A teacher who has the wisdom, skill and compassion to teach it;
- A teaching that sheds illumination on the subject. Microbiology is not that subject;
- A Community—the Physics Department of the University, and not its Physical Education Department.

For a Buddhist student, the Buddha is the Teacher. He represents the Buddha Mind of all sentient beings, a mind free of obscurations, beyond dualism, a wisdom that has realized the bliss of the emptiness of all phenomena.

The Dharma is the body of his teachings and their Commentaries. It also represents the speech of the Buddha, and the discriminating wisdom of his mind.

The Sangha are the community that study and practise the Buddha's Teachings. It consists of ordained monks, nuns and the laity.

When you find that Buddhism is the path that is best suited to you, then you take refuge in the Three Jewels. There is no Creator God who demands it, but your own logic, reason and investigations. For, the Buddha teaches the doctrine of Emptiness— that no phenomena or persons have inherent independent existence.

You don't take refuge in the Three Jewels because they are some permanent, solid, independently self-perpetuating objects of God and the One Truth; you take refuge because the Buddha's path allows you the blissful freedom to modulate the path to your self-awareness at your own rhythm, and in accordance with your mental disposition. But also, to take the responsibility of your suffering on yourself and not to pile the blame on 'another', 'my enemy', 'religion', and so on.

In Buddhism, truth is not the exclusive revelation available through some Special Being only. The view of dependent origination and emptiness of inherent existence of all phenomena is a profound and radical one. In terms of a religious view, it is the only one that dispenses with the existence of a Creator God or Superior Being. The view is taught not as an article of faith or as an exclusive revelation to a Special Being or Messiah or Prophet, but is one that can be ascertained by study, debate and direct experience. The methodology of investigation is as thorough and rational as those of physics and mathematics. Like Science, this can only be studied under a qualified and experienced teacher and not through books or rote memorization.

His Holiness the Dalai Lama says that crucial to the hermeneutic approach is the Mahayana principle of the four reliances. These are:

i.   reliance on the teaching, not on the teacher;
ii. reliance on the meaning, not on words that express it;

iii. reliance on the definitive meaning, not on the provisional meaning; and

iv. reliance on the transcendent wisdom of deep experience, not on mere knowledge.[2]

The guru is the living embodiment of the Buddha. A Mahayana guru must have the ten qualities of:

1. Ethical self-control;
2. Serenity and meditation stabilization;
3. Mental peace derived from wisdom of the nature of ultimate reality;
4. Should have more knowledge than the disciple;
5. Enthusiasm in practice;
6. Richness of scriptural learning;
7. Realization of reality;
8. Skill in the art of teachings;
9. Loving concern and compassion for his disciples;
10. No sense of discouragement when working for his disciples.

The disciple should be:
1. Honest;
2. Intelligent and sensitive to distinguish between good and bad;
3. Have strong interest in learning.

The Buddhist view is integrated through the three practices of listening, reflecting and meditating. There are profound and deep methods of practical education that can lead the student into the direct experience of ultimate reality. In the Mahayana paths, the uniqueness of Tantra practice is that it is an accelerated vehicle that can give realization of the view in our lifetime. This can only be obtained through direct transmission by a Realized Master who has travelled the path. The preciousness of the Lama's teachings includes oral instructions, initiation into the Tantra, and its teachings.

A lama is not ordained or nominated by a church or a counsel. A monk is accepted as a lama when disciples feel he has the qualities for being one.

In Buddhism, all monks have to undergo rigorous training and education from an early age. These studies can take up to twenty years for attaining the highest degree of Geshe—Doctor of Divinity. The monasteries are primarily educational institutions that prepare future teachers. Since the Buddhist view has no blind belief but has to be taught by logic and reason, the preservation and dissemination of the teachings depend on the teachers and the monasteries that educate them.

The Buddha's teachings have been transmitted, right from their inception, directly from a living teacher to his disciple in a tradition known in India as the Guru-Shishya Parampara. One cannot learn driving by studying it only on the Internet. Similarly, these profound teachings cannot be imbibed unless a Realized Master imparts them.

Taxila, Nalanda and Vikramshila, till their destruction in the thirteenth century, were premier Buddhist universities of India. The resident monks-yogis-scholars held all the major lineages of the Buddhist teachings. Fortunately, from the eighth century CE, with a fortune that seems almost prescient, a vigorous exchange of pundits from India and yogis from Tibet had already started. All the major lineages had been safely transported to Tibet, also called the Land of Snows. The Dharma kings of Tibet not only restructured their language but also that of the whole society to serve just one thing: preserving and propagating the Teachings. At any given time, about 20 to 25 per cent of the entire population were in monasteries and nunneries. Based on the model and methods of the famous Indian monastic universities, the renowned universities of Samye, Sera, Drepung and Ganden were built to nurture, teach and preserve the teachings and their lineages.

There, on the roof of the world, sheltered from the greed of covetous powers, Dharma flourished for over a thousand years. Not only were the teachings preserved but they were also enhanced and honed by the realizations of a steady stream of outstanding wisdom beings.

The Chinese occupation forced His Holiness the Dalai Lama and the High Lamas to flee to India. A similar millenarian ideology of intolerance and absolutism that destroyed the great Buddhist universities in India in earlier centuries also destroyed nearly 12,000 monasteries and nunneries in Tibet, including those of Samye, Sera, Drepung and Ganden. Tens of thousands of monks and nuns were imprisoned, tortured and killed as had happened in India in earlier times.

In an amazing and heroic feat, the lamas and the Tibetan exiled community have rebuilt Samye, Sera, Drepung and Ganden in south India. The Guru-Shishya Parampara tradition has again been brought back to the land of its origin. Among the exiled community, nearly 15 per cent of the Tibetan population is again monks and nuns. If this percentage is translated to India, it would amount to an astounding 150 million, and if translated to the world population an astronomical 1.2 billion!

In the prophetic traditions, there is no direct link between a seeker and ultimate reality. God reveals himself through a single favoured medium that alone has been revealed the truth. The authority for the message and union is the prophet or the messiah, and only his 'revelation' is the truth about God and ultimate reality. He and, after his demise, his church or ulema, are the sole receivers, translators and interpreters of the word of God. It sets a contrast between God and man, and accepts no other belief than itself as legitimate. Every seeker has to submit to the authority of both spiritual and temporal conduct. There is no direct access to God, and this exclusion automatically shuts out alternate paths of exploration.

In contrast, Buddhism is dominated by an inwardness that seeks direct union with the ultimate nature of reality. The Buddha says that every sentient being is capable of Buddhahood. The lama is not a specially favoured person who has a hotline to Buddha and whose pronouncement must be accepted blindly because he alone has been 'revealed' the truth. He is the aspect of the pure mind (Buddha-mind) and has by his three disciplines of morality, concentration and wisdom travelled and experienced the path. His compassion and loving-kindness, enthusiasm, effort and patience can guide and help you to find and experience it. As His Holiness the Dalai Lama teaches,

> I normally recommend to Buddhist practitioners not to see every action of their spiritual teacher as divine and noble. There are specific, very demanding qualities that are required of a spiritual mentor. You don't simply say, "It is good behaviour because it is the guru's." This is never done. You should recognize the unwholesome as being unwholesome, so one might infer that it is worthwhile to criticize it.[3]

The Buddhist-view does not rely on a Creator or a God. The view of impermanence, dependent origination and emptiness of any inherent existence in phenomena requires not just intellectual studies and diligent learning but also moral discipline and the practice of Bodhicitta—the altruistic wish to separate all sentient beings from their suffering and take them to Buddhahood. If the wisdom-realizing emptiness is not in union with Bodhicitta, it will remain a bird with only one wing, incapable of the flight to enlightenment. The method can be learnt with a Realized Master who is a supreme yogi of the art.

A mechanistic view of the world had its roots in Democritus and Leucippus, the Greek philosophers of the fifth century BC. This view gave rise to the dualism between spirit and matter, between mind and body, which became the characteristic part of Western thought. Descartes, in the seventeenth century, based his view of nature on a fundamental division of mind and matter into two separate and independent realms. The material universe was only a machine that worked according to mechanical laws. Everything in the universe could be explained in terms of the arrangement and movement of its parts. This view was extended to living organisms as well. Plants and animals were inhabited by a rational soul, but the human body was indistinguishable from an animal-machine.

Descartes' method of reasoning consisted of breaking up problems and thoughts into tinier pieces and arranging them into logical order. This approach, which became an essential part of modern scientific thought, led to enormous developments in scientific theories and technological marvels. Simultaneously, it also led to fragmentation and the widespread attitude of reductionism in science, and a belief that all complex phenomena can be understood by reducing them to their constituent parts.

Newton triumphed in developing a consistent mathematical model of the mechanistic view of nature. Till the end of the nineteenth century, the Newtonian model of the universe dominated all scientific thought. Along with the natural sciences, the humanities and social sciences accepted this view as the correct description of reality and modelled their theories accordingly.

At the beginning of the twentieth century, as the atom was studied in its aspects of electrons, protons and neutrons, totally unexpected and sensational observations were made. Classical theory that believed that atoms were discrete, solid and self-existent things could not explain the new experimental data. Instead of being the least indivisible solid entity, atoms were found to be regions of empty space in which extremely small particles called electrons moved around a nucleus. The quantum theory, by the late 1920s, invalidated atoms to be the solid objects of classical physics. They are very abstract entities that change their appearances depending on the way we look at them. Sometimes they appear like waves spread out in space and sometimes as solid particles.

A further blow was delivered to the very foundation of the mechanistic world view when it was discovered that at the subtle sub-atomic level, the existence of matter is merely a probability in space but not a certainty in a specific location. At this level, the solid classical entities dissolve into wave-like probabilities and can only be understood as inter-connectedness between the process of observation and measurement. Heisenberg's famous Uncertainty Principle gave mathematical formulation to the strangely mystical equation that states that when the location of a particle can be pin-pointed, its velocity cannot be determined and vice versa. As the Buddhist thinker and physicist Alan Wallace asks, 'How can an electron, whose wave and/or particle state is nebulous, have an intrinsic mass, charge and spin, when it does not have intrinsic location or velocity?'*

Heisenberg states in the twentieth century:

*The world thus appears as a complicated tissue of events, in which connections of different kinds alternate, overlap or combine and thereby determines the texture of the whole.***

Echoes Nagarjuna in the second century CE:

Things derive their being and nature by mutual dependence and are nothing in themselves.

Matter is just an interplay of dependencies exposed to our own conceptuality.

The Prasangika Madhyamika school of Buddhist thought accepts the existence of the two truths—that of a conventional reality as we know it through experiences of the six senses, and that of an Ultimate Reality that is the ground from which these hallucinatory and deluded images arise. It postulates that conventional reality is devoid of all inherent existence of persons and objects. It comes into being as a dependant arising out of the

---

* B. Alan Wallace, *Choosing Reality*, Snow Lion, Ithica, N.Y., p. 73.

** Fritjof Capra, *The New Vision of Reality*, India International Centre of Quarterly, Winter 2002 Spring 2002, p. 76.

causal nexus between causes and conditions that result in their manifestations. Conventional existence is merely imputed, designated and labelled by the mind, and when one attempts to discover an unchanging, permanent solid existence in the object, then nothing there is findable. Conventional existence uses three criteria for its affirmation:

1. The object is renowned among conventions.
2. In its apprehension, there is no contradiction from a valid conventional cognition.
3. There is no contradiction from a valid cognition analysing its ultimate nature.

In this centrist view, all physical and mental things are devoid of an intrinsic and inherent nature. In a conventional sense, they exist on a relative and dependant manner which makes it possible for them to react with other entities on the same conventional level. All physical and mental events are neither more real than the other nor do they possess absolute, independent or inherent existence. They are dependant on causes and conditions, parts, directions, moments and mental labelling and imputation. They interact with other phenomena only because they are neither immutable nor inherently existent.

Heisenberg has asserted, 'What we observe is not nature itself but nature exposed to our method of questioning.'* This was a startling and 'mystical' statement to be made by one of the fathers of quantum physics, and rocked the Western scientific establishment. More so, because it was supported by experimental observations.

The physicist, John Von Neumann, posed this interesting query: 'If the unmeasured electrons are described by the Shroedinger equation as mere "potentia", the same must be true of the

* B. Alan Wallace, *Choosing Reality*, op. cit.

unmeasured elementary particles of which the measuring device is composed.'*

We can use external instruments and devices to extend the range of our senses to determine the nature of physical reality. This approach is inherently limited because each system of measurement creates its own bias. It measures those aspects that it postulates and leaves out others. It measures only the part and not the whole, which remains immeasurable. In the interior journey, observations cannot be made by using external measuring devices. His Holiness the Dalai Lama says:

> *Today our knowledge has expanded greatly with the help of science and technology. But knowledge regarding our mind, our deep nature, is still limited in the Western world. This is because consciousness is formless and cannot be touched and so cannot be measured with instruments. It can only be known through medication and other methods.*[4]

The traveller has first to make himself both a tool and a laboratory by training himself to observe extremely subtle states of the mind. Like certain processes and experiments in conventional reality require 'clean-room' conditions, similarly, experiments and experiences in the inner laboratory require the purging and discipline of unruly and powerful forces in the seeker's mind.

For a Buddhist, conventional reality is merely a labelled and designated entity whose definitions and functions we agree upon by mutual consent. In its ultimate nature, this reality is not as solid and permanent as it appears to be, but is empty of independent inherent existence. To see reality in its ultimate nature, you need to get rid of the gross states of mind and be in those very subtle states that can experience and see it non-conceptually. This is not possible by mere book learning and intellectual

---

* Heisenberg, *Physics and Philosophy: The Revolution in Modern Science*, Harper and Row, N.Y., p. 58.

gymnastics; the seeker has to undertake a radical inner transformation of the poisonous states of attachment, hatred, pride, jealousy, doubt and ignorance. Only a being of pure morality and wisdom can guide you on that path.

In Buddhism, there is no concept of original sin. Negative states of mind are a result of the ignorance of the nature of reality. These states, like physical acts, are habits that we, as individuals, cultivate and nurture because of attachment to objects we like and an aversion to those we dislike. As we can train our bodies to become great athletes, similarly, it is possible to habituate our minds and emotions to wholesome acts and views. The mind, in the Buddhist view, is something quite different from its corresponding meaning in the Western sense. Even in Western languages, there is a great difference between the English word 'mind' and the German word 'Geist'. 'Geist' also has the connotation of 'spirit', which is not included in the English concept of 'mind'.[5] In the Western languages, the mind is associated with intellect, rationality and the heart, with the intuitive and emotional. In the Sanskrit 'citta' and the Tibetan word 'sem', both functions are incorporated and no gap is created between the emotional and the intellectual. 'Citta' and 'sem' include 'as well in the scope of its meaning all sense perception, such as hearing, seeing, smelling and so on'.[6] Perhaps the closest English word would be 'experience', which is whatever happens to us and whatever occurs.

The mind is not just an organ like the brain or a space in the head. Mind is 'that which has an object'. As Berzin writes, 'There is an arising of something and an engaging with it in cognitive way. There is the arising of a sight and the seeing of it, the arising of a thought and the thinking of it, and so on . . . Mind gives rise to something and apprehends it. Not understanding something is as much a form of engaging with an object as is understanding it. Whether we are conscious of something or not, we can still experience it. Mind gives rise to a thought and thinks it simultaneously.'[7]

The mind itself is devoid of any independent and inherent existence. This emptiness is no more a 'thing' than the mind; it is not nothing either. It is empty of existing in this impossible way. A deluded mind perceives objects and the contents of its cognition as equally permanent, existing from their side, and solid. It creates duality. Then it tends to cling onto those that give it pleasure, in both a sensory and mental way, and acquire abhorrence for those that are inimical to its hedonistic pursuits. This self-clinging and self-grasping are the root of all negative emotions such as anger, hatred, pride and so on. In its delusion, a being creates acts that leave an imprint on the mental continuum which ripen into their corresponding results of happiness and sorrow.

> This chronic disease of cherishing ourselves
> Is the cause giving rise to our unsought suffering.
> Perceiving this, we seek your blessings to blame, begrudge,
> And destroy the monstrous demon of selfishness.
>
> The mind that cherishes all mother beings and would secure them in bliss
> Is the gateway leading to infinite virtue.
> Seeing this, we seek your blessings to cherish these beings
> More than our lives, even should they rise up as our enemies. *

Lama Zopa teaches us that all results are equal to the cause— negative causes and conditions will produce negative results, as positive actions will produce happiness and joy. To be free of the suffering of samsara, one has to create those causes and conditions that will give us freedom from suffering and an abundance of happiness. But since all of creation is a seamless web, where all sentient beings are dependent on all others, an individual's

* *The Guru Puja*, Library of Tibetan Works and Archives, Dharamsala, p. 37.

happiness and liberation from suffering is possible only by wishing to free all of them from their suffering. Liberation is not possible by just an intellectual understanding but has to be practised through compassion and loving-kindness.

How wonderful it would be if all sentient beings were free of suffering and its cause.
May they be free of suffering and its cause.
I myself will free them from suffering and its cause.
Please, guru-deity, bless me to be able to do this.
How wonderful it would be if all sentient beings had happiness and the cause of happiness.
May they have happiness and its cause.
I myself will make them have happiness and its cause.
Please, guru-deity, grant me blessings to be able to so this.

How wonderful it would be if all sentient beings were never separated from the happiness of higher rebirth and liberation.
May they never be separated from these.
I myself will cause them never to be separated from these.
Please, guru-deity, grant me blessings to be able to do this.

How wonderful it would be if all sentient beings were to abide in equanimity.
Free of hatred and attachment.
May they abide in equanimity.
I myself will make them abide in equanimity.
Please, guru-deity, grant me blessings to be able to do this.[8]

On the Mahayana path to enlightenment, the seeker has to fly with both the wing of Wisdom and its method, which is Compassion. Trying to fly without these two wings would be an impossible endeavour.

The Lama is empty of all inherent and permanent existence. He is an aspect of the pure mind of enlightenment—the Buddha Mind. Wisdom may be grasped intellectually, but method has to be taught by one who has seen the path. That is why we pray:

*You are our Gurus; you are our Yidams; you are our
Dakinis and
Dharma Protectors.
From this moment until our Enlightenment, we need seek
no refuge
Other than you
In this life, the bardo and all future lives,
Hold us with your hook of compassion.
Free us from samsara and Nirvana's fears, grant all
attainments,
Be our unfailing friend and guard us from interferences.* *

1. *Praises to Shakyamuni Buddha*, Prayers for the Teachings of HHDL, Compiled and partially translated by Gelongpa Jampa Jamyang Choki.
2. *The Path to Tranquillity*, HHDL, compiled by Renuka Singh, Penguin, p. 161.
3. *The Path to Tranquillity*.
4. *The Path to Tranquillity*.
5. *The Gelug/Kagyu Tradition of Mahamudra*, HHDL & Alexander Berzin, Snow Lion Publications.
6. Ibid.
7. FPMT *Prayer Book*.
8. Ibid.

* Ibid. p. 19.

Path to Transformation

Karma Lekshe Tsomo

I have always been fascinated with the question, 'What happens to us after we die?' The ministers at the churches my family attended when I was a child had the usual stock answers, 'If you are good, you go to heaven. If you are bad, you go to hell.' Since I was quite naughty, this answer worried me. It scared me and also seemed simplistic. Are heaven and hell, good and evil, the only two alternatives? Aren't matters of life and death more complex than that? These questions have continued to intrigue me ever since.

To make problems more complicated, I grew up in the 1950s in Malibu and California surrounded by sun, sea and sand—surfing, exploring, and getting into mischief—which made the whole business of being philosophical very difficult indeed. In addition to asking my all-time favourite, 'What happens to us after we die?' I was curious about things like, 'If a God exists, why can't I see one?' 'Jesus told his followers to give up everything and follow him, so why are there millionaires at church?' and 'Why are people so unkind to each other?' My brother and I used to debate the question, 'How do we know that what I see and call "red" is the same as what you see and call "red"?' Only years later did we learn that my brother is colour-blind.

When I was about twelve, I became a Buddhist. The transition was very natural because although I was born and raised in the US, my German family name was Zenn. Like a birthright, my name led me directly to Buddhism. The children at school used to tease my brother and me, calling us 'Zen Buddhists,' so I went to the public library to find out what that meant. One day I opened a book called *The Way of Zen* and felt like a light bulb had been switched on in my head. For the first time, I learned about Amitabha, the Buddha of Infinite Light. Phrases like, 'life is defined by death' and 'motion is defined by stillness' leapt out of the pages toward me. My spiritual quest deepened with every page I turned. The ideas seemed to make perfect sense and gave reasonable answers to the many questions that had haunted me. To my mother's great distress I declared myself a Buddhist. In her fundamentalist interpretation of Christianity, everyone but Protestants was destined for hell.

Getting reliable information on Buddhism was very difficult in those days. Very few Buddhist teachers had arrived in the West, so there were no centres of learning that I could go to. By the age of nineteen, I was thoroughly disillusioned with the lifestyle of people in my prosperous community. I felt completely alienated from the college students of my age. My greatest joy was surfing, but the beaches were becoming crowded and many surfers were becoming competitive and aggressive. Around that time, I made friends with several Japanese-American surfers who I found were kind, loyal and generous. Eventually, I decided to drop out of college and began to work with the intention of saving money so that I could go to Japan to surf. Carrying my surfboard and little else, I took a ship from San Francisco to Yokohama and began surfing the waves of the sea in eastern Japan. When winter came and it was too cold to surf, I found my way to a small monastery on the outskirts of Tokyo and began meditating. The fragrant incense, deep quietude and the peace of the meditation hall filled the spiritual vacuum within me.

However, a million questions still plagued me but I was unable to find the right mentor. So I read voraciously. And after a year or so, I set out on a journey to India with the intention of combining adventure with spiritual quest. One night aboard the ship, somewhere between Saigon and Singapore, I dreamt that I was a being of light; I was clad in robes and surrounded by a wondrous spiritual community. The peace, luminescence and purity of that vision brought me great joy. Inspired by what I had seen, I wanted to become a monk, but alas, my gender was against me. It took many years for me to accept the idea of becoming a nun and still more years to examine why becoming a monk had sounded so much more attractive than becoming a nun.

For a year I travelled through Malaysia, Thailand, Cambodia, Nepal, India and Sri Lanka. In Nepal, I met Tibetans who had arrived from beyond the Himalayas. I learned the famous mantra, 'Om Mani Padme Hum,' which translates to, 'May I achieve enlightenment for the benefit of all beings.' In all the countries I travelled, I visited temples and met monks, but never found a monastery that welcomed women. Disappointed, I returned to study Japanese at the University of California at Berkeley, where I also took classes in Buddhism.

During the turbulent 1960s, I marched to protest the injustices of racism and war, and filled with idealism, I pledged to relieve the sufferings of the world. And then the Vietnam war broke out and I began to feel even more intensely the painful nature of human condition. This experience led me to realize that genuine compassion is the only worthy response to the sufferings of humanity. Watching the war played out in the media, I became disheartened with political solutions, which seemed heavily weighted towards the wealthy and powerful. Spiritual transformation seemed a better solution.

Then one day, while I was still at Berkeley, I found my way to the home of a Tibetan lama who had just arrived from India. Along with a group of other Americans, I studied Buddhism, learned Tibetan, went on picnics and did hundreds of full-length prostrations to purify my mind and create good karma. On a lark, I applied for an East-West Center grant to study at the

University of Hawaii and to my surprise, one fine day I found tickets to Honolulu in the mailbox. The grant gave me an opportunity to learn more about Buddhist philosophy and also to practise meditation at the local Zen centre. After completing a Master's degree in Asian Studies, I set off to Japan and India for higher studies. Eventually, I landed up in Dharamsala.

When I first arrived there in 1972, His Holiness the Dalai Lama and about 1,00,000 Tibetans were living as exiles in India and Nepal, having fled the Chinese invasion of their country. The Library of Tibetan Works and Archives had recently been constructed to preserve Tibetan literature and culture; it also offered courses on Buddhism in English. The very first day I entered the library, breathless from running down the mountain, I encountered a small lama wearing a pointed hat, sitting on a cushion at one end of the room. He was describing the stages of dying in elaborate detail, 'at the second stage of the dying process, you will see a faint smoke . . .' Here, I thought, was the perfect teacher. Hardly daring to believe my good fortune, I sat at his feet for five years, studying the classic texts of Indian Buddhism.

The people who studied at the library in those early days comprised a motley crew of aspiring scholars and spiritual seekers from many nations and backgrounds. The local Tibetans were surprised and somewhat amused that Westerners could sacrifice their comfortable lifestyles and live in such misery and poverty, but His Holiness has vision and compassionately arranged for us to study with some of the best Tibetan Buddhist scholars of the time. Many students and researchers from this pioneering group have since become famous translators and interpreters of Buddhism for the West.

Over the next five years, I made many journeys back and forth between India and the US. I would study in India as long as I could, then return to Honolulu to work and save money, then go back to India to continue my studies. These years were filled with countless blessings but also many difficulties. Western students in Dharamsala attended wonderful classes, met frequently with His Holiness, and received knowledge from many remarkable teachers. The sounds of ritual horns, drums, and chanting filled the crisp mountain air and we had plenty of time to practise what we had learnt. At the same time, we also struggled to get visas, to learn Tibetan, to cook over kerosene stoves in mud huts in impossible weather, and to survive many debilitating illnesses. When visa, health and money were exhausted, I had no choice but to return to the US to work. Along the way, I often halted in other Buddhist countries because it gave me an opportunity to discover the richness of their cultures.

Although all Buddhists accept certain fundamental teachings of the Buddha, the traditions of each country are markedly different. Based on the same basic set of Buddhist values and philosophical principles, each tradition has developed its unique cultural statement in response to different social and geographic conditions. Captivated by the beauty of the temples, the serenity of the Buddhas and friendliness of the people, I became totally committed to Buddhist thought and practice.

Since the 1960s, many spiritual seekers like me have made journeys to Asia. Although we came independently and had unique experiences, our quests have culminated in the successful planting of Buddhism in North American soil. For one thing, there was a remarkable degree of social and intellectual freedom which provided a fertile climate for religious and philosophical exploration. Universal education and new means of communication provided greater access to information, including books on Buddhism and other Asian traditions. Economic prosperity gave people more leisure to read and explore these traditions.

The prosperous 1960s led many thoughtful people to reflect that greater wealth and material happiness did not necessarily bring greater joy or inner peace. The American dream—with its three-bedroom house, a two-car garage and an avocado green washer/dryer combo thrown in for good measure—was not as exhilarating as many people had hoped. Families had become nuclear, moved away from the security offered by the extended family and community, and this often led to a profound sense of loneliness and alienation. As family structures began to change, women more than men began to question traditional gender expectations and reassess their human potential. Space exploration, artificial intelligence and new scientific technologies gave rise to new questions about what it means to be human. Seeing the earth from orbiting satellites gave us a new perspective and led many Americans to question their place in the universe. Some of us began to look in new directions for answers to the perennial questions of life. Buddhism offered some intriguing ideas and possibilities.

Experimentation with consciousness-altering substances also served to change perspective. For some, this experimentation led to substance abuse; for others, it led to an exploration of non-Western, especially Asian, systems of thought. Books like *Siddhartha, The Dharma Bums, Autobiography of a Yogi, The Way of the White Clouds, I Ching*, and *The Tibetan Book of the Dead* opened up new vistas of philosophical inquiry. Many people sought psychological help and spiritual guidance to cope with the accelerating pace of life and the horrors of war, the threat of nuclear destruction, the disintegration of family life, disillusionment with political institutions and other social changes.

While many people remained content with mainstream religions, others began exploring alternative traditions, Tai Chi, yoga and meditation. For some, the quest led to Buddhism.

A rich diversity of Buddhist traditions greeted these spiritual seekers: from Burma, Cambodia, China, Japan, Korea, Sri Lanka to Thailand, Tibet and Vietnam. The people who took up Buddhism were also a diverse lot, from many different ethnic and religious backgrounds: Christian, Jewish, Native American, African American, Asian American, Anglo-American, to name only a few. This diversity is a distinctive feature of Buddhism in the West.

The spread of Buddhism to North America was facilitated by immigration from Asia, beginning with the Chinese in the 1860s and the Japanese in the 1890s. Buddhist temples were established in California and Hawaii, and Buddhism became a headliner at the historic Parliament of World Religions held in Chicago in 1893. People who travelled to Asia and returned with Buddhist ideas and teachers also facilitated the transmission of Buddhism to the West. Mid-century, the work of writers such as Jack Kerouac and Gary Snyder resulted in an upsurge of interest in Eastern philosophy, while the work of teachers such as Shunryu Suzuki and Hsuan Hua resulted in the setting up of the Tassajara Monastery and the City of 10,000 Buddhas, the first monasteries in North America. With the advent of modern technology, information about Buddhism has spread quickly and left a deep impression on the popular consciousness, and made inroads into mainstream American culture through music, literature, film and advertising.

Buddhism's multiracial character may help explain its popularity in the West. Just as the US is composed of people from different religious, ethnic and socio-economic backgrounds, Buddhism is also a cloth of many colours. Buddhism teaches tolerance and understanding. Because of their different affinities and karma, people are inclined towards different religious ideals. The many different Buddhist traditions available in the West allow people to find a path that suits them the best.

Some Buddhist traditions are highly structured, while others have very little. Some are highly intellectual, others are mystical. Some practise many rituals, others have none. Some teach reliance on one's own inner resources, while others teach dependence on Kuan Yin or Amitabha Buddha. With such a rich variety of approaches to choose from, newcomers to Buddhism can select the one that best suits their needs and temperament.

Buddhist teachings fill a basic human need by addressing uncomfortable aspects of the human experience and proposing solutions. Buddhism offers practical methods for dealing with anxiety, depression, loneliness, anger and other sources of stress. The Buddha gave straightforward advice about how to cope with the sufferings brought on by sickness, impermanence and death—topics that are studiously avoided in Western cultures. Buddhist insight on these subjects has become more popular than ever, especially in light of the AIDS epidemic.

Another reason for Buddhism's increasing attractiveness is that it requires no adherence to dogma and is, therefore, compatible with logical reasoning. Blind faith is discouraged. The Buddha spoke from his own experience, and then enjoined his followers to verify his insights through their personal experience. He offered reasonable explanations to the big questions of life: Where do we come from? What is the purpose of life? Where do we go after death? Buddhists are free to adopt whatever teachings they find useful and encouraged to discover the meaning of life for themselves. For modern people educated in the scientific method, this empirical approach is refreshing.

It is not the custom for Buddhists to evangelize or recruit members. The wisdom is accessible to all, without charge or obligation. Practising Buddhism is more like a personal journey into one's mind. Looking for the right mentor or a spiritual home is like discovering one's spiritual affinities. A person who is interested in learning more about Buddhism has to make the effort to seek out a teacher or a community. The fact that Buddhism is 'low-key' and does not seek to convert is part of its appeal.

Buddhist methods for understanding the mind and dealing with conflicting emotions are growing in popularity and are beginning to have a major impact on the practice of psychology, counselling and psychotherapy. In fact, some consider Buddhism closer to psychology than to institutionalized religion. Because words and actions proceed from the mind, the Buddha suggested many methods to develop mindfulness and concentration. Mindfulness, the practice of cultivating awareness of every moment, helps us live keenly and fully in the moment. Mindfulness helps us create skilful actions rather than unskilful ones, creates causes for happiness rather than misery and dissatisfaction. Improving the quality of our actions ('karma') will help avoid unpleasantness now and in the future. Corporations, schools, and even the US military, are recognizing the benefits of mindfulness practice for controlling anger, reducing stress, and achieving mental health. The practice can also do a lot for interpersonal relationships.

Ethics is another aspect of Buddhist practice that is enormously attractive to a practitioner. Undoubtedly, there is a crisis of values in contemporary society about what constitutes moral integrity and what role society plays in upholding it. The Buddha laid out clearly reasoned guidelines for living, including upholding the universal values of honesty, integrity and kindness. Instead of divine retribution, his law of cause and effect talks about responsible human conduct to prevent suffering and promote happiness. These guidelines serve as ethical benchmarks to help one cultivate an integrity that will guide one in everyday life. The Buddha's moral integrity set the standard for principled, trouble-free living.

Buddhist meditation is a powerful means to achieve inner transformation. Faced with stressful modern living, many people have turned to meditation as an effective means of coping with their chaotic world. Buddhist meditation helps reduce stress by revealing the way the mind creates dissatisfaction and misery for itself. Turning away from distractions like shopping, entertainment, gossip, sports and, instead, turning inward to discover the nature of the mind itself, we soon see the tricks our mind plays on us by creating unrealistic desires and expectations that make us unhappy, tense and angry. The closer we pay attention, the better we understand the destructive cycle of desire and dissatisfaction. Unmasking the cyclical process of expectation and disappointment is crucial for achieving a peaceful and happy life.

Counselling and ritual are important aspects of Buddhism. In Western countries, many Buddhist monks, nuns, priests and teachers share their understanding of life in what works out as a formal or informal counselling relationship. The advice is sought to tackle all sorts of psychological, spiritual and emotional problems. In addition to counselling, Buddhist teachers may be asked to perform blessings, chants and other ritual practices. Thus, they function in a multidimensional capacity; they are community-oriented, adept at adopting culture to suit modern-day needs. Even in modern societies, seeking blessings and spiritual guidance have become part of meeting basic human needs, and Buddhists are often expected to fulfil them.

The burden of expectations that rests on Buddhist teachers—even ordinary nuns and monks—has raised questions about authority, authorization and qualifications. There are few fully qualified teachers of Buddhism in Asia and there is as yet little encouragement or support to train people in the West. What we do have in this part of the world are university courses on Buddhism without the practice component and Buddhist practice centres minus the education component; few programmes offer adequate courses for both studies and practice. What led me to India was my wish to pursue intensive studies in Buddhism and practice what I learnt in a conducive environment. Though centres are evolving and changes have occurred, I believe that nurturing a generation of fully qualified, indigenous teachers of Buddhism is the most pressing challenge for Buddhism in the West.

I have had Asian Buddhists tell me, 'You are so lucky to find Buddhism, since there is no religion in your country.' It is not true that Western people are godless, despite the way our culture is represented in the media. The US is still a deeply religious country, but tumultuous events in recent years have caused many people to explore new options, including Buddhist philosophy and meditation. Although sometimes belittled as 'feel-good Buddhists' or 'nightstand Buddhists' (because they read Buddhist books before dropping off to sleep), many people today draw spiritual nourishment and practical advice from the teachings of the Buddha, the Dalai Lama and Thich Nhat Hanh.

A passing interest in Buddhism is one thing, but a lifelong commitment to an Asian religious tradition is quite another. My family was distressed at my decision to become a nun, but when I returned to the US five years after I had been ordained, the reaction from the general public was even more striking. Devout Asian Buddhists seemed delighted to see a Western nun, but many ordinary folks appeared shocked. On the streets, children stared and adults gasped, 'Oh, my God!' Asian monks and nuns are usually tolerated since 'they don't know any better,' but a Caucasian who elects to follow a 'pagan' faith can elicit shock, fear or blatant disapproval. Twenty-five years later, I find people more accepting of Westerners in Buddhist robes.

In one sense, the commitment to a simple celibate lifestyle in itself implies a criticism of consumerism and worldly indulgence. But embracing the teachings of the Buddha does not necessarily mean rejecting the teachings of Jesus, since both faiths advocate the same ethics of compassion, peace and contemplation. My monastic lifestyle is not intended to criticize the lifestyle of others, but is my attempt to find meaning in life. In aspiring to live with honesty, generosity and kindness—values common to all religious traditions—I have created a cross-cultural spiritual identity that is a blend of East and West.

There were a good thirteen years between my actually wanting to become a nun and the time when I finally did. There were a million worldly preoccupations demanding my attention: education, career, relationships and varied interests. During those years I yearned to become a nun, I went from surfing to painting, poetry to tai chi, aikido and yoga to astrology. I found myself constantly struggling to juggle my spiritual life with these more worldly involvements and relationships, which were the most time-consuming of all.

Gradually, I realized that if I was ever to go below the surface, I would need to really concentrate on spiritual practice, and to do that, I had to simplify my life. It was impossible to be immersed in all these activities and also find time for meditation. I had never been too interested in starting a family or following a career, but I now recognized that spiritual practice ultimately meant putting worldly things aside. I began to devote more and more of my time and energy to cooking for visiting teachers and learning Tibetan. Gradually, everything but Dharma began to fall away.

In 1977, after simplifying my life to the bare essentials, I was finally ready to become a nun. Working as a Japanese interpreter in Honolulu, I saved enough money to live for two years in India so as to concentrate on Buddhist studies and practice. When I approached Gyalwa Karmapa in southern France to request ordination, he greeted me with the words, 'Ah! The cook from Hawaii!' He asked what I planned to do after ordination and I told him I would go to study in Dharamsala. 'Perfect,' he said. As his monks cut my hair and the long curly blond locks fell into my lap, I felt an indescribable joy and freedom. The next morning five of us—three monks and two nuns—were ordained in a simple, very beautiful ceremony. Before noon, I was back in the kitchen cooking for Gyalwa Karmapa.

From 1977, I studied at the Library of Tibetan Works and Archives in Dharamsala. In 1983, by a stroke of good fortune, I was admitted to the Institute of Buddhist Dialectics. This is a non-sectarian institute established by His Holiness the Dalai Lama that offers a traditional monastic curriculum, with classes in history, poetry, languages and debate. For a good part of the time I spent there, I was the only nun and the only Westerner, struggling to comprehend the voluminous Buddhist philosophical texts that were explained with the aid of equally hefty Tibetan commentaries. We would have impromptu debates on the nature of ordinary consciousness, the nature of enlightened awareness and the stages on the path to liberation.

As a solitary nun among eighty monks in a monastery, I began to recognize that other nuns living nearby did not enjoy the same opportunities for philosophical studies as the monks did. The traditional assumption has always been that nuns are more inclined towards contemplative practices while monks are more disposed to philosophy. When I talked with the nuns, I found that many were completely unlettered, especially those who had fled from Tibet. Some were content to recite prayers and mantras, but others, having dedicated their lives to Buddhist practice, were keen to learn more about the philosophy that sustained it.

I felt compelled to help these nuns realize their potential. In the beginning, it was not easy to convince them of their own abilities, nor was it easy to find teachers for them, but gradually there was an attempt to develop a series of study programmes for women in the Himalayan region. Despite the initial difficulties, fifteen years later, study programmes for women continue to multiply and the benefits of training women as teachers and community leaders have become obvious. In many Himalayan areas, women still lack literacy, yet there are many courageous nuns who have clearly demonstrated women's intellectual and leadership capabilities, dispelling centuries of preconceptions. The pioneering efforts of these nuns have confirmed my belief in the power women wield in social transformation.

One day I was bitten by a snake while looking for a place near Dharamsala to build a new school for the nuns. I clearly remember the ominous sensation my companion and I felt as we approached an overgrown tract. I had a sense of foreboding as I felt something fall directly onto my right shoulder from an overhanging branch. I immediately knew that a snake had bitten me; I became nauseous and disoriented and, on getting back to the monastery, I collapsed.

Over the next week, my right arm swelled with gangrene and my condition started to deteriorate. The local hospitals were not equipped to treat me and after eight days, a friend and her husband arranged for a taxi to drive us to Delhi that was over 500 kilometres away. This incident occurred at the height of the terrorist activity in Punjab; vehicles were prohibited from travelling through the area by night for fear of attack. The only way to go through Punjab after daybreak was to leave Dharamsala at midnight. The journey was agonizing. My arm was like a huge open sore and the taxi careened and ricocheted over the rough mountain roads, making the pain unbearable. We arrived in Delhi in the middle of peak hour traffic; it was very hot though it was monsoon. After a few days we realized that the hospital I had been admitted in was not a good one—in fact, it did eventually face charges of incompetence and mismanagement and had to close down operations. When it became clear that I would die for lack of treatment there, my friend arranged for an ambulance to take me to another hospital where the timely treatment saved my life.

My three-month stay in the hospital was tortuous. The nurses and doctors provided the best care they could, but none of them expected me to pull through. My chances became even dimmer because a malaria epidemic was raging at the time and I had mosquitoes buzzing around me all the time. The hospital staff had all contracted the disease. Then there was the fear of AIDS. Most hospitals did not have the means to test blood the way they do today and there I was, needing repeated transfusions.

I was lying in pain, uncertain whether I would survive the ordeal. It was a great lesson for me. I learnt first-hand the fragile nature of human condition; that death comes to us all is something I had accepted, but the suddenness with which it had loomed upon me taught me not to take anything, most of all life, for granted. I learned how utterly dependent we are on the kindness of others, whether it be a glass of water or blood from an absolute stranger.

An equally important lesson was the value of meditation. Years of meditation had trained my mind and prepared me to face death with dignity and clarity. Simultaneously, I became intensely aware of how difficult it is to control the mind while one is medicated or reeling in pain. I learnt that before facing death again, I would need even greater control over my mind. These months of suffering were a gift that shook me out of my complacency and awakened me to the reality of how precious life really is. Equally important, I developed boundless sympathy for the sufferings of the sick, dying, disabled and bereaved. When I teach Buddhism and talk about death, meditation or compassion now, these topics are not mere academics to me. On a very practical level, I now know through experience that the Buddha's teachings on the urgency of death, the value of cultivating the mind to prepare for it, and the inner joy produced by love and kindness are a fact, rooted in reality.

7

The Buddhist Way of Life
Dharmakirti

I grew up in Shangrila. This was the Himalayan kingdom of Sikkim in the 1970s, one of the last bastions of Mahayana Vajrayana Buddhism in the world. At that time, it was an 'independent' country, a 'protectorate' of India, and ruled by one of the last 'Dharma-rajas' (Tib: CHO-GYAL) of the Indian subcontinent—the last Chogyal Palden Thondup Namgyal. As a school-going teenager, I was witness to the demise of the Namgyal dynasty as the government of Indira Gandhi made short shrift of the Chogyal, deposing him and taking over Sikkim as the twenty-second state of India. I was also witness to the passing away of the 'Patriarch' of Dharma in Sikkim—the previous incarnation of the Karmapa-lama. With the demise of these two institutions, I saw the sun set on Dharma in that land; the degeneration and corruption that are part and parcel of the Indian system took over in the name of democracy and development.

It was undoubtedly due to my good karma from previous lives that despite being born into a Sikh family from Himachal Pradesh, my parents were progressive and 'secular' and did not impose the Sikh faith on me; and that even though not a Buddhist, I grew up surrounded by the symbols of the Dharma—monasteries, maroon-robed monks, monastic rituals, prayer-flags, 'lama-dances'; and then there was the Chogyal, a friend of my father's. I must thank my Tibetan-Buddhist karma that I grew up in the midst of Tibetans, as my father was, at that time, the principal of the Tibetan Refugee School in Gangtok. Thanks to my powerful karmic link with the Buddhist Deity MANJUSHREE, at the age of eleven, I received his mantra from a roguish Tibetan boy called Tamding, who was the son of the Tibetan Machen-la (cook). This is how it happened.

In the winter of 1970, my father decided to take a group of Tibetan students on a pilgrimage tour to Bodhgaya and some other neighbouring holy sites. He managed to wangle a government grant and, with the intention of providing some pocket money to the students, he got his friend Bill Dickson, the Scot manager of the government tea estate in Kewzing, to hire the group as daily-wagers on the estate for a month. I too was part of this group. We were put up in tin-shed dormitories where we slept on the ground. I was mortally afraid of the dark, and every time I wanted to pee in the middle of the night, I used to wake up my 'caretaker', the cook's son Tamding, to accompany me outside.

He bore with me for a few days but then one night as I poked him in the ribs, he sat up and looking gravely at me, said he was going to teach me a very powerful secret mantra that would protect me from all fears, all fearful THINGS. My ears perked up. I trusted him because he was older and because his father, the cook, was a part-time Tibetan sorcerer who occasionally held public performances of his sorcery-dance. He would wear a strange skirt made of long strings that hung from a belt fastened around his waist. The strings were held down with small black weights that were tied to their ends. He would tap his foot to the beat of his hand drum and sing in a high cracking falsetto, go round and round, and jump so high into the air that we thought he would just take off or something. His skirt twirled and flared out, whirling like the propeller of a helicopter, his two pigtails also whooshing around like a couple of fans. So, a mantra from his son Tamding was to be taken seriously. Obviously, when he told me he had this special mantra, I was all ears. I remember clearly the words he intoned that night in the dorm at Kewzing in the light of a flickering kerosene lamp. The mantra was short and simple—OM-A-RA-PA-CHA-NA-DHIH. He made me repeat the words till I got it right and then imperiously commanded me in his strong baritone voice to go outside and pee fearlessly.

The command was almost hypnotic—his eyes prodded me to obey, and the pressure in my bladder told me I would not be able to delay the inevitable—that I did indeed rush outside and relieve myself, albeit not fearlessly, furiously chanting the mantra all the while. Thereafter, it became a nightly routine. The power of the mantra was such that it stayed with me and I began using it whenever I faced fear of any kind. One night, several months after we had returned from the trip, I was all alone at home when the house was plunged into darkness due to power failure. Instantly, I began chanting the mantra and that night a change came over me. There I was, all of twelve years, walking down the pitch-black road to an isolated Buddhist cremation ground that was a kilometre from my place. I sat awhile in that cylindrical crematorium, continuously chanting the mantra. I felt as if I had been bathed in a faint, calming luminous light as I sat there. Maybe it was the moonlight. But I became quite a daredevil after that.

Fifteen years later, when His Holiness the Dalai Lama accepted me as a disciple, the first thing he asked me to do as the beginning of my 'practice' was the Guru-yoga of Arya Manjushree, which involved visualizing the Deity and reciting the mantra—OM-A-RA-PA-CHA-NA-DHIH—6,00,000 times.

Manjushree, is the first name of His Holiness.

I have lived my life in the backdrop of Tibetan Buddhism. And it was undoubtedly due to the blessings of the Great Guru Manjushree that this religion took centre stage when, at the age of twenty-four, I encountered, head-on, the Prasangika Madhyamika system of Arya Nagarjuna, which is the heart of Manjushree, and the philosophical core of the Buddha-dharma.

When I was studying biochemistry in college, I realized that science had no understanding of the human mind. It did not even address the problem of consciousness. Science often confuses the idea of consciousness with a study of the brain and they are just not the same things. An analytical subject, it limits itself strictly to whatever is quantifiable and in doing so, naturally excludes the realm of consciousness—that quality of the brain that makes it essentially an observer. In fact, in its confused philosophical underpinnings, it tried to reduce (the 'reductionist' approach) consciousness to matter—claiming that it was an 'epiphenomenon' of highly organized matter. Through my experiences and observations, I began to realize that consciousness could not be reduced to matter.

Through a series of unexpected and terrifying encounters with the supernatural, I became convinced that there was more to mind than matter. That there is more to this world than met the scientific eye.

Then one day, my father pointed out the philosophical inconsistencies in my scientific world view when we were in the middle of a dialectical debate. Our arguments usually lasted well into the night and, at the end of this particular session, he sort of 'called me aside' and admonished me not to piddle around but to seek out the Buddhist doctrine of Emptiness. He did not explain himself further, leaving me nonplussed. A week later, he suddenly died. He was forty-nine.

Devastated by his death, I began seeking out the doctrine of Emptiness as if my life depended on it. I found it tucked away in a book that I chanced upon in a bookstore in New York. It had an exquisite line drawing of Arya Manjushree and contained a definitive modern English translation of the Prasangika Madhyamika system of Buddhist philosophy as practised by the Geluk-pa school of Tibetan Buddhism. That was it. Over a period of two years, I studied this book intensely, during which time I gradually divested myself of all entanglements. When I was twenty-seven, I found my way back to the lotus feet of my guru— the head of Tibetan Buddhism, Gyalwa Tenzing Gyatso—the fourteenth Dalai Lama.

Having gained a clear intellectual understanding of the profound doctrine of Emptiness, I realized that it was imperative that I now follow through on my discovery with meditation, the only process that could lead to a complete, direct, 'non-dual' realization of the profound Emptiness. It was with the intention of receiving instruction on the meditative techniques that I sought out the Great Guru, who immediately recognized my need and proceeded to give me the necessary instruction in a structured manner.

Thereafter, the cultivation of these extremely tough meditative states became the sole focus of my life. My life became profoundly meaningful; I now had a direction and a definite great goal in my life.

In order to comprehend the future impact of Buddhism on global society, one should examine its historical record. It did not conquer by the sword, and it did not remain a practically confined religion; its aim was not subjugation and economic exploitation or slavery of 'other' people. Its spread all over Asia was entirely peaceful and it brought peace in its wake, even in ancient civilizations like China. That it was able to 'subdue' without military might even people like the Mongolians and Tibetans and the so-called 'rakshasas' of Lanka, transforming them into peaceful gentle people, is an indication of its profound spiritual power. The third Dalai Lama—a peaceful Buddhist bhikshu—actually brought the Mongol Khan to his knees in reverence. The Chinese Emperor, Chien Lung, accepted the fifth Dalai Lama as his guru. The Tibetan Lama, Chogyal Phakpa initiated Kublai Khan into the Hevajra Tantra.

The reason why Buddhism spread far and wide in the past and why it continues to win people over today, especially in developed countries, is because, unlike other religions, it is based on a rational, analytical investigation of reality and not on belief in seemingly impossible miracles. Its analytical philosophy has tremendous appeal. The first disciples of the Buddha were brahmins who could easily comprehend the extremely subtle philosophical view that the Buddha advanced. It is this philosophy that forms the framework for the meditative path. Even Adi Shankara, who outwardly did everything to suppress Buddhism, borrowed heavily from its philosophy, so much so that even his peers called him a closet Buddhist.

The Western mind took a little longer to catch on. It took the philosophies of such luminaries as Nietzsche, Wittgenstien, Eliot, Jung and the existentialists, to get them to develop a sufficiently sophisticated conceptual vocabulary to contain the profound Dharma. Buddhism appeals specially to the scientific mind because without entering into any conflict with scientific theory on matter, it deals with the mind—a subject about which science continues to be clueless; it goes beyond mere scientific knowledge when it comes to the topic of the ultimate nature of reality, the reality that is accessible only through meditation. There is no god to confuse issues because Buddhism places the individual in the centre of his or her universe by making the individual completely responsible for his or her condition. Furthermore, not only are you wholly responsible for the *world* that you experience, but you are also totally competent to transform yourself into a perfect being, who, by completely transcending the cycle of birth–death–rebirth, is able to guide other beings through their continuum of lives, and thereby bring them the ultimate benefit of the same transcendence.

8

The Human Mind
Lama Thubten Yeshe

The subject of mind is not the exclusive domain of lamas; it concerns all living beings. When I talk about mind, I'm not only talking about mine; I'm talking about yours as well. If your mind has an implicit faith or belief that happiness comes from material things alone, and your life is dedicated to these, you are suffering from a misconception. This attitude of mind is not simply an intellectual thing. Your immediate reaction will be, 'Oh no! I don't have that kind of mind; I don't have total faith in material things.' But if you check deeper within your psychological mirror, you will find that within you there is such a belief, and that it manifests itself in your daily activities. You must check for this. If you are bound by faith in the external world, my interpretation is that you have a narrow mind: without space, sick and unhealthy. In Buddhist terminology, this narrow, limited mind is called 'dualistic.'

In the West, the authorities are so afraid of people doing unusual things, like taking drugs. But interest in taking drugs comes from the mind—that's the very first thing; it doesn't come from the drug itself. Hence, the authorities' psychology is strange: they don't worry about the influx of polluted ideas and wrong philosophies that drive people crazy, but they worry so much about the entry of drugs and things like that. Misconceptions that disturb people's minds cause a country far more difficulties than a few people taking drugs. But because they don't know the nature of the mind, they can't see the polluted ideas and misconceptions entering the country; all they see are external phenomena. Drugs don't spread throughout the population, but wrong ideas can affect everybody so that the whole country has no peace. All that comes from the mind.

All mental problems, such as depression, come from the mind. Thus, we have to treat the mind itself, not interpret, 'Oh, you are unhappy—it's because you are weak. Better buy yourself a powerful car. Then you'll be happy.' That sort of advice is not very wise. The basic problem of dissatisfaction does not come from not having a car. Another patient has insomnia, 'I can't sleep.' 'Oh, you'd better take these pills.' Pills are no solution. You see, there's a big difference between Western Psychology and that of Lord Buddha.

The patient comes back to the psychiatrist, 'I bought a powerful car but I'm still unhappy.' 'Ah, you must have bought the wrong type of car. Buy a more expensive one, or at least paint the old one a different colour.' Again, the patient returns, 'I'm still unhappy'—and again the psychiatrist suggests some superficial change. Problems get sublimated but they never stop.

If a car is really a factor in producing agitation, Buddhist Psychology would prescribe giving it up altogether for a time and observing what happens to the problems then. This is much better than retaining the issues that cause agitation so that problems keep changing from one to another but never really go away. The patient thinks he is better, but he's not; one problem has simply changed into another. Thus, recognizing the nature of the mind is the most important thing.

We are human beings: we always want satisfaction. By knowing the nature of the mind, we can find internal—and possibly eternal—satisfaction. Knowing the nature of the mind is very important. That's why I say it's strange how we see things so clearly with our sense perception and give them our full attention, but are so unaware of our internal world—the wrong conceptions that run continuously, keeping us under the control of dissatisfaction and unhappiness. You don't know that? You have to know that; it is so important. Make sure you don't believe that external objects alone can satisfy you and make your life worthwhile. Such a belief is rooted deeply in your mind. Many things in our mind are deeper and stronger than those at the intellectual level.

Some of you might think, 'My way of thinking is not based on faith in material things; I have learned many religious philosophies and doctrines.' Simply learning a few theories doesn't make your mind spiritual. There are many Western professors of Buddhism, Hinduism and Christianity who can explain these philosophies intellectually but that doesn't make them spiritual people. They are just like tourist guides—they can take you through the ideas but they don't have the key to the philosophies they discuss; they don't know how to put them into effect, how to put them into experience, how to unify the philosophy with the mind. Thus, there is a big difference between talking about a spiritual path, putting it into experience and gaining the results.

So don't think that simply learning some philosophical theories makes you spiritual. A cup of tea is of more use than that. When you drink a cup of tea, at least it quenches your thirst, but a dry philosophy devoid of the key cannot support your mind and is no solution to anything. Learning it is a waste of time and energy.

'Spiritual' means searching for and investigating the nature of the spirit or mind. There is no outer spirit— the spirit is the mind. Those who correctly analyse the nature of the mind are spiritual: if they understand the actions of their body, speech and mind, their analysis has been effective. Those who do not have this understanding, waste whatever they have learned of philosophies and doctrines; it doesn't help them. One who has begun to know his mental attitudes and perceptions has entered the spiritual path.

If you are obsessed with atoms—the limited phenomena of

the external world—you will find it impossible to enjoy life; your mind becomes as limited as the objects to which it is attached. I'm not talking philosophy: external energy is limited; your mind gets caught up in it; your mind becomes narrow. When your mind is narrow, when you don't have an ocean-like mind, small things agitate you. Whenever religion is discussed, the subject of morality arises. What is morality? It is understanding the nature of the mind. Such wisdom automatically gives rise to positive action. That is morality. The basic nature of the narrow mind is ignorance or, in other words, negativity. When you know your psychology, your mind's nature, depression and so forth automatically disappear. All beings then become friends instead of enemies and strangers. The open mind accepts whatever comes; the narrow mind rejects it.

Just look at your mind to see how it is. Imagine that you had every pleasure in the universe: still you wouldn't be satisfied. True satisfaction comes from within you, not from without. Sometimes, we marvel at the progress in material and technological development. We think that things new to the world are so wonderful. But look at their nature. In America, for instance, many of these advances have turned upon their creators; instead of helping people, they are destroying them. Don't look only at your immediate environment—check as widely as you can. External energy offers limited benefits: it helps at first, but its nature is to degenerate, to destroy itself. This is the nature of the four elements: earth, water, fire and air. Your body shows the same thing; at first it grows, but eventually an imbalance of the elements destroys your life. This is because of their natural limitations. When their power to cooperate has dissipated, they fall into conflict. Thus, our bodies age, get sick and die. Internally and externally, the limited nature of material substances is the same. This is not something you just have to believe; as long as you are born into a body of flesh and bone, it happens automatically, whether you believe it or not. This is the inevitable evolution of the body. But the human mind is capable of infinite development. If you can discover, even a tiny bit, that satisfaction derives from the mind, you will recognize its potential for unlimited development to everlasting fulfilment.

This is quite simple. You can ask yourself right now where the feeling of satisfaction lies. In your nose? Your eyes? Your head, your heart, your stomach? Where is it? In your hands, in your legs? It is in your mind! If you think it is in your brain, why is it not in your nose or your leg? When your leg hurts, do you say the pain is in your brain and not your leg? Anyway, every painful or pleasurable feeling is an expression of the mind.

We always say things like, 'I had a good time today.' That means that you have had the experience of a bad time before; thus, today's experience is called 'good.' If tonight's dinner is good, it means you've had a bad one before; without the experience of a bad dinner, it's impossible to have a good one—unless you have discovered the absolutely good or absolutely bad dinner. But it's impossible for food in your kitchen to be inherently good or inherently bad; these are just projections of the mind.

Likewise, 'I'm a good husband' or 'I'm a good wife' are simply expressions of the mind. One who says 'I'm bad' isn't necessarily bad, and one who says 'I'm good' isn't necessarily good. The man who says, 'I'm a good husband' may be saying it with incredible pride, his limited, inflated mind stuck in the external world. Although he says he's a good husband, perhaps his narrow mind is disturbed. That makes his wife's life very difficult, doesn't it? How can he be a good husband? Being a good husband does not depend on words but on attitude: creating a peaceful environment where he and his wife can understand and help each other and be happy together. All this depends on the mind and on understanding the psychology of human problems. On this basis, one can truly generate loving kindness for others. This is not simply an intellectual thing: one can talk for hours, months and years about loving kindness without it changing the mind one bit. I'm sure you've heard about loving kindness a hundred times, but perhaps your mind is completely the opposite. It is not simply philosophy and words; if you know how the mind functions, your attitude can become loving, kind and spiritual. Just holding the notion that we are spiritual—believing it like a man believes he is a good husband—may be simply make-believe.

To make your precious human life worthwhile, control the continual confusion of your mad elephant mind and direct your powerful mental energy into satisfied enjoyment. Be as wise with your mind as you possibly can.

The way we live and think—everything is dedicated to the pleasure of the senses. We consider material objects to be of utmost importance and materialistically devote ourselves to whatever makes us happy, famous and popular. Even though all this comes from our mind, we are so totally preoccupied by the external objects themselves that we never look within, we never question what makes them so interesting. However, this mind is an inseparable part of us; as long as we exist, our mind is there within us. Thus, we are always up and down; it is not our body that goes up and down, it is our mind—the mind whose way of functioning we do not understand. Therefore, sometimes you have to examine yourself; not just your body but your mind: which is the thing that is telling you what to do. You have to know your own psychology or in religious terminology, perhaps, your inner nature. But no matter what you call it, you have to know your mind.

Don't think that examining and knowing the nature of your mind is only an Eastern trip. That's a wrong conception; it's not an Eastern trip, it's your trip. How can you separate your body, or the picture you have of yourself, from your mind? You can't say, 'I have the material power to separate my body from my mind.' That's impossible. You think you are free—a free person in the world, enjoying everything. That's what you think, but you are not free. I'm not saying that you are under the control of someone else; it's your own mind, your own attachment, your own uncontrolled mind that you are oppressed by. If you can discover how it oppresses you, the uncontrolled mind will disappear automatically. Thus, knowing your mind is the solution for your mental problems.

One day the world is so beautiful; the next day it is so bad. How can you say that? Scientifically, it's impossible for the world to change radically like that. It's simply your mind that makes this happen. Don't think that this is religious dogma; your going up and down is not religious dogma. I'm not talking about religion; I'm talking about the way you lead your daily life, which sends you up and down. The people and the environment don't change radically; the changes are in your mind. Surely, you can understand that—it's so simple.

Similarly, one person thinks that the world is beautiful and people are wonderful and kind, but another thinks that everything and everyone is horrible. Who is right? How do you explain that scientifically? It's just their minds' projection of the sense world. Hence, you feel, 'Today is like this, tomorrow is like that; this man is like this; that woman is like that.' But where is the absolutely fixed, forever-beautiful woman? Who is the absolutely forever-handsome man? They are non-existent; they are simply creations of the mind.

Also, you should not expect material objects to satisfy you and make your life perfect; that too is impossible. How can you be satisfied by even vast amounts of material objects? How can you be satisfied by sleeping with hundreds of different people? It's impossible—satisfaction comes from the mind. Your dissatisfied mind wanting to keep changing from one person to another, from one trip to another, can never satisfy you. This is just your mind. So you see—if you don't know your psychology, you might ignore what's going on in your mind until it breaks down and you go completely crazy. People go mad through lack of inner wisdom: the ability to examine their mind. They cannot explain themselves to themselves; they don't know how to talk to themselves. Thus, they are constantly preoccupied with external objects while their mind within is running down until it finally cracks. They are ignorant of their internal world: their minds are totally unified with ignorance instead of being awake and engaged in self-analysis. It is necessary to examine your mental attitudes and it is essential that you become your own psychologist.

You are intelligent: you know that material objects alone cannot bring you satisfaction. However, you don't need to embark on some emotional, religious trip to examine your mind. Some people think they do; they think that this kind of self-analysis is something spiritual or religious. To do this, it's not necessary to classify yourself as a follower of this or that philosophy or religion. But if you want to be happy, you do have to check the way you lead your life. For this, you don't need to put yourself into some religious category—your mind is your religion.

When you check your mind, you should not rationalize or push. Relax. Do not be upset when problems come—just be conscious of them and their origin, knowing their root. Introduce the problem to yourself, 'Here is this kind of problem. How has it become a problem? What kind of mind has made it a problem? What kind of mind feels that it's a problem?' This is so simple, and when you check thoroughly, the problem automatically disappears. That *is* simple, isn't it? For that to happen, you don't have to believe in something. Don't believe anything. All the same, you can't say, 'I don't believe I have a mind.' You can't reject your mind. You can say, 'I reject Eastern things'—I agree. But can you reject yourself? Can you reject your head, your nose? You can't reject your mind. Therefore, treat yourself wisely and try to discover the true source of satisfaction.

When you were young, you loved and craved chocolate and cake, and thought, 'When I'm old like my parents, I'll have all the chocolate and cake I want, and be happy.' You made that kind of decision. Now you have so much chocolate and cake, but you're bored; you don't like it. So you decide that since this doesn't make you happy, you'll get a car . . . a house . . . television . . . a husband or wife; then you'll be happy. So now you have everything, but there are more problems. The car is a problem; the house is a problem; the husband or wife is a problem; the children are a problem. You realize, 'Oh, this is not satisfaction.' Then, what is satisfaction? Go through all this mentally and check; it's very important. Examine your life from childhood to the present—meditate. This is meditation; analytical meditation. 'At that time my mind was like that . . . now my mind is like this . . . it has changed this way, that way . . .' You see—your mind has changed so many times but still you have not reached any conclusion as to what really makes you happy. My interpretation of this is that you are lost. I don't care that you know your way around the city, that you know how to get home, that you know where to buy chocolate; as far as I'm concerned, you're lost; you can't find your goal. Check honestly, you'll find that this is so.

Therefore, Lord Buddha is saying that you only have to know what you are, how you exist; that's all. You don't have to believe anything. Just understand your mind: how it works; how attachment and desire arise; how ignorance arises; where the emotions come from. It is sufficient to know the nature of all that; just that gives you so much happiness and peace. Your life changes completely; everything gets turned upside down; what you interpreted before as horrible, becomes beautiful. It's truly possible.

I'm sure that if I told you that all you were living for was chocolate and ice-cream, you'd think I was crazy. 'No, no, no,' your arrogant mind would say. But look deeper into your life's purpose. What are you here for? Gaining a good reputation? Collecting possessions? Trying to be beautiful? I'm not exaggerating—check for yourselves, then you'll see. Through thorough examination, you can realize that if your entire life is dedicated to seeking happiness through things like chocolate and ice-cream, there is no significance in your having been born human. Birds and dogs have the same kind of attitude to life. If you think you're intelligent, you should dedicate your life to goals higher than those of a chicken! I'm not deciding your life for you but you, check up. It's much better to have an integrated life than to live in mental disorder. Otherwise, your life is not worthwhile, not beneficial to yourself or others. Ask yourself what you are living for—for chocolate? For steak? Perhaps for education. But that comes from the mind. Without the mind, what is education, what is philosophy? A philosophy is somebody's way of thinking, his thoughts put together in a certain way. Without the mind, there's no philosophy, no doctrine, no university subjects. All these things are mind-made.

How can one check the mind? Just watch how your mind perceives or interprets any object that it contacts; what feeling—comfortable or uncomfortable—arises. Then you check, 'When I perceive this kind of view, this feeling arises; that emotion comes; I discriminate in such a way. Why?' That is how one should check the mind; that's all; it's very simple.

When you have checked your mind properly, you stop blaming others; you recognize that false actions come from your own defiled, deluded mind. When you are preoccupied with material, external objects, you always blame them and others for your problems. Then you become miserable because you project that view onto external phenomena instead of seeing their reality. So you can realize your view of false-conception—the attitude, or nature, of your mind.

You might think that this is all very new for you, but it's not. Whenever you are going to do anything, first check whether to do it or not and then make your decision. Since you do this already, I'm not telling you something new; the difference is that you are not doing it enough. You have to do more checking. This doesn't mean just sitting in some corner doing nothing—you can check your mind all the time: even while talking or working with other people. Also, you shouldn't think that examining the mind is something only for those who don't have a job or who are on an Eastern trip.

You should realize that the nature of the mind is different from that of the flesh and bone of this body. The mind is like a mirror, reflecting everything without discrimination. If you have understanding wisdom, you will control the sort of reflections you allow in your mind-mirror. If you totally ignore what is happening in your mind, it will reflect all kinds of garbage—things that make you psychologically ill.

Your checking wisdom should distinguish between reflections that are beneficial and those that bring psychological problems. Eventually, when you realize the nature of subject and object, all your problems will dissolve.

Some people think they are religious, but what is being religious? If you do not examine your nature, do not gain knowledge-wisdom, in what way are you religious? Just the *idea* that you are religious— 'I am a (something)'—does not help at all; it does not help you; it does not help others. If you have knowledge wisdom, you can really help others.

The greatest problems of mankind are psychological, not material. From birth to death, people are continuously under the control of their mental sufferings. Some people never keep a watch over their minds when things are going well, but when something goes wrong—an accident or some other terrible experience—they immediately say, 'God, please help me.' They call themselves religious but they're just joking. In happiness or sorrow, a serious practitioner maintains a constant awareness of God and his own nature. You're not being realistic or even remotely religious if you forget yourself when you are having a good time, surrounded by chocolate, and preoccupied with pleasures of the sense, and turn to God only when something awful happens. That doesn't help.

No matter which of the many world religions we consider, their interpretation of God or Buddha or whatever is simply words and mind; only these two. Therefore, words don't matter so much. What you have to realize is that everything—good and bad; all kinds of philosophies and doctrines—comes from the mind. The mind is very powerful; therefore it requires strong direction. A powerful jet needs a good pilot; your mind's pilot should be wisdom: understanding the nature of the mind. Then its powerful energy can be directed to benefit your life instead of being allowed to run uncontrollably like a mad elephant, destroying yourself and others.

Now, instead of talking more, perhaps I can answer some questions. You don't have to agree with what I have said; I'm not a dictator ordering you to do this or that. You have to know my attitude; I like people to contradict me, 'You said this—I think you're wrong.' I'm simply making suggestions; I'm satisfied if you just examine what I've said, and tell me if you disagree.

Q. *What are the aims of Buddhism—superconsciousness, nirvana, universal love, enlightenment? Which of these?*
A. All of them. Superconsciousness: the awakened state of mind. Nirvana: beyond wrong conceptions and mental agitation; everlasting, fully satisfied, integrated wisdom. Universal love: all beings are equal in wanting happiness and not wanting unhappiness, but our dualistic mind discriminates, for example, 'This is my close friend; I want to help him and not share him with others.' You understand what I mean. So, of course, universal love, which is beyond the narrow mind, is one of our aims. Enlightenment: the highest and ultimate goal. Thus, all Lord Buddha's teachings were given so that we could gain realizations such as these.

Q. *When you say 'everlasting' do you imply that the mind transcends the death of the physical body?*
A. Yes. And if you have wisdom, even if negative physical energy arises at the time of death, it can be transformed into wisdom.

Q. *Does generating universal love bring you to enlightenment, or do you first reach enlightenment and then generate it?*
A. First you generate universal love. Then your mind reaches the state of equilibrium, free from emphasizing 'this' and 'that.' The mind is balanced, beyond duality. Enlightenment follows.

Q. *Many religions claim that theirs is the only way to enlightenment. Does Buddhism recognize all these as having the same source?*

A. There can be absolute and relative answers to this question. I think that the various approaches to enlightenment proclaimed by different religions are helpful, even though some religions may be based on misconceptions. For example, some early Hindus of India 2,000 years ago believed that the sun and moon were God. Some still do. I think these are wrong conceptions, but still I say they are good. Why? Because even though the philosophy is wrong, at least those practitioners accept morality— that one should be a good human being and not harm others. Through following this, they may one day reach the point where they discover for themselves that their belief in external lights as God was wrong. Mental development is gradual; you can't change the mind suddenly, like you can the colour of cloth by dyeing it. A slow evolution purifies the mind of defilements; it takes time. Not all people are ready for such a broad concept as universal love, or the idea that you should care for others just as they care for you. Many would say that's impossible. So others have to be approached according to the amount of space in their minds, and various religions can gradually bring a person up to the right view of perfect wisdom. Hence, different religions are necessary.

Q. *Why do we need a teacher to reach enlightenment?*

A. Why do you need a language teacher? To help you communicate. Like language, enlightenment is also a form of communication. Even if you go to buy a box of matches, you need language to communicate with the shopkeeper. This is the same sort of thing: you have no experience of the path to enlightenment in this life or the past, it's an entirely new experience, therefore you need someone to guide you, to make sure you are understanding correctly and not hallucinating.

Q. *Who taught the first teacher?*
A. Wisdom is the first teacher . . . but there is no beginning! Wisdom is universal wisdom.

Q. *How can we recognize our teacher?*
A. By using your wisdom and not following anyone blindly. Check as much as you can if the person is good for you or not. Don't grab a teacher like a hungry dog grabs meat. Check very carefully. As I said before, mental pollution, wrong conceptions, do a lot more harm than drugs. They waste your time and life and cause you many problems. Be wise.

Q. *Is it true that the mind can only take you so far on the spiritual path and that at some point, in order to go further, you have to give up your mind?*
A. How can you give up your mind? It's impossible! While you are a sentient being, you have a mind; when you are enlightened, you have a mind. Your mind runs continuously; you can't reject it intellectually, 'I don't want my mind.' It is stuck karmically to your body. If the mind were a material object, perhaps you could give it up, but it is not. Some intellectually spiritual people think that since they are bored with their mind, they can reject it. There's no way to reject the mind.

Q. *What is a dualistic mind?*
A. Since you were born, there have always been two things complicating your mind. That is duality. You have never found just a single thing. Whenever you see one thing—'this'—your mind automatically says, 'But what about *that*?' This innate tendency to compare things unbalances your mind. We call this sort of mind 'dualistic.'

Q. *How does one check the mind?*
A. As I said before: examine how you perceive and interpret

things; for example, your girlfriend. One morning you feel nice towards her; that same afternoon your feeling is foggy. Ask yourself why—has she changed radically in those few hours? No, she hasn't. Then, why has your feeling changed? This is how one should check; it's so simple.

Q. *What is a lama? What does the title mean?*
A. The Tibetan connotation of a lama is someone who is very well educated in the internal world; someone who is not preoccupied with the present as we are, but who knows the past and the future as well; who knows where he has come from and where he is going; and who has control over his mind and can give psychological treatment to others. We consider someone like that a lama.

Q. *Is there a Western equivalent?*
A. I'm not sure. Psychologists? Priests? A lama has realized the nature of his own mind and that of others. He has the perfect solution to mental problems. I'm not criticizing, but I don't think Western psychologists are that well qualified. I don't think they really know the nature of the mind or the basis of mental problems. Many times they give external interpretations of internal disorders—'When you were a child, your mother did this or that, therefore, you now have this neurosis.' I disagree with that sort of analysis. Of course, external factors can aggravate mental disorders, but they are only co-operative, not principal causes. Perhaps, Western doctors are afraid to give this type of interpretation. So I don't think psychologists are Western lamas. And priests? I have met many, and many are my friends. But they don't seem to deal too much in the here and now; they are not so concerned about everyday life and its problems from the practical point of view. They emphasize the religious aspects of God and faith, but people today are very sceptical about these matters and don't want to 'believe.' Therefore, they reject the methods of treatment by the priests.

Q. *Would you say something about karma, please?*
A. Karma? You are karma, that's all. It is very simple. Actually, 'karma' is a Sanskrit word that means cause and effect. For example, yesterday something had happened in your mind, today you feel the effect of that. Your life, your parents, your environment—these are all karmic results. Every day, all the time, whatever you do, within your mind is cause and result, cause and result, cause and result. As long as you have this body, observing the world of the sense, making discriminations of this and that, good and bad, your mind automatically creates.

Karma is not a philosophy—it is the Buddhist equivalent of Western science. It explains what makes your life: form, colour, feeling, sensation, discrimination and so forth. It explains what you are and the relationship of all this to your mind. Karma is the Buddhist scientific explanation of evolution: 'If this happens, that results.' So although karma is a Sanskrit word, what it actually comes down to is that you are karma, you are living within the confines of karma. Your energy is the result of previous energy and causes further reactions. Then that reacts again, and so mentally and physically, your life goes on. That is all karma.

Therefore, karma is not something that you have to believe in. Whether you believe in it or not, the innate nature of your body and mind causes you to cycle. Just as the four elements combined bring forth a spontaneous result in association with the environmental circumstances, so does your mind act and react in contact with the world of the sense. Last year, you enjoyed chocolate, but since then, you haven't been able to get any—you miss it so much through the memory of the previous experience. This reaction is karma: the previous experience is the cause; your present longing is the effect.

Q. *How can one recognize the true nature of the mind?*
A. To understand the true nature of the mind, you have to know the two truths: relative and absolute. When the mind has a correct sensory perception of the sense world, that way of knowing is the

relative truth. When your mind sees beyond the this-and-that of duality, when its view is unified, you see the absolute nature of the mind, totally pure. In our everyday mundane life's usual dealings with the sense world, there are always two things manifest. Two things always create problems. Even with children: one is okay, but put two together . . . you know what I mean. It's the same thing with the mind: we dualistically interpret the world through our five senses and feed this information to our mind. The mind grasps this view and automatically is in conflict and is agitated, a state which is completely the opposite of inner peace and freedom. When you reach beyond that, you experience the perfect, peaceful realization of the mind's absolute true nature. Yours is a very big question: I'm sure this small answer hasn't satisfied you. But it's an introduction; if you have some background, you can understand.

Q. *When you check your mind, does it always tell you the truth?*
A. No—sometimes your wrong conception answers. But you don't listen to that; you tell yourself, 'I'm not satisfied with the answer my mind has given me; I want a more truthful answer.' Then you check deeper. In this way, finally, the wisdom of your fundamental nature will emerge. It is good to question yourself. If you are a person who does that, as soon as a problem starts, the solution to it starts simultaneously. Those who don't question, don't get answers. But you shouldn't question in an emotional, hysterical way, 'What is that! What is that! I want to know this! I want to know that!' Instead, when a question comes, write it down. Sit there; think. The answer will come; it just takes time. Even if you don't get the answer today, post your written question on your wall. Sometimes, answers come through experiences. If your question is strong, the answer might come in a dream: WHAM! Why? Because wisdom is your basic nature. Don't think that you are totally, hopelessly ignorant; there are positive and negative sides to human nature.

Q. *What is the definition of a guru?*
A. A guru is one who can really show you the true nature of your mind and offers perfect treatment for your psychological problems. But one who doesn't know his own mind cannot know the minds of others and therefore cannot treat their problems correctly. He cannot possibly be a guru. Therefore, be careful. In the West, the problem of self-proclaimed gurus often arises. Anybody can say, 'I'm a guru; I'm a yogi. Come, I'll give you knowledge.' Young Westerners are very earnest, they easily take such people seriously and really believe they can teach them something. They are gullible and easily led astray. Easterners are much more sceptical than that because they have had much more experience with these things. You should relax, and check carefully.

Q. *Is it more difficult for Westerners to attain knowledge-wisdom, given the environmental distractions and pressures of the West?*
A. The gaining of knowledge-wisdom depends on the individual, not on where he comes from. It does not necessitate abandoning the material comforts of the Western environment. But you do have to develop a clear understanding that such objects are not the only thing in life. What makes them a problem is the grasping and attachment we have for them. The objects are not the problem. You can lead a wonderfully luxurious life but at the same time be completely detached from your surroundings. What is perfect is enjoying things without attachment. You can turn Western material development to your advantage; you can get things here very easily. Getting such things in the East often takes much time and effort and is often accompanied by much clinging and suffering. The problem is attachment—try to let go of your attachment while you have everything. You can still gain knowledge-wisdom.

9

Working with Emotions
Bhikshuni Thubten Chodron

People worldwide want to know how to work with their emotions—how to prevent being overwhelmed by painful ones and how to enrich the wholesome and loving ones. As a young person, I had no idea how to do this, and it was Buddhism's perspective on this that first attracted me. So I will begin with my journey leading to the Buddha's teachings, continue with the methods the Buddha recommended to work with emotions, and conclude with a few observations about the future of Buddhism.

I came to Buddhism rather unexpectedly, or so it may seem. As a child, I was curious about religion, and as a teenager, my mind teemed with spiritual questions: Why am I alive? What is the purpose of life? What happens after death? Why do people fight and kill each other if they want to live in peace? What does it mean to love others? Growing up in a Jewish family in a predominantly Christian suburb in the US, I asked my teachers and the religious leaders around me these questions. The answers that satisfied them nevertheless left me dry.

Studying history at university, I came to learn that during almost every generation, for hundreds of years, wars were fought in Europe in the name of God. Disillusionment with organized religion overcame me, for wasn't religion supposed to make people more peaceful and harmonious? In reaction, as a young person in the 1960s, I took part in some of the social protests of the times, as well as turned to the various distractions offered to my generation.

I graduated Phi Beta Kappa from UCLA and, after working for a year, travelled in Europe, North Africa, the Middle East and Asia. I wanted to learn about life through experiencing it instead of reading about it. After a year and a half, I had learned a lot, but still lacked understanding of the meaning of life. Nevertheless, feeling that the purpose of life must have to do with benefiting others, I returned to the US, taught elementary school in Los Angeles, and graduate studies in Education at USC.

One summer vacation, I saw a flyer about a meditation course taught by two Tibetan monks, Lama Thubten Yeshe and Zopa Rinpoche. One of the first things they said at the course was, 'You don't have to believe anything we say. You are intelligent people. Listen to the teachings; think about them logically; test them out in your own life experience. Use the teachings that help you in your life and leave those that don't make sense on the back-burner.'

'Whew,' I thought. 'Now, I'll listen.' If they had said they would tell us the Truth, I would have left. I liked Buddhism's open-minded approach and began to listen and to practise the teachings. As I did, I was surprised to find that what the Buddha taught over twenty-five centuries ago in ancient India applied to my modem American life. I wanted to learn more.

During a retreat after the course, I realized that if I neglected this opportunity to learn the Dharma—the Buddha's teachings—I would regret it at the end of my life, and dying with regret never appealed to me. Thus, instead of resuming my teaching post that autumn, I went to Kopan monastery, Lama and Rinpoche's monastery outside Kathmandu. My parents were hardly thrilled about their daughter again putting on a backpack to visit a Third World country. But for me, the spiritual urge was strong, and I had to follow it.

Once there, I attended the teachings that the lamas gave in broken English to the variety of Western travellers passing through

Nepal in the mid-1970s. In addition, I reflected on them, practised them as best I could, and participated in the community life at Kopan. After some months, I decided I wanted to become a nun. Why? I wanted to focus my life on spiritual development and knew that to do this effectively, I needed to direct my energies. Living while following vows provided that conducive lifestyle. In addition, as I reflected on the vows, I saw that I really didn't want to do the things they proscribed. Thus, the vows were a protection against acting upon my attachment, anger and ignorance—emotions and attitudes that Buddhism sees as the origin of our suffering and state of dissatisfaction. In addition, the vows helped me to clarify my ethical values and to live by them.

I requested Lama Yeshe for permission to ordain. He said yes, but asked me to wait. This waiting period, which lasted nearly a year and a half, was a wise move, for it helped me become clear about my motivation. I had to face the questions and challenges posed by my family and friends, which strengthened my motivation. In the spring of 1977, in Dharamsala, I was ordained by Kyabje Ling Rinpoche, the senior tutor of His Holiness the Dalai Lama.

What attracted me to Buddhism? I was taken by its ideas, perspectives, views and practices. In particular, the Buddha's teachings on how to work with emotions—how to subdue disturbing emotions and enhance positive ones—provided both logical framework and practical techniques with which I could work. What, then, is the Buddha's perspective on emotions?

Each of us wants to be happy and to avoid suffering. From a Buddhist viewpoint, our mind—specifically its attitudes, views, and emotions—are the primary factors contributing to our experience of happiness and pain. This view flies in the face of our usual perception of things. For example, most of us instinctively feel that happiness is 'out there' in an external person, place or object. We think, 'If only I lived in this house . . . had this career . . . married that person . . . moved to that place . . . bought this car, I'd be happy.' We are taught to be good consumers—not just of possessions, but of people, ideas, spirituality, and everything else as well—in our search for happiness. However, no matter what we have or how much we have, we are perpetually dissatisfied.

Similarly, we feel that our problems have been thrust upon us from outside. 'I have difficulties because my parents yelled at me, my boss is inconsistent, my children don't listen to me, the government is corrupt, others are selfish.' Thus, we devise wonderful advice for others to follow and believe that if they only did what we suggested, not only would our problems cease, but also the world would be a better place. Unfortunately, when we tell other people how they should change so that we can be happy, they don't appreciate our sagacious advice and instead tell us to mind our own business!

This innate world view that happiness and suffering come from external sources leads us to believe that if we could only make others and the world be what we wanted them to be, then we would be happy. Thus, we endeavour to rearrange the world and the people in it, gathering towards us those we consider happiness-producing and struggling to be free from those we think cause pain. Although we have tried to do this, no one has succeeded in making the external environment exactly what he or she wants it to be. Even in those occasional situations in which we are able to arrange external people and things to be what we want, they don't remain that way for long. Or, they aren't as good as we thought they would be and we are left feeling disappointed and disillusioned. In effect, the supposed path to happiness through external things and people is doomed from the start because no matter how powerful, wealthy, popular or respected someone is, he or she is unable to control all external conditions.

This supposed path to happiness is also doomed because even if we could control external factors, we would still not feel fulfilled and satisfied. Why? Because the source of true happiness lies in our mind and heart, not in possessions, actions of others, praise, reputation, and so forth. But we must examine this for ourselves, so the Buddha asked us to observe our experiences to see what causes happiness and what causes misery.

For example, we have all had the experience of waking up on the wrong side of the bed. Nothing in particular happened to cause us to be in a bad mood; we simply feel lousy. But, interestingly, just on those days we feel grumpy, we encounter so many uncooperative and rude people. Just on the day when we want to be left alone, so many obnoxious people descend upon us! Suddenly, the way our spouse smiles appears sarcastic, and our colleague's 'Good morning' seems manipulative. Even our pet dog no longer seems to love us! When our boss comments on our work, we take offense. When our friend reminds us to do something, we accuse him of being controlling. When someone turns in front of us on the road, it feels that person is deliberately provoking us.

Conversely, when we are in a good mood, even if our colleague gives us some negative feedback on a project, we can put it in perspective. When our professor asks us to redo a paper, we understand her reasons. When a friend tells us that he was offended by our words, we calmly explain ourselves and clear up the misunderstanding.

That our interpretations of events and responses to them change according to our mood says something important, doesn't it? It indicates that we are not innocent people experiencing an objectively real external world. Rather, our moods, perspectives and views play a role in our experiences. The environment and the people in it aren't objective entities that exist from their own side as this or that. Instead, together with them, our mind co-creates our experiences. Thus, if we want to be happy and avoid suffering, we need to subdue our unrealistic and non-beneficial emotions and perspectives and enhance our positive ones.

Let's look at some of the methods the Buddha prescribed to transform specific emotions. Reflection on impermanence and the unpleasant aspect of a person or thing counteracts attachment.

Cultivating patience and love opposes anger, and wisdom demolishes ignorance. Thinking about a difficult topic or reflecting that all we know and have comes from others eliminates pride. Rejoicing prevents jealousy. Following the breath diminishes doubt. Contemplating our precious human life dispels depression, while meditating on compassion counteracts low self-esteem.

Reflection on Impermanence and Unpleasant Aspects Counteracts Attachment

When our mind is under the influence of attachment, we cling to people, things or circumstances, thinking that they have the power to bring us happiness. However, since these things are transient— their very nature is to change moment by moment—they are not safe objects to rely on for long-term happiness. When we remember that our possessions do not last forever and our money does not go on to the next life with us, then the false expectations we project upon them evaporate, and we are able to cultivate a healthy relationship with them. If we contemplate that we cannot always remain with our friends and relatives, we will appreciate them more while we are together and be more accepting of our eventual separation.

Contemplating the unpleasant aspect of things we are attached to also cuts false expectation and enables us to have a more balanced attitude towards them. For example, when we have a car, we will definitely have car trouble. Therefore, no benefit comes from getting too excited about having a new car, and no great catastrophe has occurred if we can't get a car. If we have a relationship, we will undoubtedly have relationship problems. When we first fall in love, we believe that the other person will be everything we want. This skewed view sets us up for suffering when we realize that he or she isn't. In fact, no one can be everything we want because we are not consistent in what we want! This simple process of being more realistic cuts attachment, enabling us to be more happy.

Cultivating Patience and Love Opposes Anger

Having exaggerated certain negative aspects of a person, thing, idea or place, we become angry and are unable to bear it. We want either to harm what we think is causing our unhappiness or to escape from it. Patience is the ability to bear harm or suffering. With it, our mind is calm, and we have the mental clarity to figure out a reasonable solution to the difficulty. One way to cultivate patience is by seeing the disturbing circumstance as an opportunity to grow. In this way, instead of focusing on what we don't like, we look inside and develop our resources and talents to be able to deal with it.

Seeing the situation from the perspective of others also facilitates patience. We ask ourselves, 'What are this person's needs and concerns? How does she see the situation?' In addition, we can ask ourselves what our buttons and sensitive points are. Instead of blaming the other person for pushing our buttons, we can work to free ourselves from them so that they cannot be pushed again.

Cultivating love—the wish for sentient beings, including ourselves, to have happiness and its causes—prevents as well as counteracts anger. We may wonder, 'Why should we wish those who have harmed us to be happy? Shouldn't they be punished for their wrongdoing?' People harm others because they are unhappy. If they were happy, they would not be doing whatever it is that we found objectionable, because people don't hurt others when they are content. Instead of seeking punishment or retaliation for harms done to us, let's wish others to be happy and thus free from whatever internal or external conditions precipitate their negative actions.

We cannot tell ourselves we must love someone; rather, we must actively cultivate this emotion. For example, sitting quietly, we begin by thinking and then feeling, 'May I be well and happy.' We spread this thought and feeling to dear ones, then to strangers, and to people we find disagreeable, threatening or disgusting, and say again and again to ourselves, 'May they be well and happy.' Finally, we open our heart and wish happiness and its causes to all living beings everywhere.

Thinking about Complex Topics and Recognizing Our Indebtedness to Others Eliminates Pride

When we are proud, we cannot learn or develop new, good qualities because we falsely believe we have attained all there is. When a Buddhist student becomes arrogant about his scholarship or practice, his teacher often instructs him to meditate on the twelve sources and eighteen elements. 'What are those?' people ask. That's the point—just hearing the names, let alone understanding their meaning, makes us realize we have a lot to learn and thus dispels arrogance.

When we are proud, we have a strong feeling of self, as if whatever qualities we are proud about are inherently ours. Reflecting that everything we know and have has come from others quickly dispels this arrogance. Any abilities due to genetics came from our ancestors; our knowledge came from our teachers. Even our artistic, musical or athletic abilities would not have surfaced had it not been due to the kindness of parents and teachers who encouraged and taught us. Our socio-economic status is due to others who gave us money. Even if they gave it to us in the form of a pay-cheque, it was not ours to begin with. Our education came from others. Even our ability to tie our shoelaces came from those who taught us. Looking at our lives in this way, we are indebted to the kindness of others. We have much to be grateful for and nothing to be arrogant about.

Rejoicing Dispels Jealousy

The jealous mind cannot endure the happiness of others and wishes that happiness for itself. Although we want to be happy, jealousy is a painful emotion, and we are miserable when we are under its influence. Rejoicing, on the other hand, celebrates goodness. We always say, 'May everyone be happy,' so when someone is, we might as well rejoice in it, especially if we didn't even have to make any effort to bring it about.

We may start by rejoicing in the happiness we already have, enabling us to realize that we are not completely bereft of joy even though we may not have what we want at the time. Then we focus on the goodness and happiness of others and rejoice in them. While this initially may seem uncomfortable due to the force of jealousy, if we persist in recounting the goodness and happiness of others, our mind will, in time, become joyful. 'Isn't it wonderful that Susan excels in sports? How great that Peter was promoted and that Karen got a new car! Bill and Barbara have a caring relationship; I'm happy for them. Jane's meditations are going well, and Sam has a lot of contact with his spiritual mentor. That's great.'

Thinking positive thoughts in this way automatically makes our mind happy. It shifts our perspective from focusing on what we don't have to the richness in the world.

Following the Breath Diminishes Doubt and Anxiety

When our mind is turbulent, spinning in doubt or anxiously imagining worse case scenarios, the Buddha recommended that we focus our attention on the breath. Sitting comfortably, we breathe normally and naturally. We place our attention either at the nostrils, feeling the touch of the breath on our upper lip and on the nostrils as it passes in and out, or at the belly, being aware of the rise and fall of our abdomen as we inhale and exhale. Should our attention shift to doubts and anxious thoughts, we recognize this and then patiently but firmly bring our focus back to the breath. By doing this continuously, the runaway thoughts begin to calm down, and the mind becomes clear and calm.

Contemplating Our Precious Human Life Dispels Depression
Often, we take our opportunities and fortune for granted and instead focus on what we lack. This is tantamount to ignoring all the delicious food in a large buffet and complaining, 'There is no spaghetti.' Instead of becoming depressed because we are ill, we can remember that we are fortunate to have others who help us when we don't feel well. Even if they don't help us as much as we would like to, they still are there for us, and we would be hard put if they weren't. Something is always going well in our lives, and it's important to remember those things that are.

In addition, we have human intelligence and the opportunity to encounter a spiritual path. This opportunity in itself is cause for great rejoicing. No matter if we are sick, lonely, imprisoned, or going through hard times financially, we still can take refuge in the Three Jewels—the Buddhas, Dharma and Sangha. We can practise our spiritual tradition no matter where we are, who we're with, or what the state of our physical body is, for genuine spiritual practice does not depend on certain external implements or actions but involves redirecting our mind towards constructive emotions and realistic attitudes. Thus, for as long as we are alive, we can be happy about what is going right in our lives and at the opportunities we have for spiritual practice. Even when the time comes to die, we can rejoice at a life well-spent and dedicate all the goodness we created for the benefit of all sentient beings.

Meditating on Compassion and on Our Buddha Nature Counteracts Guilt and Low Self-esteem

When we suffer from guilt and low self-esteem, we concentrate all attention on ourselves. There is little space in our mind for thoughts of others, and everything related to ourselves is overblown. Guilt is an inverted feeling of self-importance, 'I'm the worst one in the world, unforgivable,' or 'I'm so powerful that I can make all these things go wrong.' This is totally unrealistic.

Compassion is the wish for sentient beings, including ourselves, to be free of suffering and its causes. Meditating on it works in two ways. First, we think, 'I am a sentient being, worthy of happiness and freedom from pain, just like everyone else. I have the Buddha nature—the underlying purity of mind—just as all living beings do. Therefore, I can wish myself to be happy and to be free of suffering, and I know that these are achievable goals because the basic nature of my mind and heart are pure. The clouds that cover them can be dispelled.' Thinking in this way helps overcome depression.

In addition, spreading our love and compassion out to others alleviates the pain of the self-preoccupation lying behind guilt and low self-esteem. By taking the focus off ourselves, compassion enables us to realize that everyone is in the same position. Thinking of others and reaching out to them pulls us out of the isolation of guilt and low self-esteem.

Wisdom Demolishes Ignorance

From a Buddhist perspective, the ignorance misapprehending the nature of reality is the root of all other disturbing attitudes and negative emotions. To dispel it, we cultivate wisdom, which is of three types: the wisdoms of learning, thinking and meditating. First we must learn from qualified teachers, either by listening to talks or reading books. Then we think about what we have learned, examining it thoroughly to test it logically and to make sure we have understood it properly. Finally, we integrate the meanings of the teachings into our lives through meditation and continuous practice.

For example, we listen to teachings on profound reality, the emptiness of inherent existence. We read about and study these concepts, and then discuss them with our friends as well as think about them ourselves. When our understanding is correct and refined, we then familiarize ourselves with emptiness in meditation, first by investigating the nature of reality and then by focusing single-pointedly on it. When we arise from meditation, we try to hold this newfound meaning in mind as we go about our daily activities, so that this wisdom will be integrated into our mind and life.

Since all other disturbing attitudes and negative emotions are rooted in the ignorance misapprehending reality, developing this wisdom is a general antidote to all these. However, since cultivating the correct view is difficult, takes time and requires effort, we practise the antidotes explained earlier, which are unique to each particular emotion. By pacifying these emotions even a little, our mind becomes clearer and more tranquil, which makes the development of wisdom easier. For this reason, we learn not only the specific methods to counteract each disturbing attitude, but also wisdom as the antidote to all of them.

Our Responsibility

Subduing and transforming our mind is a process we alone must do. While we can pay someone to clean our house or fix our car, hiring someone to get rid of our negative emotions doesn't work. I can't ask you to sleep late so that I'll feel refreshed or to eat so my hunger will go away. Just as we must sleep and eat to experience their benefits, we must practise in order to let go of our harmful emotions and to nourish our constructive ones.

The Buddha's teachings explain many techniques for subduing our disturbing emotions and for cultivating positive ones. Just learning these techniques does not transform us. Reading a book with instructions on how to type does not give us the ability to sit down at a computer and type perfectly. We need to practise and train ourselves. In the same way, we must reflect on the techniques taught by the Buddha and then practise them consistently over a long period. The Tibetan word for meditation, *gom*, has the same root as the word meaning 'to familiarize.' Familiarization takes place with effort and over time. Similarly, we say we 'practise the Dharma,' meaning we train ourselves in certain attitudes and emotions over and over again. In short, there is no shortcut for transforming our mind.

However, since the disturbing attitudes and negative emotions are not the very nature of our mind and because they are based on misconceptions, they can be eliminated through cultivating realistic views and constructive emotions. Our mind and heart are a stable base for this transformation, and if we cultivate wisdom and compassion over time, they will increase infinitely. It is our responsibility, for our own as well as for the happiness of others, that we engage in the practice to do so.

Over a period of many centuries, Buddhism spread throughout Asia. Now, with modern transportation and communication facilities, it is quickly coming to Western nations. Nevertheless, it faces many challenges both in Asia and in the West.

In Asia, Buddhism is widely accepted, but not widely practised among its adherents. In some places people have neglected to learn the meaning of the ceremonies and rituals. In others, the religious hierarchy could be reinvigorated by broadening educational opportunities for nuns and laypeople. Buddhist institutions need to be more engaged in helping society.

In the West, Buddhism risks becoming another consumer good, tailored to suit the tastes of the public. The Buddha's teachings have always been a challenge to society and to our egos. We must be careful not to dilute their essential power in the name of spreading them to more people. In addition, we must abandon our hidden wishes for an 'instant fix' and be prepared and happy to practise for a long time. His Holiness the Dalai Lama says that one of the biggest hindrances for Westerners is the expectation to gain realizations quickly and easily. This attitude makes some people give up practice when their fanciful ideas are not actualized.

While Buddhism has much to offer in Asia and the rest of the world, the extent to which it is able to do so depends on the quality of its practitioners and teachers. Thus, we must try to improve our learning and practice as well as support others who are doing so. As individuals and as Buddhist institutions, we must take responsibility, create and maintain harmony, and look out for the common good.

10

The Reformist's Role
Vivek Kumar

An aspect of Buddhism which is of great interest to me is its revival and development among the Dalits in India. Dalits are referred by various names in the Indian society viz. Untouchables, Scheduled Castes, Harijans, Parayans, Adi-Dravida, and occupy the lowest position in the caste hierarchy—the hub of Hindu Social Order. Owing to their positioning in the social structure, Dalits have had to suffer 'cumulative deprivation'—social, economic, political, religious and so on. As this deprivation was legitimized by the sacred scriptures, Dalits could not challenge it and remained subjugated, exploited and isolated. But as time went by, they started waging a war for the amelioration of their condition. Though history testifies that Dalits have asserted their legitimate rights in different realms of society since time immemorial, I will restrict my narration to my experiences about the assertion of Dalits in the religious realm.

As a young Dalit, I grew up in the fold of Hinduism. Members of my family, though treated as untouchables, followed the practices of Hindu religion, and most of them still do so. They observed the same Hindu festivals and rituals as the so-called Upper *Caste* Hindus did and spent their time, money and energy on them. They took holy dips on different occasions in river Gomti, undeterred by the fact that it has been polluted to such an extent that even the Lucknow Water Works Department finds it hard to treat it. The social ceremonies from birth to death via marriage

saw a half-baked priest reciting *Sanskrit shlokas* incorrectly and
going scot-free, proving my family members' total submission
to, and blind faith in a process about which they knew nothing.
The lavish expenditure they incurred on these religious festivals
and ceremonies could easily incapacitate a rich man. But the
pathetic part is that this expenditure has become indispensable
among the Dalits. Come what may, they will have to spend it,
even if they have to borrow. And borrow at a higher rate of
interest.

The continuous cycle of festivals in India kept my relatives
and my family in perpetual debt. Caught in the debt trap, they
could never come out of their economic drudgery. They could
not accumulate any surplus capital to invest in the future of the
younger generation. I still remember, though faintly, the
'Brahmin-Bania' nexus—a proverb quite popular among the
literate Dalits who often blamed this nexus for their poverty. I
could not relate to it in those days, but now I can understand the
mechanism of Dalit exploitation. The *Bania* lends, and the
Brahmin legitimizes. The paradox of subjugation of my people
on the one hand, and exploitation on the other, within the system
started vexing me as I grew up. Gradually, I became disillusioned
with the Hindu Social Order.

I cannot state precisely when exactly I became a Buddhist but
it is certain that my education and the Dalit assertion in Uttar
Pradesh helped me gain an insight into Buddhism. As I grew up
and did my graduation, I started attending the small meetings
and talks organized by the Dalits. Each meeting started with
Buddh Vandana (Prayer of Buddha) *Tisaran* and *Panchshila,
Buddham Sarnam Gachhami, Dhammam Sarnam Gachhami,
Sangham Sarnam Gachhami* (I take refuge in Buddha; I take
refuge in the Dhamma; I take refuge in Sangha) . . . as a layman
I used to repeat the prayer, in the crowd, without knowing its
meaning. For long, I used to think that the prayer is in Hindi. I
later read in a book that the language of the prayer is Pali and
not Hindi. Another thing which attracted me to Buddhism was a

string of conversion ceremonies organized by Dalits in different parts of the country. I attended many of them, particularly in Uttar Pradesh. Gradually, I started reading more about it and learnt about the role of Iyothee Tass and Babasaheb Ambedkar in reviving the ancient religion of India and using it as an emancipatory tool for the Dalits. Buddhism became a natural choice for me as it was becoming increasingly popular among educated Dalits in contemporary Indian society.

Buddhism touched my life deeply when as a rebel, in my family, I married according to Buddhist rituals. My family and relatives witnessed such a ceremony for the first time in their lives and were amazed by the simplicity and minimal expenditure involved in it. The second incidence, which shocked them, was the funeral procession of my mother. In Hindu society, whenever a funeral procession starts, the people accompanying it chant *Ram Nam Satya Hai* (Ram's name is truth). But somewhere I had heard that according to Buddhist rituals, on such an occasion, people chant '*Buddham Sarnam Gachhami, Dhammam Sarnam Gachhami, Sangam Sarnam Gachhami*' (though still I have not referred any text for this). Therefore, I started chanting these words and so did the others. I do not claim that these practices of Buddhism have become established in my family and community, but I am sure they made many of them conscious about these elements being present in Buddhism. I came to know afterwards that many other people have also tried it. In this manner, a silent revolution is taking place among Dalits which is leading to the revival of Buddhism. But this revival of Buddhism in India has a history too.

The revival of Buddhism in India is synonymous with Ambedkar's conversion to Buddhism in 1956, which is misleading. Evidence proves that Buddhism was used by Dalits to enhance their self-esteem and change their identity in Tamil Nadu way back in 1898. Aloysius (1998) reports that Pandit Iyothee Thass (1845–1914) with other Dalits organized the *Sakya Buddhist Society* in Madras in 1898. Their decision to seek out and reclaim their lost religious identity was unambiguously aimed at moving Dalits from their present enslavement towards future emancipation. He narrates that in 1907, the society began a weekly newsmagazine to educate fellow Dalits. In this magazine, Buddhism was presented as the religion of the oppressed. Branches of the society were opened, initially, in Bangalore and the Kolar Gold Fields, and then elsewhere in northern Tamil Nadu. This movement spread primarily among urban Dalits and remained small. It rejected the rituals, beliefs and traditions of the Hindu caste system, which was guided by Brahminism. In its place, it propagated Buddhist ceremonies, weekly meetings and celebrations for the community. Right conduct was consistently upheld as the essence of religion, the goal of which was *mukti* or emancipation (Aloysious 1998: 134). This movement withered away because of the emergence of Dalit politics and the rigid British policies not to extend the facility of reservation to the Buddhist converts from Dalits. Moreover, this movement could not spread in other parts of the country. Though it is difficult to say at this point in time that this movement had any influence on Ambedkar or not, but it did play an important role in keeping Buddhism alive in India.

According to many Dalits, it is a myth that Babasaheb Ambedkar converted to Buddhism on 14 October 1956 in Nagpur along with *lakhs* of his followers. They argue that it is true that he took *deeksha* on the said date, but it was a happy homecoming for him because he always maintained that Dalits were originally Buddhists and because of their rivalry with Aryans, who practised *Brahminism*, they were forced to leave their original religion. In 1948, he published *The Untouchables: Who were They and Why They Became Untouchables* (Ambedkar 1990: 239–370). His book asserts that the Untouchables (now Dalits) were originally broken men, stray survivors of the indigenous tribes conquered by invading sedentary agriculturists, the Brahmans. These men came to live on the outskirts of villages as labourers for the conquering agriculturists. They were hated by the Brahmins in the villages because they were Buddhists, and Buddhism was antithetical to Brahmanic religion, which at that time practised cow sacrifice. When Brahmins saw that they were losing masses of non-Brahmins to Buddhism, which forbade the slaughtering of the cow but not meat-eating, they were forced to engage in one-upmanship to regain their leadership from the Buddhists.

They gave up meat eating, became vegetarians, and declared the cow sacred, which it was not to the Buddhists. Thereafter, the broken men became Untouchables. Because of their poverty, they were forced to eat carcasses of the now sacred cow and by doing so, they became polluted outcastes. In this way, we can say that Ambedkar identified the contemporary Dalits with the ancient Buddhists. Ambedkar also supplied the rationale for this identification. Lynch observes, 'The Untouchables, descendants of the Buddhists or broken men are the true autochthons, carriers of true and only valid Indian tradition. Their destiny then demands that they revive their cultural heritage and that they regain their ancestral patrimony' (Lynch 1974: 142). That is why, it is believed by the Dalits, that Ambedkar not only appealed to the Indian Dalits to convert to Buddhism, but also did so to the Sri Lankans as well. Keer writes, 'Ambedkar then addressed a meeting in the town hall at Colombo and appealed to Untouchables there to embrace Buddhism. He told them that there was no necessity of their having a separate organization. He also urged Buddhists in Ceylon (as Sri Lanka was known at that time) to accept the Depressed Classes in Ceylon and look after their interests with paternal care' (Keer 1990: 423).

In Ambedkar's article entitled 'Buddha and Future of his Religion' which he contributed to the Mahabodhi Society Journal, Ambedkar summarized his thoughts on Buddhism as follows: (1) The society must have either the sanction of law or the sanction of morality to hold it together. Without either, the society is sure to go to pieces. (2) Religion, if it is to function, must be in accordance with reason, which is another name of science. (3) It is not enough for religion to consist of a moral code, but its moral code must recognize the fundamental tenets of liberty, equality, and fraternity. (4) Religion must not sanctify or ennoble poverty (Keer 1990: 421). With this core thought on Buddhism, and foreseeing the future of the Dalits in it, Ambedkar declared that he would dedicate himself to the propagation of the Buddhist faith in India. And he succeeded in doing so when he got the chance. In this regard, Keer (1990: 481-2) argues, 'Ambedkar also declared that he would propagate Buddhism in India when equipped with proper means for the task. As maker of the Constitution, he had already achieved several things to that end. He described the provision for the study of *Pali* made in the Constitution, the inscription of a Buddhistic aphorism on the frontage of the imposing Rashtrapti Bhawan in New Delhi, and the acceptance of the Ashok Chakra by Bharat as her symbol, as personal achievements. Government of India had declared Buddha Jayanti a holiday mainly through his efforts . . . Besides, he had established two Colleges, one at Bombay and the other at Aurangabad, where about 3,400 students were studying and where he could encourage Buddhism.'

Last, but not the least, no one can forget Ambedkar's conversion along with his huge army of followers, which gave a fillip to the religious conversion to Buddhism later on and a jolt to everyone at the helm of affairs. To keep the Dalits and followers of Buddhism, he wrote a book named *Buddha and His Dhamma* and along with *Tisaran* and *Panchshila*, he added twenty-two oaths as the part of the prayer. These oaths embodied the total rejection and renunciation of Hinduism and the complete acceptance of the Buddhist creed. Since then, we can see that Buddhism has been spreading among Dalits in India, slowly but surely.

Since Ambedkar converted to Buddhism, more and more Dalits are being attracted towards this religion, shedding their previous religious faith. Today, according to a rough estimate, Buddhists number approximately seven million, that means in forty years i.e. since 1961, their population has doubled. *Bodh Viharas* of different shape and size have been established in different parts of the country. In 1960, especially in Agra, such was the enthusiasm among the Dalits that they converted twenty to twenty-two Hindu temples into Buddhist temples (Lynch 1974: 164). Today, their number is increasing day by day. Not only that, a number of organizations have mushroomed in the name of Buddha where Dalits come together and debate on various issues relating to Buddhism or the Dalit community. A noticeable feature of this conversion to Buddhism by the Dalits is that, except in the initial period when Babasaheb converted to Buddhism, it attracts more and more educated Dalits. This is in contrast to Hinduism and other religions in India where the illiterate masses are subsumed for salvation. It is also true that the conversion to Buddhism takes place without any allurement and force from any outside agency.

The impact of Buddhism has grown in the daily lives of Dalits. Today, even marriages are solemnized in accordance with the Buddhist rituals. The religious choice of Buddhism has become so overpowering that Dalits have broken the marriages of their daughters if the bridegroom's side has refused to comply with it. The portrait of Buddha has become a must among Dalits, whether it is a seminar or a birthday party or a marriage. In fact, garlanding the Buddha's statue or portrait and the recital of *Buddha Vandana* in the beginning of every programme has become an established ritual among Dalits. Further, you can find Buddha's idol in the drawing rooms of most of the literate or semi-literate Dalits. Soon after Ambedkar attained *Nirvana* on 6 December 1956, a fair is held every year on the day of Dussehra in the same venue where Ambedkar took *Deeksha* on 14 October 1956 along with lakhs of his followers in Nagpur, Maharashtra. The number of Dalits visiting this fair is increasing every year. Dalits—rich or poor, literate or illiterate—throng here in large numbers from different parts of the country.

Though Gokhale (1993: 187) eloquently portrays the impact of Buddhism on the Mahars of Maharashtra, but the same can easily be said about other sections of Dalits living in different parts of the country in order to understand its growing influence. According to her, 'The conversion thus has created a new set of symbols and myths and produced a new consciousness within the Mahar-Buddhist community. It has instilled a sense of pride and self-affirmation' among the former Mahars. They felt released from the tyranny of the caste-Hindus. They have acquired the *manuski* (humanity, self-worth), denied to them as Untouchables. This newfound sense of equality and dignity has had repercussions 'particularly in the villages.'

Similarly, Wilkinson (1972: 98), argues, 'Change of religion has liberated them (Mahars) from the stigma of untouchablity, thus enhancing their self-confidence to a great measure. Many of them explained that the economic benefit after conversion was mainly due to their giving up the rituals and ceremonies for which a considerable amount was spent. Not being burdened with all these conventional expenses, they could use the money thus saved for bettering their economic condition.' But this does not mean that after embracing Buddhism, Dalits have abandoned Hinduism completely. Yes, there are evidences where Dalits practise Hindu rituals along with Buddhism. It has only been forty-five years since Dalits started reasserting their faith which they were forced to abandon centuries ago. With time, they are shedding their Hindu rituals.

Significantly, the spread of Buddhism among Dalits has transcended national boundaries. In ancient India, King Ashoka, after the Kalinga war, sent his son, Mahendra, and daughter, Sanghmitra, to different parts of the world for spreading the message of Buddha. And since then, Buddhism has been flourishing in many Asian countries like China, Japan, Thailand, and South Korea, along with the Indian subcontinent. In the recent past, with the Dalit migration to different parts of the world, Buddhism has spread to other countries as well. One can observe a steady migration of trained Dalits to countries like the US, the UK, Canada, Malaysia and so on. They celebrate *Buddha* and *Ambedkar Jayanti* regularly in these countries. A Dalit non-resident

Indian emphasized that these rituals have inculcated solidarity among Dalits who have migrated. For example, in the UK, over one lakh and fifty thousand Dalits, approximately, celebrate *Buddha and Ambedkar Jayanti* (*www.ambedkar*.org). Similarly, after the 'First Dalit World Conference: A Vision Towards a Casteless Society' held in Malaysia on 10 October 1998, Dalits world-over feel that among the Dalits, Buddhism can be a uniting force.

Recently, in India, Lord Buddha Club is deeply involved in the conversion of Dalits to Buddhism. The club has organized a number of programmes of conversion throughout the country. This was an exercise to galvanize the Dalits at the grass-roots level and to prepare at least one million Dalits to convert to Buddhism on the famous Ramleela Ground at New Delhi in 2001. But it is stated that, because of the state intervention to avoid any collision, the ceremony could not take place on the scale propagated. But it is true that a few thousand did convert to Buddhism. Recently, Kanshi Ram, the president of Bahujan Samaj Party (BSP), the only party with a national stature led and dominated by Dalits, has announced that he will organize a 'Conversion Rally' to Buddhism in 2006.

This can be a significant event in the history of Buddhism because BSP has a substantial following in the country, especially in the northern part. And even if a small portion of its supporters convert to Buddhism, it would boost the numerical strength of Buddhists in the country. We can conclude that the future of Buddhism among Dalits in India is taking deep roots as time is passing by. On the basis of the above analysis, we can say that it will spread further, as the level of education, politicization, and consciousness among Dalits grows proportionately.

Importantly, the Dalits have made various efforts to enhance their social status. Three major strands can be seen in this regard. One, they took refuge in different religions by the process of conversion. They converted mainly to Islam, Christianity, Sikhism and Buddhism. Secondly, they tried to establish their independent religion with the plea that they were the original inhabitants of the Indian society and different from Hindus (Aryans). Hence, the Dalits launched a number of movements such as the Adi-Hindu, Adi-Dravid, Ada-Dharm in the first half of the twentieth century. Lastly, Dalits tried to develop their own sects in the name of Dalit Saints and declared themselves different from the Hindus. They called themselves *Raidasis* or *Ravidasis, Kabir Panthis* and *Satnamis*. But their sects were not considered outside the fold of Hindu social order and remained more or less within it. A striking feature about these efforts for the enhancement of social esteem by the Dalits is that conversion to Buddhism was chosen as the last resort. Despite this, it has come to stay among them and is spreading day by day. We hardly hear about Dalits converting to other religions and establishing new sects in India.

❖

Aloysius, G., 1998, *Religion as Emancipatory Identity: A Buddhist Movement among Tamils under Colonialism*, New Age International Publishers, New Delhi.

Ambedkar, B.R., 1990, 'The Untouchables: Who were They and Why They Became Untouchables', *Dr Babasaheb Ambedkar Writings and Speeches*, Vol. 7, Education Department, Government of Maharashtra, Bombay.

Gokhale, Jayashree, 1993, *From Concessions to Confrontation: The Politics of an Indian Untouchable Community*, Popular Prakashan, Bombay.

Keer, Dhananjay, 1990, *Dr Ambedkar: Life and Mission*, Popular Prakashan, Bombay.

Lynch, O.M., 1974, *The Politics of Untouchability: Social Mobility and Social Change in a City of India*, National Publishing House, New Delhi.

Wilkinson, T.S., 1972, Buddhism and Social Change among Mahars, in T.S. Wilkinson and M.M. Tomas (eds.) *Ambedkar and the Neo-Buddhist Movement*, Christian Literature Society, Madras.

11

Maitreya Project
Peter Kedge

I was raised a Christian in England. My family was involved in our church to the extent that it was the entire focus of our life, both spiritually and socially. I grew up going to church several times a day, singing as a choirboy at weddings and funerals several times a week, and later, ringing bells and organizing a youth club. Nevertheless, I never felt completely satisfied that all the inevitable questions about life, death, heaven and hell had been clearly or satisfactorily answered by those who raised me in the Christian faith. Later on, after training as an engineer, I travelled to the East not realizing it would turn my whole world upside down and change my life forever.

Only when I came in contact with Tibetan Buddhism did I begin to find answers. At a short meditation course, led by two Tibetan Lamas at Kopan Monastery in 1972, the many questions I had were answered precisely, logically and clearly. Moreover, the answers were substantiated by meditation techniques that I was told I had to experiment with in order to fully validate for myself the explanations that were being given. The experience was sufficiently satisfactory and profound so that my main interest in life became the study and practice of the Buddha's teachings as explained by the lamas who became my teachers.

There were two major factors I found very compelling about Tibetan Buddhism as it was presented by Lama Thubten Zopa

Rinpoche and Lama Thubten Yeshe. The first was the logic of it. There were no gaps. Then there was a well-structured process of meditation, which gave one the opportunity to validate what was being presented. The meditation was quite scientific. There were meditation exercises for developing concentration. The concentration was then used as a tool to analyse certain aspects of the mind, mental activity, one's behaviour, relationships and the nature of the mind itself.

Then, there was the admonition, which always came—'Don't accept this because I said so. Analyse it.' Doubt is positive if it is investigated and a conclusion is reached. Doubt is negative when it is allowed to fester.

Furthermore, and in a sense more importantly, is the concept of the unbroken lineage of the teachings. I found it extremely powerful that the lineage of oral tradition we were receiving had been unbroken since the time of Shakyamuni Buddha. Each time a teaching was given by a lama, it was prefaced by an introduction to the origin of that teaching. From the Buddha to his disciples and down to our teachers, who would pass this unbroken tradition to us.

The second important credential was the experiential lineage which is based on the oral lineage but represents the meditational experience that each teacher/disciple received before passing it on to their disciple. That leaves one with the responsibility of investigating any doubt, bringing it to a conclusion, and doing so through the meditational tools that had been presented.

Having trained as an engineer, the logic, method and process were very satisfactory. Very quickly, this led me to the conclusion that to investigate this further was critical. After some weeks of reflection, this appeared to be the only thing to do in my life and the perfect way to do that was as a monk with no concerns other than to study, to meditate, to seek and realize the truth. With my parents' blessing, this is what I did for seven years.

In time, as Dharma began to develop in the West, there seems to be a great need for organization and funding to help the many centres that were beginning to grow and develop in Europe, America and Asia. I found myself becoming involved in this process. I wanted to help share this very complete and satisfactory set of explanations and methods with others, and that idea began directing all my activities. I soon became fully immersed in the commercial world, developing and running a high-pressure business to try and generate funds for translating, publishing, organizing, facilitating and administering Dharma activities such as meditation courses, world tours for the lamas and so on.

Now thirty years later, I am privileged to be responsible for the development and execution of one of the world's most incredible projects. This great endeavour was initiated almost twenty years ago by the late Lama Thubten Yeshe, now reincarnated as a Spaniard, Osel Hita Rinpoche, whose wish was to build a large statue of Maitreya, the embodiment of loving-kindness and the next Buddha to appear in this world.

Over the years, Lama Yeshe's principal disciple, Lama Zopa Rinpoche, continued to develop the vision of what has become known as the Maitreya Project. The current plan is to build a 500-foot statue of Maitreya, the archetypal form representing the quintessentially important quality of loving-kindness. The statue will be a building housing prayer halls, shrine rooms and other facilities for pilgrims and visitors, and will be located in a beautifully landscaped park with circumambulation paths, stupas and statues. The project is being designed to last a thousand years. To date, the preliminary design is complete and a detailed design phase is soon to commence. It is expected that construction will begin in approximately twelve months with completion in five years.

It took me several months before I realized just what an extraordinary project it is. When Lama Zopa Rinpoche first asked me to work for the Maitreya Project in April 1997, I was on the verge of starting a new business. It was too far down the road to stop it at that point, so for the first few weeks, I agonized over how could I possibly manage both?

For that first year and a half, I ran the new business in London and simultaneously tried to come to terms with the financial and logistical challenges of the Maitreya Project. However, it became clear that the project had to take precedence. The vision and scope of the project had become all encompassing. So in January 1999 I decided to sell my interest in the business and focus all my efforts and energy on the Maitreya Project.

What makes working for Maitreya Project so compelling is that at the core of the project is loving-kindness. As embodied by Maitreya Buddha, this is the quintessential quality at the heart of all true religions. It is the only cause for inner peace. Peace can be brought about externally by various means such as disarmament, pacts, treaties and so on, but only temporally. Inner peace is the only true cause for lasting external peace.

Given the situation of our world today, I cannot think of any other way of working towards a lasting solution than to promote a culture of loving-kindness. I now live in a small rural community. It is such a delight. It is so harmonious and whether or not it is achievable on a global scale, it does not matter. The fact that it could work and that we believe it can work, must be sufficient for us to try and implement it to the extent possible, and Maitreya Project will go a long way in doing this. The project has the potential to bring about an enormous, meaningful and far-reaching change in people's thinking, promoting this quality of loving-kindness.

Initially, I was thinking only about a statue, and something from my Christian upbringing baulked at it. I was not especially enthusiastic. Gradually, as I have lived with, thought about and dreamed about the project, it has become clear that it is the most brilliantly conceived method to bring benefit to living beings.

There is nothing on this planet I would rather do. I cannot imagine a more powerful way to exert my efforts. I'm truly grateful for this enormous privilege.

The first task for the development of the project was to develop an understanding of how to construct such an enormous monument.

While researching it in travels around the world, meeting with engineers, architects and builders of other great statues and monuments, it became apparent that the challenge was tremendously exciting in terms of the technology required.

Then we conducted an economic impact study, and it became even clearer that the construction and then the operation of the Maitreya Project site, even in the near term, is going to have an enormously positive impact upon what is a desperately poor part of India.

A social work programme had to be fully integrated in the project as well. We investigated and identified the need for education and healthcare facilities, and as we began planning a school and a hospital, we realized that the potential for bringing relief to a situation where most cannot even afford education and healthcare was enormous.

Interestingly, even now, the Maitreya Project Universal Education School in Bodhgaya is helping to develop the minds of children of those who would otherwise have no opportunity to educate them in such a poor rural community.

Environmental considerations and impact studies showed us how the Maitreya Project could become a benchmark in sustainability and environmental protection.

As I became more and more familiar with the scope of this project, I could see a vast potential for every form of major benefit: spiritual, inspirational, medical, educational, economical and environmental.

From the beginning, we have made it one of our main concerns to adhere to the highest ethical principles in all our dealings: with employees, authorities, government, contractors and benefactors. Personally, I am confident that our way of dealing with everyone can only have a positive ripple effect on the entire region.

Maitreya Project is dedicated to sustainability—'Improving the quality of life of the present population without compromising the ability of future generations to achieve the same or higher quality of life' and environmental contribution—'No energy or natural resource-hungry installation will be provided where a passive solution exists.'

The purpose of the project is to benefit living beings in the most extensive possible way. To understand what 'the most extensive possible way' means, we have to understand something about Buddha's teachings on karma. Benefit in this context means benefit for living beings over many lifetimes—many lifetimes for which the project will remain and many lifetimes for individuals that come into contact with the project.

As to why Maitreya Project will bring benefit, one of the simplest reasons is that great monuments inspire. From my experience, I know that to be the case. With three friends, I drove from England to India in 1971. The journey took us about six months and, at one stage, we had driven through the night from Kabul in Afghanistan and were headed towards a place called Bandarimir. Not knowing where we were in the rugged countryside, we stopped in complete darkness, and pitched tents beside our Landrover. I still recall the exhilaration I felt that morning putting my head out of the tent and seeing the great Buddhist statues of Bamiyan carved into the cliff about a hundred metres from where we had unknowingly stopped. At that stage, I certainly was not a Buddhist. As we climbed through the great tunnels and passageways that were carved into the cliff and the statues, and through what at one stage had been part of a monastery, I recall being moved and inspired by what those statues represented.

There is no direct link between the Buddhas of Bamiyan and the Maitreya Project but just as those Buddhas inspired people for hundreds of years, so it is the wish of all who are involved in the Maitreya Project that this magnificent, contemporary, Buddhist cathedral building will last at least a thousand years. It is our intention that this will be a source of awe, inspiration and hope for a countless number of beings.

To some, religious monuments may almost seem like a

medieval phenomenon. There are few current religious monuments being built for the future. The Maitreya Project is one. In engineering terms, it will become one of the wonders of the world. Its beauty and the artistic statement that it will present will make it one of the major architectural wonders of the world. In terms of its symbolism, emphasizing as it does the crucial importance of loving–kindness in this world, it will verbalize the aspirations of millions around the world. Doing so will make a positive difference in the world.

The need for Maitreya Project to do this is most apparent in the current situation as the world order seems in danger from a part of the world where Buddhism at one time flourished. The great Buddhas of Bamiyan were a wonder of the world. The hatred, anger, misunderstanding and perversion of religious thought that resulted in their destruction, is a force that endangers the entire planet.

When we look at the holy places around the world, whether it be Lourdes or Mecca or Borobudur or the Lotus Temple in New Delhi, it is interesting to note that they attract such a huge number of people. I believe that most people want to have an enriching spiritual experience and the Maitreya Project is going to offer them that.

In a short time, I firmly believe the silhouette of the Maitreya statue will be as well recognized as those statues at Bamiyan, the Eiffel Tower, the Taj Mahal, the Statue of Liberty, the Pyramids and other symbols that represent great human aspirations from our past.

The statue of Maitreya Buddha is the embodiment or archetypal representation of the qualities of loving-kindness and compassion. So when sentient beings see the statue of Maitreya Buddha, something will happen in their consciousness, whether they are Buddhists in any one of the traditions or are from another religion or they are non-religious.

These qualities represent potential and can be developed in any living being. A seed is planted inside the mind, and on that basis, Shakyamuni Buddha explained there's incredible benefit in creating Holy Objects.

The size of the Maitreya Buddha is important, and as seen from the outside, the Maitreya is going to be huge. Inside, it is going to be the most stunningly beautiful Buddhist cathedral that one can image, and our architects are working on that. It is going to be spectacular in the sense that it will be inspiring and will contain many Holy Objects. The Maitreya Buddha will attract millions of people from all around the world who will come and make contact with a Holy Object of the future Buddha.

It is important to understand what a Holy Object is. Buddha Shakyamuni explained that Holy Objects, such as statues of the Buddha, stupas, tangkas, all have a uniquely powerful quality. This makes it possible for something to happen in the mind of sentient beings. This occurs when one comes into contact with these objects and is inspired by them, venerates them, makes an offering to them, makes circumambulations or prostrations, or in other ways makes contact with the Holy Object. The consciousness receives an imprint from the object, and that imprint imbues the consciousness with the positive qualities that the object represents.

As Buddhists, we understand that in order to generate virtue or to create positive imprints in the mind, we need a positive motivation, and then we have to undertake a positive action. That's really hard. Even to do this for the duration of one breath during meditation is challenging for most people. It is difficult to create virtue on any sort of ongoing basis.

So this is where the Holy Objects come in. Because of the power of a Holy Object, we create this virtue or this enhancement of the mind or consciousness—even without a motivation. With the correct motivation, it becomes much more powerful; either way, virtue is being created. So, in Buddhist terms, the creation of a Holy Object is the greatest, easiest and best way to benefit others, because we are facilitating and providing them with the means of imbuing and enhancing their consciousness.

Many of us are not going to complete the path to enlightenment in this lifetime, and possibly not even during the time that Shakyamuni's teachings exist and flourish on this earth. By making a connection with the future Buddha, just by seeing a picture of the project, and even more so by visiting the Maitreya statue, one will really make a huge connection, a hook. With that hook, we have a chance in future lives to meet Maitreya Buddha, to hear his teaching, and the possibility to attain enlightenment. That's a huge benefit and part of the rationale behind the project. If there is a panacea for all ills in the world, it is loving-kindness. It has the potential to solve virtually all the problems in the world, and the more people receive the positive imprints of Maitreya's qualities, the greater the benefit to the world.

The incredible significance of Maitreya is what it represents. Maitreya and the Maitreya form is the archetypal symbol of the vital human qualities of loving-kindness and a kind heart. It is crucial for individual peace, peace in the family, in the community, for all nations and the world. It is crucial for spiritual development.

Sometimes, I wonder if we should be calling the statue a Buddha since for many, the term Buddha has become synonymous mainly with the teachings and practice of the historical Buddha, Shakyamuni. I sometimes worry that it may appear exclusive to Buddhists, whereas in fact, it is not. Maitreya has the aspect of universality. Loving-kindness is the quality which is at the heart of any true religion. It is in essence, a completely universal quality. The Maitreya 500-foot statue that we are building is for all of humanity. It is a symbol to remind everyone—Buddhists, Christians, Jews, Muslims, Hindus and even the non-religious— of the benefit and crucial importance of loving-kindness.

Engaged Buddhism
Adriana Ferranti

'Engaged Buddhism' is the new battle cry. It stands for 'a Buddhism engaged in social activities'. Unknown to the masses twenty years ago, disregarded until a few years back, it owes its name to His Holiness the Dalai Lama's relentlessly repeated appeal throughout the years for Buddhists to be 'engaged in social service like Christian brothers and sisters'. Finally, more and more people seem to hear—the 'born' Buddhists with unquestioning devotion, the older students (mainly Westerners) with hardly concealed amazement, the new students with wonder and interest—all with absolute certainty that a 'new' Buddhism has come to life. But has it?

Throughout their individual histories, religions, born out of inspiration and knowledge, develop along lines akin to cultures they sprang from to such an extent that centuries later they come to symbolize only some aspects of the original message, thus making it rather hard at times to trace the other aspects, that is to say the inspiration and knowledge in its entirety. As each religion seems to develop towards one aspect, it inevitably ensues that a religion becomes identified to that aspect only. This is how Christianity is now identified with 'engagement in society' and as wanting in ascetic detachment, and conversely Buddhism with mystical peace and serenity and as wanting in compassionate action.

In reality, compassion has always been one of the major aspects of Buddhism, since in the Mahayana tradition, it is the union of wisdom *and* compassion that brings about enlightenment. But the twist lies in the stress on the added quality of compassion 'that seeks enlightenment for the benefit of all sentient beings'. Real benefit can ultimately be only enlightenment itself, compassion turning to the immediate relief of worldly suffering comes to be perceived as diverting both the seeker's energy from enlightenment and the beneficiary's attention from it and, therefore, becoming 'non-Dharma'. Seen in this light, the assumption makes sense; the question therefore is whether I have dedicated myself to social work 'regardless of such view' or, conversely, given that social work *was* meant to be my path in life, on what basis could I become involved in Buddhism at all. Such questions are quite legitimately asked by people coming across MAITRI and myself. I shall try and answer it in a way that I hope will give credit both to the intellect and to the heart.

'Start from the beginning', the old voice of wisdom suggests. And my beginning starts in 1972, at the time when I was turning thirty, a milestone for everyone and certainly the main turning point in my life. That was when I opted for life, as opposed to death—either the slow, numbing destruction of the mind or the quick, physical self-annihilation, which was what I was heading for.

Although I had been endowed with a healthy and attractive body, a keen intellect and a tender heart, I had never been happy, except for some moments when persons akin to my nature would communicate appreciation and empathy, providing a sense of security and hope in the future. Unfortunately, early in my twenties, I ran out of such hope and accepted society's ways to have, in turn, acceptance of myself by society. That was a sure recipe for disaster for an inquisitive, questioning mind like mine. And so it was. I managed to waste my twenties, although by society's standards, I was the quintessential successful young lady: attractive, educated, elegant, well mannered, sociable, intelligent.

Intelligent always comes last in society's list of a young woman's assets, which would cause me unbearable agony when my intellectual skills and potential would be rudely disregarded. Since this was most of the time, I grew neurotic and slid into a trap of self-inflicted physical disorders.

Until self-preservation prevailed. A long journey then started, an inner search which would ultimately reveal my scope in this lifetime. I was not moved by any apparent sense of spirituality, let alone religion—it was a bare, desperate wading through the murky waters of existence in a quest for truth and light. It was long and lonely, at times painful, punctuated by moments of exhilaration and others of desperation. But I never gave up, because I knew that my life was at stake.

The first dim light at the end of the tunnel appeared soon after the start, when I understood that if my life was to be meaningful, it had to be dedicated to others. But lacking in any professional skill in that direction, I had to keep moving on, trusting that one day it would be revealed. I pushed on more by instinct, at times some 'inner voice' suggested which book to read, which place to go to, which turn to take. And it worked all the time. I can say that I was definitely guided, which provided me a sense of security. Thus, when I underwent a totally unexpected spiritual experience in an old cathedral in Italy in October 1977, I accepted the summons from the faith I was born into, although such 're-conversion' did not deter me from continuing my 'search for truth' as many were the questions that still troubled me.

My first encounter with Buddhism was through a book by a Tibetan Master, Ven. Chogyam Trungpa Rinpoche, whose ability to communicate with the Western mindset is very well-known. The book appealed to my inner need for a higher scope and to my intellectual quest for answers, as it was a censure of the search for 'feel-good solutions', i.e. a temporary, albeit immediate, release from life's miseries. This helped me get the taste, which awoke the appetite, at one point made keener by a cassette of Tibetan tantric rituals that I 'discovered' in a bookshop in Milano. In retrospect, it is clear that I was heading towards Tibetan Buddhism, but at the time, such a thought would never consciously arise. It was 1978.

That was also the year when I discovered Gandhi, and it was love at first sight. The Mahatma's 'experiments with truth' gripped me and inspired me to continue my quest; they also led me to first get acquainted with, and later personally meet, his great disciples, Vinoba Bhave and Lanza del Vasto, a.k.a. Shantidas. Gandhi's and his disciples' thought drew me to the Indian soul and set the basis for my future 'love affair' with the country.

I kept moving, though, and so another year went by, during which I came across several 'spiritual' centres where I would spend a few hours and from which I would end up walking out with the clear knowledge that 'it was not it'. Again, what this 'it' was supposed to be was still intellectually unclear, but my inner voice had no doubts and I let it lead me. Until one day I came across Ge.Pel.Ling, Geshe Rabten Rinpoche's centre in Milano. As soon as I walked in and saw Ven. Gonsar Rinpoche, Geshe Rabten's closest disciple, I knew I had finally arrived. That was the heart speaking. The intellect got its share at the following week's lecture by Geshe Gedun Zangpo from the Tibetan monastery in Rikon, Switzerland. His lecture on the nature of the mind presented a new perspective of the area I had been investigating for seven years with the tools of Western Psychology. It made me keen to know more about it and energized me into attending lectures by Ven. Alan Watts and Steven Bachelor, excellent scholars and dedicated teachers, whose rational, clear expounding of the Buddhist philosophy captivated me completely.

However, this was still at a very intellectual level. I would accept sitting on cushions and stoically bear unknown-of pains in the knees but would not prostrate or chant, let alone take any religious commitment. I managed like that for about five months, until I answered 'the call of Pomaia' and went to Istituto Lama Tzong Khapa to attend Lama Yeshe's and Lama Zopa Rinpoche's one-month teachings. This is how the guru entered my life and I became a Buddhist.

Thus, I found myself with two religions on my lap—Catholic Christianity and Tibetan Buddhism—so apparently dissimilar and discordant. However, never in my mind did the doubt arise that they could be conflicting; besides, at that time my existential problem, i.e. how to be of help to others, was still unsolved. It was only in November 1980 that my search for a way out of the stalemate finally ended in the inspiration of my lifetime. In that revelation, both the Christian and Buddhist realities contributed in distinct and yet complementary ways to that rare and most precious moment of mine.

An example of selfless dedication to leprosy patients in the African jungle triggered the storm that raged in me for three days, at the end of which the blinding light of realization 'So can I' struck, bringing in the image of Asanga's act of compassion towards the dog and the maggots infesting its leg. Along came the understanding of the self-inflicted boundaries in our existence—all that in an instant. Even if I had suspected that reconciliation between vocation to social service and Dharma practice was not possible, which I had not, that very revelation would have justified it.

My tale shows that there was no conscious decision-making from my side, but rather an acceptance of what destiny/*karma* had in store for me. The decision came next, when I saw that I had to try and extract the marrow from these two religions, which were now crowding my life. Rather unorthodox procedure, I agree, but there was no option.

After taking stock, it was apparent that there could be no duality, i.e. labelling my urge to do social service as a Christian alone was a contradiction in terms. But then, if such activity is commendable also by Buddhist standards, there may be a spiritual dimension to it as well.

The Middle Path of the Mahayana Tradition confers meaning to any action based on its motivation. Hence, even the action of drinking a glass of water may be meaningful from a spiritual perspective—mentally dedicating the water to the Guru as Buddha and drinking it as if it were holy water can become a profound action. This being the case, it ensues that when offering something to someone who needs it, we practise the virtue of generosity, and when this has the added ingredient of loving-kindness, it becomes an act of compassion. Thus, even the action of giving a pill can be transformed into pure Dharma action.

As compassion seems to be the hub of the matter, it may be useful to define it. The Webster's says 'COMPASSION— *Sympathetic consciousness of others' distress together with a desire to alleviate it*', and, in turn, '*SYMPATHY—a) the feeling or mental state brought about by the act or capacity of entering into or sharing the feelings or interests of another—b) an affinity, association, or relationship between persons or things wherein whatever affects one similarly affects the other.*'

By definition itself, we can then see the whole process evolving before our eyes: sympathy generates compassion, which feeds on interdependence, since the giver cannot exist without the recipient. This condition, in turn, further delves into and enhances sympathy, and so forth, in a perpetual spiralling energy of love, becoming purer, stronger and powerful and shedding its beneficial action onto everything and everyone it touches. It is thus that an act of compassion becomes, or better *is*, a spiritual practice as far as the giver is concerned. What about the recipient?

In terms of the 'Dharma content', the bone of contention, so to say, lies on the validity of the service provided to the recipient, since few would argue against the presence of a Dharma aspect in the giver's action—they may in principle rather debate its relevance or degrees of importance. The recipient may or may not be aware of the value of what they are receiving: if they are so, their hearts are open and ready to receive and give gratitude in exchange. Gratitude comes from humility, the acknowledgment that one is in need and is not ashamed of it. In such a mental condition, the recipient is performing a spiritual act, i.e. surrender, whereby a profound communion can be established between giver and recipient: such is the optimal donor-recipient relationship and on a higher level, the guru-disciple one.

We can say that, when both giver and recipient fulfil the requirements, there is spiritual content in every act of compassion.

In fact, Catholicism recognizes two paths to achieve union with the Divine: the vertical or direct path through ascetic practice, and the horizontal or indirect path through service to mankind. In 1980, I heard it explained by a former Italian Carmelite, who after spending some twenty years in the cloister under the name of Suor Maria dell'Immacolata Concezione (Sister Mary of the Immaculate Conception), had answered a call to re-enter the world in order to dedicate herself to fellow mankind. She saw them as the reflection of God and therefore wanted to serve out of her boundless love for God. This example of selflessness paved the way to that momentous milestone of mine.

The motivation expressed by Sister Mary could also be found in Mother Teresa, who repeatedly explained how she saw Jesus Christ in every destitute person and how by taking care of such brothers and sisters she was serving Christ and manifesting her love for Him. Incidentally, Sister Nirmala, Mother's appointed successor, was the leader of the 'mystical branch' of the Missionaries of Charity. There is no doubt that the Mother had achieved, what in Christianity is called, 'union with God' and that in every act of hers, she manifested such spiritual experience.

I have tried to step beyond cultural archetypes and have drawn the above parallel intending to show the philosophical similarities, though from different standpoints, between the two religions concerning compassion, with particular regard to its manifestation in action.

Feelings of compassion can fail their aim without due consideration for the actual mental and physical conditions of the 'beneficiaries', i.e. their *karma*. One aspect of Dharma practice is the development of the so-called skilful means, which will enable one to offer others relief from suffering in a way they can understand. Undeniably, people weighed down by absolute poverty very rarely have the capacity to raise their eyes and minds to higher objects; their thoughts being fully engaged in the fulfilment of their primary needs. By helping out in this area, one may be able to create a pathway that may allow into their hearts words and concepts of higher liberation.

In 1988, at the time when without apparent success, I was pursuing the Bihar government's authorization which would allow MAITRI, the newly set-up organization, to run the leprosy eradication programme in Gaya district, I met Rinpoche in Delhi. He encouraged me to persevere in my efforts and expounded his vision of leprosy patients doing 'Dharma practices' at the future centre. To my objection that perhaps that was more within the range of Rinpoche's responsibility and I should rather limit myself to taking care of their material problems, Rinpoche responded, 'Yes, provided you keep in mind that it [leprosy] is their *karma*.' Those words slowly sank in and a few months later I was in a full-fledged crisis: believing as we do that our sufferings come from our ripening *karma* from past lives, what good can it do to leprosy patients to be healed from leprosy in terms of their future lives? In other words, assuming that my work would help *me* in my spiritual progress, what use would it be to *them*? Since I could not consider working only on my behalf, I was about to give up, when Rinpoche reassured me that such work would be worthwhile and beneficial and I should go ahead.

Seeking the profound meaning of Rinpoche's advice, i.e. in what way my activity could be truly beneficial, I could find it in a 'dynamic' view of karma, which I have been striving to apply.

Given that whatever we are is the product of our past actions, our lives have manifestations of both positive and negative *karma* in the physical, mental and spiritual components of our existence. Thus, we are afflicted with handicaps, ailments, deficiencies, delusions and, conversely, we are endowed with skills, good health, perfections, clarity, which are all impermanent and can therefore be modified through the power of new actions. The results may be reaped in next lives as well as in the present one, as in the specific case of leprosy patients who are generally regarded as 'cursed by God'—this is where the stigma lies. In fact, since someone, i.e. MAITRI, has come along to take care of them, the *karma* of hopelessness and neglect attached to the disease is clearly being purified. In the process, that positive *karma* of ours that has empowered us to do the action of care, shall further increase and ripen.

Feeling compassion for and helping fellow beings who in this lifetime experience a harsher *karma* has been one of His Holiness the Dalai Lama's main exhortations to all Buddhists. Whether He is believed to be the embodiment of Avalokitesvara by Buddhist followers, or is regarded as a holy person by the international community at large, there cannot be any doubt in His Holiness's ability to experience true compassion and to dedicate His life to serve others. His unpretentiousness and humility are witness to His inner wealth and high spiritual qualities. All this was revealed again during His speech at the 1999 Dharma Celebration held by Tushita Mahayana Meditation Centre in Delhi, where His Holiness went so far as to identify actual Dharma practice with social service, while 'he, being a Buddhist monk, all he can do is just talk about compassion'. Such words gave me great encouragement to continue my work and, if possible, further increased my veneration for Him.

I believe that His Holiness's example is showing us how to approach *karma*. Be it negative or positive, it should be taken with the utmost humility, when it is ours we are dealing with, and boundless compassion, when it comes to others'. Our positive *karma* should be seen as a powerful tool to use skilfully in order to benefit others, and the negative one as our opportunity to purify and hence proceed to unhindered liberation. The negative *karma* of others should be the object of our compassion for their suffering, and the positive one should be taken as a model for us to imitate and rejoice about. This way, Dharma's purpose shall be fulfilled— from just providing enlightened assistance *to rather become* one's own way of life. It is at such a point that the pieces of the puzzle start falling into place, and one is swiftly and yet gently carried along by the current of existence.

Striving to achieve *bodhicitta*, the mind aiming at enlightenment for the sake of all beings, is the higher practice of a follower of the Mahayana tradition. How to achieve such 'great compassion'? There are meditational practices, whose aim is to develop compassion in one's heart and purify, refine and uplift it to the superior motivation.

When in 1982, I set foot on Indian soil, I immediately realized that I belonged to it. Thus, when soon afterwards I had the opportunity to speak to Rinpoche about my determination to work for leprosy patients, I expressed the desire to do so in India. Rinpoche supported my plan and wrote a full meditation for a special retreat on 1,000-Arm Chenrezig [Avalokiteswara] that should enable me to perform healing. The whole meditation is based on the development of such compassion towards all sentient beings as to make the practice of '*tong-len*' the natural, unavoidable way to try and bring some relief to them. In the beginning, I felt rather uncertain and afraid of taking up other people's negative energy, fearing the development of some disease or ailment. But the meditation was so powerful, reaching to the core of my heart, that very soon taking in negative energy did seem as the only way to do it. Although this is not intended to be *bodhicitta*, it should slowly lead to it.

The retreat showed me how in this lifetime, my nature, though craving equally for asceticism and for social engagement, has to be dedicated to the latter while being supported by the former. This is a very delicate balance, never to be neglected. It may, ideally, be maintained through wisely alternating a condition of retreat and activity in order to keep awareness alive and prevent the overachievement energy from prevailing. In actuality, the condition of retreat keeps eluding me; therefore, I have had to learn to make do by simply withdrawing into myself in times of stress and crisis and 'watch and feel' my heart to see if the core motivation is intact or is showing some signs of wearing off, and whether the work I have been doing is still relevant to the 'beneficiaries'. Such self-questioning must be utterly honest or else disaster would ensue. Should the answers be negative, it might indicate that a time for major change has come, hence persisting would bring about disastrous results both to me and to my activity. So far, my motivation has proved to be unmarred and the soul-searching has left me energized while strengthening the bond with the people I am working for.

However, many times when, confronted with human delusions and an uncompromising *karma*, I see the futility of striving for the actualization of my heart's vision, let alone seeking recognition of its worth, and visualize a life in seclusion as the only way to be at peace. Although it is but a fleeting moment, it takes me back to the gritty reality of craving for the worldly *dharmas* and I surrender to the fact that in this world seldom do recognitions match the worth of their object. This generally lies hidden and requires effort to be detected and appreciated.

Over ten years ago, MAITRI underwent a severe crisis that almost destroyed it—the doctor tried to take over and manipulated the field staff to get their support. Heartbroken by the accusations they hurled at me, during a conversation with Rinpoche, I cried out, 'How can they accuse me—I never did anything like that!' Rinpoche's reply was, 'If you have gold and people see it as brass, still it *is* gold.' At the time those words somewhat heartened me and boosted my determination to continue my work. Later, they have acted as reminders of *samsara*'s ways, of our tendency to miss the true value and be bewitched by pretension, reminders that our primary obligation is to be true to ourselves, which thus forces me to ruthless soul-searching to determine whether my original motivation, *my gold*, is still pristine.

Having been able to accept that my mind is still quite far from the state of the 'great *bodhicitta*', such harsh realization has been tempered by the example of the Bodhisattva Avalokitesvara, with His vow never to achieve enlightenment until all sentient beings are enlightened. The image of Chenrezig/Avalokitesvara, associated by Tibetan Buddhists with His Holiness the Dalai Lama, makes my connection with the Deity, who is so important for my practice, a physical reality, a superior companion in this lifetime.

The picture would not be complete without representing the role played by animals in my vision of life and in my commitment to a meaningful, compassionate way of life.

Although I was not born with keen feelings of empathy for the existence of animals, the perception that they have a mind much like our own was awakened in me by a dog, Lucky, that was adopted by my family over forty years ago. At the time, I was not pursuing any spiritual path or any conscious investigation into life's multifaceted expressions. It was the anguish of his look at times staring into my eyes that made me see the sentient being within the animal form and made me wonder about the possibility of animals 'having a soul'.

Since then, every relationship I have had with animals of any size and type has confirmed that initial understanding that animals, like humans, have a mind capable of thinking and a heart capable of feeling. Buddhism has lent me the philosophical, rational explanation to such a perception which is contrary to the general attitude in Western societies and in many others as well. The next natural step for me was to renounce meat in the name of Buddhist non-violence and Gandhian *ahimsa*. I have been a vegetarian for over twenty-two years since I took my first Buddhist vows. Although there is no such specific vow as being vegetarian, my decision followed taking the vow of not killing. My reasoning being that, since I was not inclined to kill in order to feed myself, I should not lay the responsibility of the killing onto somebody else's shoulders, who would thus gain negative *karma* on my behalf.

I used to be disturbed by the Christian Church's view of animals, which to me does not reflect any of Christ's precepts. My perception is that His submission as 'the sacrificial lamb' proscribes ritual sacrifices and equates human and animal life.

But this is debatable, whereas the Buddhist vision unreservedly acknowledges the right to life and dignity to *all* sentient beings.

My concern is not only for dogs but for all animals. Dogs, however, carve a separate niche for themselves in our existence, because their connection with human beings appears to entail the closest emotional symbiosis. Their response to human presence and vice versa appear to be the closest to mutual pure love that you can get in this confused world of ours.

Dogs in this part of India live a rather pitiful life. They are stray, unattended for, and have very short lives. They are generally semi-wild and, when grown up, difficult to approach. But the puppies, lonely and sick, crave to be cared for; we pick them up and try to restore them to health. We provide a place where they can feel safe and, if terminally ill, where they can pass away peacefully. When I am around at the time of their death, I perform Amitayus Buddha meditation with the recitation of the Medicine Buddha's mantra and the sprinkling of a special powder received from Rinpoche. In my absence, MAITRI staff request some senior monks at the Tibetan monastery to come and recite some prayers. We then bury the dogs in the graveyard in our campus and light candles for them at the stupa for forty-nine days. My hope is that through their close association and bond with human beings and through their exposure to mantras and other religious practices, they will obtain a higher rebirth.

I have narrated a somewhat philosophical representation of inspirations, compulsions, drives, motivations that may trigger, feed, heighten, or ultimately sublimate humanitarian actions or activities. It is hard to describe in words personal contents and experiences that lie at the core of one's being. Some are better kept to one's self, as words would not do them justice and, besides lending an uncomfortable sense of exposure, might lead to misinterpretations and controversy, all very destructive.

What I have written is a matter for experience rather than speculation, meant for readers from any spiritual position or preference, be they lay or ordained, Buddhist or Christian, Hindu or Muslim, animist or shamanist, theist or atheist, believer or agnostic. It does transcend belief and differences as it is based on a genuine desire to benefit others. Such desire can be inspired either by religious piety or by an instinctive urge and can either spring out occasionally under special circumstances or be the primary motor of one's own existence. In the case of the latter, one is moved by a compelling call or, as they say, a sense of mission. Hence, the particular religion practised shall make no difference; it all being in the name of 'humanity' or, in His Holiness's words, *'universal responsibility'*.

I believe that the 'environment' created by such a mental state and the commitment ensuing from it is highly conducive to a better understanding among people from all walks of life. Bridges of love are built over chasms of intolerance and division, many times created by religious bigotry. And the bridges shall be made with the bricks of persevering compassion and strengthened with the mortar of tolerance.

13

In Harmony With Nature

K.T.S. Sarao

I spent a good part of my childhood in my village in the company of my grandmother, a very religious lady. I accompanied her whenever she went on a pilgrimage and, during the course of these travels, met many a recluse and holy person. My grandmother's guru was a *sanyasi* who would come to our village once in a while and stay at a small abandoned monastery. Whenever he was around, it used to be my duty to fetch him food and milk. On many such occasions, he would sit me down by his side and narrate all kinds of fascinating stories. Hence, a special bond developed between the two of us: I would fetch him food and get a 'discourse' in return. After I left to pursue higher education, I rarely ever returned to the village. The *sanyasi* has been dead for many years but his memories are still fresh in my mind. Thus, when I began a serious study of Buddhism, it was a sort of homecoming for me because now I know that most of the stories he used to tell me were *Jataka* tales.

There are innumerable reasons why I find Buddhism fascinating. The teachings of the Buddha that have impressed me the most are: the emphasis on personal wisdom, tolerance, ahimsa, and, last but not least, Buddhist attitude towards flora and fauna.

It is a well-known fact that 'development' has turned the world we live in into a dangerous place, so much so that the very future of life on this planet has become a big question mark. The gap between affluence and poverty has never been greater, and corruption in public life no longer comes as a shock. No wonder a lot of us want to leave the modern age behind and make a new beginning in a post-modern era. It is in this context that I believe the teachings of the Buddha are quite relevant.

The Buddha laid great emphasis on the right to life. A civilization that condones the killing or exploiting of other forms of life in order to sustain itself is not a civilization of mentally healthy people. How blasé we are about the atrocities perpetrated by human beings against an ecosystem that has nurtured life for millions of years. The destruction of the environment has taken place through cruel methods of hunting, fishing, butchering, deforesting, over-mining, excessive use of pesticides and pollution in various forms. Ironically, our dependence on nature has never been greater; we look to the skies for rain and wonder what has happened to the natural cycle of seasons, knowing well that it is payback time for the crimes committed against the very environment that has given us life.

Buddhism is more explicit in its concern for the natural world than other traditions. Buddhologists like Venturini have strongly emphasized the necessity of 'harmony with nature,' in the context of 'ecology of the mind' that aims at achieving a 'purified' world. Various forms of Chinese and Japanese Buddhism perceive every single animal and plant as capable of becoming a Buddha. The Buddhist texts speak of never causing harm to the plant kingdom (*bija gama bhuta gama*). The Buddhist practice of Rainy Retreat (*vassavasa*) has its origins in such a concern. Causing damage to the environment is an offence that requires expiation on the part of the monk. This may be interpreted as an extension of the principle of non-injury (ahimsa) that clearly states that animals and plants are to be treated with as much respect as human beings; Buddhist cosmology emphasizes that all sentient beings are intimately interrelated. So it is that one finds Thai monks who not only work to protect whatever remains of the virgin forests in their country but also undertake to plant trees in places where previous felling has led to disruption of water supply or flooding.

The Vietnamese monk, Thich Nhat Hanh, says, 'We classify other animals and living beings as nature, acting as if we ourselves are not part of it. Then we pose the question "How should we deal with nature?" We should deal with nature the way we should deal with ourselves! We should not harm ourselves; we should not harm nature . . . Human beings and nature are inseparable.' According to the concept of Conditioned Arising, human beings are seen as having an effect on their environment not only through the purely physical aspects of their actions, but also through the moral/immoral qualities of these. That is, karmic effects sometimes catch up with people via their environment. As pointed out in the *Anguttara Nikaya*, if a king and his people are not righteous, their action has a bad effect on the environment, leading to little rain, poor crops and compromised longevity.

Accounts of the Buddha's life are richly embellished with allusions to nature. As he took his first steps, lotus flowers sprang up. During childhood, he often meditated under a jambo tree. His Enlightenment took place under a bo tree. When he lay down between two *sal* trees to die and pass into nirvana, they are said to have burst into blossom, and showered their flowers on him in homage. The environment thus responds to the state of human morality; we are not mere performers on a stage, nor is this world a sterile container.

Every action of ours has a reaction and we cannot afford to ignore the effect of these actions on the environment. This is one of the most important messages of the *Aganna Sutta* of the *Digha Nikaya*, where there is an account of the initial stages of the development of sentient life on earth. According to this text, formerly divine beings fall from grace, and by consuming a savoury crust floating on the oceans, develop physical bodies, and sexual differentiation. At first, their environment is bountiful, but it becomes less giving when they begin to take greedily from it. They feed off sweet-tasting fungus, and then creepers, but these begin to disappear because the beings differentiate in appearance;

the more beautiful ones become conceited and arrogant. Then they feed off quick-growing rice, gathering it as and when they need it. But they soon grow lazy and begin to gather a week's supply at a time, taking more than the plants can replenish. So they start cultivation. The land is divided into fields and the system of division of property is invented; naturally there is theft.

This story illustrates plainly the relationship between man and environment. The environment ceases to remain generous when morality declines. This is just what the principle of Conditioned Arising is all about. Nothing exists on its own, and interdependence is the key to life on earth. To quote the *Avatamsaka Sutra*, 'Every living being and every minute thing is significant, since even the tiniest thing contains the whole mystery.'

Even according to the Ch'an/Zen school of thought, the traditional ideal is one of harmony with nature, and they do practise what they preach. Their meditation huts, for example, are made in such a way that they blend with the natural landscape; the food in their monasteries is never wasted; they are into landscape painting and landscape gardening in a big way, and nature poetry is always encouraged. In their paintings, human beings are an insignificant part of the natural scene, not the focus. Great attention is paid to seemingly unimportant aspects of nature because they believe that any insight is valuable. A harmony with all things natural can also be seen in the poems of the *Theragatha*. There are pretty descriptions of forests and delightful rocks, 'cool with water, having pure streams, covered with Indagopaka insects', not to mention elephants and peacocks, 'covered with flax flowers as the sky is covered with clouds', 'with clear water and wide crags, haunted by monkeys and deer, covered with oozing moss.' The Buddha's association with the environment is illustrated in the key events that took place in his life. He was born under a tree, attained enlightenment under another, gave his first sermon in an animal park, and died among trees.

In Buddhism, the forest represents the ideal place for meditation and a number of prominent Buddhist writers believe that the forest is the best way to gain insight into the theory of impermanence. In fact, Theravada monks specializing in meditation are known as 'forest monks,' whether or not they actually reside in the forest. The forest-dwelling monk, the hermit, is unafraid of wild animals because he does not threaten them. On the contrary, he offers them safety and friendship; he is happy in the solitude of wilderness because he has abandoned worldly desires and is content with little. Indeed, it seems that the attitude towards nature has played an important role in the growth of ecological movements in some Buddhist countries. In the case of one who has renounced this world and has retired to the forest (*aranya*), it is primarily the wild animals (and plants) that constitute his society. For those still embroiled in the material world, forests appear uninviting but there is good karma in planting trees for the greater good of mankind. Emperor Ashoka, for one, is known to have prohibited the random burning of forests.

The economist, E.F. Schumacher, points out that Buddhism is not as anthropocentric as most other religions, 'Man is a child of nature and not the master of nature.' He goes on to say, 'The teaching of the Buddha . . . enjoins a reverent and non-violent attitude not only to all sentient beings but also, with great emphasis, to trees. Every follower of the Buddha ought to plant a tree every few years and look after it until it is safely established. He does not seem to realize that he is part of an ecosystem of many different forms of life. As the world is ruled from towns where men are cut off from any form of life other than the human, the feeling of belonging to an ecosystem is not realized. This results in a harsh and improvident treatment of things upon which we ultimately depend, such as water and trees.'

Thus, the Buddhist concept of economic development stresses the importance of avoiding gigantism, and the use of machines which tend to control rather than serve human beings. With gigantism comes the greed that drives us to violate and rape nature. Once greed is brought under control, it will be easy to accept the Middle Path, and both industry and agriculture can cohabit in a peaceful environment.

I must clarify that Buddhism has nothing against wealth and prosperity, but all riches should be acquired and utilized in an ethical manner; killing or wounding any living creature is against the dictates of Buddhism and so is destroying their habitat. The Buddha teaches one to be content with little so that one can avoid waste. He denounces *udumbara-khadik*, shaking down an indiscriminate amount of fruit from a tree in order to eat a few. One can easily draw comparisons with modern-day drift-net fishing, where more animals are killed than utilized. The interdependence between animals and their habitat is clearly perceived in the *Jatakas*. For instance, one of the stories illustrates how the migration of tigers from a forest caused it to be felled by woodcutters, thus depriving the animals of their habitat. Elaborating on the importance of reciprocity between man and nature, Padmasiri de Silva says:

> The day to day maintenance of our life support system is dependent on the functional interactions of countless interdependent biotic and physiochemical factors. Since the inherent value of life is a core value in Buddhist ethical codes, the notion of reciprocity and interdependence fits in with the Buddhist notion of a casual system. A living entity cannot isolate itself from this causal nexus, and has no essence of its own. Reciprocity also conveys the idea of mutual obligation between nature and humanity, and between people.

Given that all life forms are part of a continuous process of creation, the end result of one's actions become supremely important. The law of karma states that one must bear the consequences of one's actions, as clearly expressed by the Buddha in the *Dhammapada*:

If a man speaks or acts with an evil thought, evil follows him even as the wheel follows the foot of the ox which draws the cart.
If a man speaks or acts with a pure thought, happiness follows him like a shadow that never leaves him.

I think it most appropriate that the final words in this piece come from His Holiness, the fourteenth Dalai Lama:

In our approach to life, be it pragmatic or otherwise, a basic fact that confronts us squarely and unmistakably is the desire for peace, security and happiness. Different forms of life at different levels of existence make up the teeming denizens of this earth of ours. And no matter whether they belong to the higher groups such as human beings or to the lower groups such as animals, all beings primarily seek peace, comfort and security. Life is as dear to a mute creature as it is to man. Even the lowliest insect strives for protection against dangers that threaten its life. Just as each one of us wants happiness and fears pain, just as each one of us wants to live and not to die, so do all other creatures. (Tenzin Gyatso, 1980: 78.)

14

Buddhist Suggestions for a Just Society

Lama Doboom Tulku

The Buddha stated in *The Dharani of the Glimmering Jewel,*

> Though I have taught the noble doctrine, if you who have
> heard it do not put it into practise, then just as a patient
> who carries a bag full of medicines without taking them
> will not be cured, my teachings will not serve their purpose.

The implication of this passage is that well-being and the
deliverance from suffering depend entirely upon practising the
Dharma, i.e., cultivating the path to enlightenment.

This also suggests that in Buddhism, the ultimate safeguard is
the *Dharma* itself.

Among the Triple Gem, or Buddhist Trinity, the Buddha is
never regarded as a final authority on any theory or doctrine.
Nor is he regarded as a Creator of the animate and inanimate
worlds. He is simply seen as a guide to the states of liberation
and omniscience.

In another sutra, Buddha advised his followers never to accept
any of his teachings merely out of respect for him, but to first
analyse and investigate them as carefully as a goldsmith scrutinizes
a piece of gold that he considers purchasing. We should accept a
teaching only after being convinced of its validity and applicability

through our reason and experience. This shows that Buddha wanted his followers to take a scientific approach toward his doctrine.

In the quotation given before, the Buddha compares himself with a doctor, whose duty is to diagnose and prescribe the proper medicine to his patients. The responsibility for taking the medicines lies with the patient and to be relieved from the sickness depends on how well one follows the doctor's advice. Similarly, we do not achieve liberation and enlightenment simply by blindly believing in the *Dharma;* we have to implement the teachings correctly.

It is useful to have examples of successful practitioners when we traverse the spiritual path. Thus, there is need of the *Sangha,* the Spiritual Community.

This is how the *Triratna*, the Buddhist Trinity of *Buddha, Dharma* and *Sangha,* is explained.

It may be useful to consider the similarities and/or the inter-applicability of the qualities attributed to Buddha in the Buddhist scriptures with those of God in theistic faiths, and to look at how the Buddhist view reflects upon the practitioner's commitment to social action and his or her appreciation of the ideal of justice.

The principal qualities of the buddhas as teachers of sentient beings in the quest to achieve liberation from cyclic existence and miserable states, are of three categories: (1) infinite wisdom; (2) immeasurable compassion; and (3) peerless strength.

We will discuss the first two of these together, as this seems more practical.

Regarding the concepts of omniscience and omnipresence, in all the Buddhist scriptures of the three *yanas* (Sravakayana, Bodhisattvayana, and Mantrayana), omniscience is attributed to the buddhas as one of the main qualifications to be teachers of the world. However, within the different tenet systems, there seems to be slightly differing interpretations of the term 'all-knowing.'

The *Abhidharma* texts seem to suggest that wherever a buddha applies his mind, the object appears as clearly as a sensory phenomenon lying directly in front of him. This mental power fulfills the requirement of a guide and teacher.

Acharya Dharmakirti in his *Treatise on Pramana*, while discussing his definition of the validity of a buddha, wrote,

> Whoever sees the nature of what is to be followed and what is to be avoided, along with their methods, he is to be regarded as valid. Whether he sees things at far distances or not is irrelevant, rather, they who see the objects of aspiration (of seekers) are the competent masters. If seeing things at a far distance makes one a valid teacher, then we should take a vulture as our spiritual guide.

Dharmakirti also wrote,

> He may or may not know the number of insects under the earth. But this matter is irrelevant to our needs.

In the Madhyamaka literature, a special quality of the buddhas is described as seeing the two truths simultaneously and directly. It is said that while traversing the *bodhisattva bhumis*, one alternates between directly seeing the two levels of reality, conventional and ultimate: in the meditational state, the ultimate truth is perceived directly; and during the intervals between meditation, only conventional truth is seen directly.

Generally speaking, most of the later Indian Buddhist philosophers tend to assert that a buddha sees every knowable thing. That is to say, he sees all things without obstacles or barriers of time and space. This theory is supported by the reason that a buddha has removed all the obstacles of knowledge through immeasurable efforts and accumulation of merits in countless aeons.

The second quality, or that of great compassion, is one of the main factors in the production of Buddha's attainment. As stated in Candrakirti's *A Guide to the Middle View*, compassion is important in the beginning, in the middle, and in the end. Here, compassion is likened in the beginning to a seed, in the middle to the nurturing of the seed through the stages of its growth, and in the end, to the final ripening of the crop. This process is a metaphor for how, at first, compassion inspires one to enter the enlightenment path; then secondly, it safeguards adherents from falling into the pitfalls of the self-peace state in the middle of the path. Finally, it is due to compassion that a buddha constantly engages in the activities that produce the happiness and enlightenment of the sentient beings, after he has achieved the completion of his own training.

Except in the case of a few *tantric* commentaries, not much Buddhist literature attributes omnipresence to the Buddha. This idea is based on the *tantric* doctrine of the subtle body and the subtle mind as being inseparable entities. The implication is that since a buddha's mind is 'all-knowing' and reaches to all existing objects, it therefore is inevitable that his body is all-pervasive. It needs to be researched whether this theory of the buddhas as omnipresent is influenced by historical contacts with other (non-Buddhist) religious traditions.

When we discuss the concept of omnipotence, the controversial concept of a supramundane creator of this world is inevitably involved. It is appropriate to analyse this point along with the third quality of a buddha, namely, his peerless strength or energy.

Here ten strengths are attributed to the buddhas. These strengths are as follows:

1. the strength of knowledge of what is possible and impossible;
2. the strength of knowledge of the karmic consequences of actions;
3. the strength of knowledge of the differing karmic predispositions;
4. . . . that of the different elements;
5. . . . that of the higher and lower mental capacities of sentient beings;

6. . . . that of the progress that leads everywhere;
7. . . . that of everything concerning the origin of all misery, and that leads to equanimity, mystic meditations, complete emancipation and *dhyana*;
8. . . . that of remembering former rebirths;
9. . . . that of birth and death; and
10. . . . that of the destruction of the afflictions.

The word omnipotent connotes being able to do anything one wishes. None of the above-mentioned strengths suggest this. Dialectical arguments may also be used here to point out that if a buddha were to have such a power, he would already have delivered all the sentient beings to the state of *nirvana* and there would be no misery in the world. It is clear that there is no place in Buddhism for omnipotence in this sense.

The previous assertions do not imply that the world comes into being without any prime factor.

A verse from *A Guide to the Middle View* of Acarya Candrakirti is relevant here,

The mind itself creates the various animate and inanimate worlds.
All the living being are produced by karma,
And without mind there can be no karma.

Karma, or action, can be categorized into two principal groups: the karma created by motivation and thought, and the karma created by motivated deeds.

We should not forget that for Buddhists the main question with the concept of a Creator centres around the problem of why individual sentient beings remain in cyclic existence of suffering and why they are delivered to the state of cessation of suffering.

The focal point in Buddhism is that the tamed and untamed mind, respectively, bring about happiness and misery. Thus, the mind which is made harmonious by the acquisition of positive qualities is the basis of not only the ultimate and highest goal (i.e., *nirvana* or buddhahood) but is also the basis of our day-to-day happiness.

The Buddha prescribed the disciplines of ten negative karmic actions from which we should refrain.

Three of these are of the body: (1) killing; (2) taking what is not ours; and (3) sexual misconduct. Four are related to speech: (1) speaking untruthfully; (2) speaking slanderously; (3) using harsh and abusive language; and (4) indulging in meaningless talk. Finally, three are related to the mind: (1) allowing thoughts of greed; (2) allowing thoughts of creating harm to others; and (3) holding to mistaken opinions and beliefs.

Besides these informal disciplines, there are numerous formal precepts of restraint. These are placed in three categories: the *pratimoksa* disciplines (Hinayana); the *bodhisattva* disciplines (Mahayana); and the *tantric* disciplines (Vajrayana). Here the essence of the first of these is to avoid harming others; that of the second is to avoid self-interest; and that of the third is to cut off ordinary perception of the world. The main effort in the *pratimoksa* disciplines is to control the body and speech against fallacious actions. Conversely, the *bodhisattva* and *tantric* disciplines are mainly concerned with controlling the mind from false activity. In the Tibetan tradition, all three are practised in union. The *pratimoksa* disciplines controls gross external faults for paving the way for the *bodhisattva*; and *tantric* disciplines control the subtle inner faults. Anyone interested in accomplishing the path to enlightenment in one lifetime should take one form of *pratimoksa* ordination in accordance with his or her personal capacity, and make this the basis for the higher trainings of the *bodhisattva* and *mantra* paths.

Without bothering to go into the various precepts of the *bodhisattva* path, we shall briefly survey the ideas behind and activities of such a being.

A person who is eligible to be called a *bodhisattva* is one who has generated a determined aspiration to accomplish the state of buddhahood, not merely for his or her sake, but for the sake of all sentient beings.

All the activities of a *bodhisattva* are subsumed under the topic of the six perfections or *paramitas*. Each of these *paramitas* is presented in a threefold manner, as follows.

The first of the six is the perfection of generosity. Its three aspects are: (a) giving spiritual teaching or imparting any useful knowledge is generosity in terms of *Dharma*; (b) giving any material thing, ranging from food and water to household items and so forth, is generosity in terms of material; and (c) giving protection to those who are threatened by any kind of fear is generosity in terms of protection.

Next is the perfection of ethics. Here, (a) learning and following the *bodhisattva* path is the ethics of accumulating merit; (b) to carefully maintain the precepts one has taken is the ethics of safeguarding against non-virtuous forces; and (c) to serve all sentient beings without discrimination is the ethics of serving others.

Thirdly, is the perfection of tolerance: (a) being tolerant in one's practice so as to bear difficulties that one encounters while engaged in spiritual application such as hunger, thirst, unfavourable weather and so forth, is tolerance against hardship; (b) to check anger towards those who cause various harm to oneself is tolerance against intentional harm; and (c) to be able to appreciate the profound teachings such as emptiness (*sunyata*) and selflessness (*anatma*) and not to be shocked by them, is the tolerance of understanding.

Then follows the perfection of effort: (a) to keep the inner resolve of achieving buddhahood for the sake of all sentient beings is the effort that is like an armour; (b) never to relent in the activities of learning, contemplation and meditation is the effort of accumulation of merit; and (c) skilfully guiding living beings in the ways of goodness is the effort of working for sentient beings.

Fifthly, there is the perfection of concentration: (a) engaging in various states of worldly absorption is concentration leading to happiness in the present life; (b) engaging in different concentrations leading to the achievement of higher qualities of a buddha is concentration for high quality; and (c) engaging in various activities for the well-being of sentient beings by means of the six clairvoyances is the concentration of working for sentient beings.

Finally, there is the perfection of wisdom: (a) to be well-versed in scriptures dealing with the spiritual path is the wisdom of knowing the means of one's well-being; (b) to be well-versed in the sciences of healing, arts and crafts and so forth, is the wisdom of knowing the means of the well-being of others; and (c) to be well-versed in the knowledge of logic, grammar, and so forth, is the wisdom of knowing the means of subduing the opposing forces.

If one honours the ideals upon which these six perfections are based, and if the ways of behaviour that they advocate prevail in society, the creation of a just social order is guaranteed. A society consists of its members and a just society is possible only when individuals learn to live a just life.

Conventional laws and regulations may best be described as attempts to bring about justice in a society. However, the ultimate factor in establishing a just society is the mind which brings about justice and injustice. And this depends upon whether an individual's mind is tamed or untamed, and whether it is spiritually mature or still spiritually immature.

15

Birth of a Buddhist Publishing Company
Nicholas Ribush

In January 1977, Lama Yeshe called me to his room in Kopan monastery and said, 'I think we need a centre in Delhi. I want you to go there and start one.'

This came as a bit of a shock to me as I had just entered my fifth year at the monastery and had no desire to be anywhere else. But perhaps that was the problem. The lama didn't like anyone to get too settled. As he often said, 'There's no security in cyclic existence. Everything changes.'

I don't know why I was so surprised. Most of my Western colleagues at the monastery had been sent hither and thither to staff many a centre in the West, and the Foundation for the Preservation of the Mahayana Tradition (FPMT). Why should I be any different? But I was not heading Westward; for me, it was India.

The reason he thought there should be a centre in Delhi, Lama Yeshe explained, was that for centuries the Tibetan people had benefited from the greatest of all Indian gifts to the world, Buddhadharma, and now that Buddhism had all but disappeared from the country of its origin, it was time to repay the kindness of the Indian people by helping bring it back home.

The Lama was my guru, there was no way I could refuse his request.

During my wanderings in Thailand in the 1960s, I had come across a book called *Buddhism* written by Christmas Humphreys, the judge who founded the Buddhist Society in London in 1924. It was my first introduction to Buddhism, and though I won't necessarily recommend it to anyone who wants to know more on the subject today, but for me it was the right book at the right time. It didn't take me long after I read it to find my way to the Kopan monastery. Lama Zopa Rinpoche taught from a locally produced book that all of us were handed a copy of on enrolment. It was titled, rather obscurely, as *The Wish-fulfilling Golden Sun of the Mahayana Practise* [sic], and had been put together, not particularly well, by students from previous batches. It had been printed on an old duplicating machine from wax stencils cut on different typewriters, had a rough rice-paper cover, and was kept bound with what looked to me like a shoelace. But what this manual lacked in production values, it more than made up for in content. The Humphreys book might have pointed me in this direction, but the *Golden Sun* really changed my life.

Rinpoche would read a sentence or two from the *Golden Sun* and then offer comments that might last anywhere from a few minutes to a few days.

One morning, I was approached by Anila Ann McNeil, a tall Canadian nun who was assisting Lama Zopa with the course. She said, 'They tell me you're a doctor.' I nodded and she asked me to follow her to see 'Lama'. I didn't know whom she meant, as Rinpoche was the only lama we'd had contact with so far. Apparently, this lama had hurt his shin on a glass-topped coffee table and the wound had got infected.

I was greeted by an incredibly warm, smiling Tibetan monk, who said, 'Thank you so much, dear; thank you so much.' I wasn't aware of anything I'd done that deserved his thanks, but I guess I said, 'No worries' or words to that effect and took a look at the wound. I decided that the best course of action would be to give Lama Yeshe, for that is who he was, penicillin injections that would have to be brought from Kathmandu. The medicine arrived the next day and I went back to see Lama to give him the first of his injections. I swabbed his skin, rolled the syringe between my hands to loosen the penicillin up, thrust the needle into Lama's buttock and pushed down the plunger. Unfortunately, I'd made the cardinal error of not tightening the joint between the needle and the barrel of the syringe; they popped apart, leaving the needle quivering in the Lama's flesh and penicillin splattered all over the place.

I was extremely embarrassed by this display of ineptitude, but he simply smiled, thanked me again and said, 'Let's try again tomorrow, dear.' That was how I met my guru.

The third Kopan course over and with a short retreat behind me, I offered my services to Rinpoche to revise the *Golden Sun*. I told him I would like to improve the quality of language and set it out more clearly, the better to make the teachings accessible to all. Surprisingly, Rinpoche agreed and over the next couple of months, Marie, who had received the name of Yeshe Khadro (YK), and I spent every day with Rinpoche, working through the book, rewriting it from cover to cover. By the time the fourth Kopan course arrived, in the spring of 1973, the new edition was ready, with an expanded title: *The Wish-fulfilling Golden Sun of the Mahayana Thought Training: Directing in the Shortcut Path to Enlightenment*. During this time, we had also reorganized the Kopan library and set up a free medical clinic for the monks in the monastery, local Nepalis and Western Dharma students, to make the best of the medical supplies that had been sent to me by friends and colleagues in Australia.

That summer, a few of us went up into the Himalayas to Rinpoche's monastery at Lawudo, not far from Mt. Everest. YK and I set up a small free clinic for the local people but, more importantly, I edited the notes another student and I had made from Rinpoche's commentaries on the *Golden Sun* during the third and fourth Kopan courses. The aim was to produce a companion volume to the root text. It was then that I realized how precious Rinpoche's teachings were and how much we'd missed by simply taking cursory notes. I resolved not to miss a word of the next course, the fifth, in the fall of 1973.

When I was working on Rinpoche's teachings on the perfect human rebirth, with eight freedoms and ten endowments, it became clear to me how precious my life and the Dharma were, and how the best way for me to completely devote myself to the practice would be to become a monk. At first, I was a little taken aback by the decision I had arrived at, but after I made a list of pros and cons (there were many pros and not one con), I told YK that I was thinking about getting ordained. She was surprised, but, with some reservations, accepted my decision.

After we got back from Lawudo, I asked Lama Yeshe's permission to become a monk, and he promptly acceded. As it turned out, YK had also decided to take ordination, as had eight other Western students at the course, and along with Lama Zopa Rinpoche's mother, we were all ordained at Bodhgaya in January 1974.

After the fifth course was concluded, Rinpoche and I worked some more on the *Golden Sun* and now that text, as well as the two volumes of commentary that I'd edited, needed to be printed, I asked Lama Yeshe if we could buy a Gestetner duplicating machine for Kopan. He agreed at once and thus we began our little printing operation at Kopan, producing not only texts for students but also many Tibetan works for the growing community of Nepali and Tibetan monks at the monastery. We didn't know it then, but this little enterprise was to germinate into what would become one of the world's leading Buddhist publishing houses, Wisdom Publications.

In the summer of 1974, Lama Yeshe and Lama Zopa Rinpoche made their first trip to the West, teaching in the US, Australia and New Zealand. The Kopan courses, which had been held twice a year, had become an annual affair. At the end of the eighth Kopan course in 1975, an American Dharma student Jesse Sartain, who ran Conch Press, a small publishing house in Hawaii, approached Lama Yeshe and asked for the rights to publish the material that the Lama had used during his trip to the US the previous year. Lama Yeshe called me over to discuss the project and suggested that Jesse's outfit and Kopan publish the book together. The next year our first book, *Wisdom Energy*, was published, and along with it, started our publishing company, Publications for Wisdom Culture.

In 1976, Lama Yeshe was offered a manuscript by a New Zealander, Brian Beresford, who'd been studying in Dharamsala and had translated a couple of teachings by Geshe Rabten and Geshe Ngawang Dhargye. We decided to publish these teachings in Delhi, and called the book *Advice from a Spiritual Friend*. This was our second book.

In those early years, it was very hard to find a decent English-language publication on Dharma, especially in the tradition of the Gelug School of Tibetan Buddhism, the one established by the Dalai Lamas of Tibet. Many of the books that had been published had been written or translated by Western scholars who basically didn't know much. The scenario has completely changed now. There are thousands of books about Buddhism that are widely available and the best part is that they have been authored by highly realized and learned masters, and the translators are people who know their subject well. Not only are specialist publishing houses like Wisdom, Snow Lion and Shambhala putting out scores of Dharma books each year, but larger mainstream publishing houses have also begun to compete fiercely to secure titles by His Holiness the Dalai Lama, other lamas, and Western writers familiar with Buddhism. I am talking only of books published in the English language.

When I first came to Delhi to start the Tushita Mahayana Meditation Centre, the lama suggested that we base Publications for Wisdom Culture too at the centre and sent a newly ordained Australian nun, Robina Courtin, to help me. Robina's family had owned a printing business and she had some experience in the field, having once worked with the London publisher, André Deutsch. While I busied myself looking for a suitable house to start Tushita Mahayana Meditation Centre, Robina started scouting around for typesetters and printers.

It took me a couple of years to find a beautiful house in Shantiniketan, New Delhi, but, meanwhile, the lama had decided to locate the publishing house in the West, and in 1978, Publications for Wisdom Culture moved into its new home at Manjushri Institute, Cumbria, England, and changed its name to Wisdom Publications.

Unable to give up my interest in editing and publishing, I soon established a publishing unit at Tushita, Mahayana Publications, and over a two-year period, we published a number of books, including an anthology called *Teachings at Tushita*, Gareth Sparham's *Tibetan Dhammapada,* as well as a number of smaller booklets. However, it seems there was a clash of interest with Wisdom Publications, which by 1981 had established a business office in London, while maintaining editorial, production and distribution offices in Cumbria. Some of the people there felt that I should be working for Wisdom instead of creating another FPMT publishing entity in New Delhi. The Lama responded by appointing me Wisdom's editorial director, stationed in India at Tushita.

Subsequently, I got involved in organizing the Lama's first Enlightened Experience Celebration—a convocation of the International Mahayana Institute (the organization of the Lama's Western monks and nuns) and FPMT lay-practitioners—that was to be held in Bodhgaya and Dharamsala. During the five-month event, I advertised for potential editors—people willing to attend a retreat where they would be trained to edit Lama Yeshe's teachings by our best editor, Jon Landaw, who had edited *Wisdom Energy.*

After Lama's 1982-83 teachings on the Six Yogas of Naropa in Italy, six of us got together with Jon at a seaside resort near Pisa for a couple of months to see what we could produce. Each of us took on one of Lama's commentaries to edit under Jon's supervision. The experiment was not a great success, but eventually two books came out of it, *Introduction to Tantra* (1987), edited by Jon, and *The Tantric Path of Purification* (1994), edited by me.

In February 1983, the director of Wisdom Publications resigned and I took over the running of the publishing house. After five years at Kopan and six in India as director of Tushita, I'd finally be leaving the East. I had mixed feelings. On the one hand, I'd very much enjoyed the past eleven years and knew it was going to be much harder to be a monk in England than it had been in India and Nepal, but on the other, I would again be in charge of FPMT publishing, the project with which I'd been so closely involved since its inception.

There were major problems to begin with. We had no money. My predecessor was a businessman who'd used his company's profits to finance literature on Dharma; and he had run Wisdom part-time. Moreover, some of the money that he'd put in was a loan. Along with Wisdom, I was inheriting significant debt. In addition, there were a number of signed contracts committing us to publish several books that year. I had no income or savings, and because of serious problems with the people at Manjushri Institute, we could not base Wisdom there, as Lama had wished, but had to set up in London, which was as Lama put it, 'not a good place for monks and nuns,' and also very expensive.

I first made a trip to Australia and the Far East in search of funding. At first I thought I'd be able to get donations, but Wisdom had, at that point, published only about six books, which wasn't enough of a track record for wealthy people to want to fund it. In the end, I borrowed about $30,000 from family and friends and, after a brief trip to Shantiniketan to bid farewell to my many Indian friends, I went back to London to see what we could do.

There were three of us there—my former girlfriend YK (who left after a few months), Robina (who'd moved to England with Publications for Wisdom Culture in 1978) and me—living and working in a tiny flat just off Baker Street, in London's West End. Our plan was to boost production so that we'd be publishing at least eight books a year, which, if they sold well enough, would generate enough income to cover our expenses. We were not getting paid; we just had a place to live in and expenses to meet our food requirements. Our biggest book that year was Jeffrey Hopkin's classic *Meditation on Emptiness*, a 1,000-page work that was financed by a $20,000 interest-free loan (all our loans were interest-free) from an American Dharma student.

However, it very soon became clear that publishing a book is one thing; selling it is another. Bigger publishers often depend on a few best-sellers to finance the rest of their list; academic presses are subsidized by the university to which they are affiliated. We could never see ourselves publishing a Dharma best-seller—certainly not back then—because in most cases, best-sellers are not born, they're made, and we had no university backing. To grab the attention of potential readers, meant hard-core marketing and that would mean having to spend more than our entire annual budget on the effort. To get copies into the bookstores, we enlisted the services of a distributor, but the discounts were so heavy that there was hardly anything left over. We realized that we would have to sell a good proportion of the books ourselves, so we set about establishing our own mail order service.

Once we had established the infrastructure to sell our publications directly, we offered to do the same for the Buddhist titles of other publishers to generate extra income. We soon realized that offering a wide range of books on Dharma was really helping the Buddhist community, since most bookstores carried few Dharma books. We decided that our mail-order catalogue must contain every authentic English-language Buddhist book in print. Even though Wisdom Publications would undergo many changes, this excellent mail-order service lives on in England under the name of Wisdom Books.

In doing so, we also made the decision to branch out from Tibetan Buddhism and represent all true Buddhist traditions in our list. In order to maintain our high production standards—the envy of editors at some of the mainstream publishing houses—

without spending too much money, we started getting our books printed in Singapore.

Early in 1984, we took on another editor, a bookkeeper and a marketing manager, and moved into a large family residence in Streatham, a south London suburb. We each now received an allowance of about $10 a week as well as food and board. We published several books, some prints and postcards and our first mail-order catalogue. We also found an American distributor in an attempt to penetrate the world's biggest market for Buddhist books. However, with even bigger discounts, increased shipping expenses and still not particularly great sales, we continued to find it impossible to break even so I started focusing more energy on fund-raising.

I wondered how other publishers involved in similar efforts were managing. There weren't that many in the first place. Shambhala Publications, which had been started by students of Chögyam Trungpa Rinpoche about fifteen years earlier, was doing well, but they subsidized their Dharma work by publishing a non-Buddhist list; only about 20 per cent of their titles were Dharma books. Also, they had gotten very lucky early by getting Random House to handle their distribution, which ensured their books came to the attention of many bookstores. In addition, they had a mega-best-selling *The Tassajara Bread Book* to their credit. All this is not to take away from Shambhala's brilliant founder and publisher, Sam Bercholz, who went all out to make a success of the venture. Then, there was Snow Lion that had started in 1980 by publishing books by the prolific translator and author, Glenn Mullin, and specialized in books on Tibetan Buddhism, politics and culture. In early 1984, the company was in dire straits and there was a possibility at that time that Wisdom might buy them out. But then Jeff Cox came on board, Snow Lion published His Holiness's *Kindness, Clarity and Insight* just in time for his extensive 1984 American tour, and the rest is history. Amongst other factors, the keys to Snow Lion's success have lain in their wonderful list, their ability to maintain low overheads, and their excellent quarterly newsletter/catalogue.

Fuelling the development of these essentially Tibetan Buddhist publishers, was the exponential rise of worldwide interest in this stream of Buddhism, which would get an enormous boost in 1989 when His Holiness the Dalai Lama won the Nobel Peace Prize and became a household name.

Why the sudden popularity? The overt support of celebrities like Richard Gere didn't hurt, but it went much deeper than that. I think many of the things that appealed to me about the Dharma, the things I had heard at Kopan, were the same things that attracted other Western-educated people as well. Also, the failure of traditional religions, dissatisfaction with material wealth, experiments with drugs, the failure of fame, power and politics to provide any lasting satisfaction sent many Westerners on a search for meaning in their lives; for many such people the search ended when they encountered the teachings of the Buddha.

Buddhism's ability to withstand analytical scrutiny, its scientific character, the clear structure of the Buddhist path and, perhaps most of all, the living example of realized masters who clearly did practice what they preached and had shown results, all contributed to its acceptance in fairly great numbers by normally sceptical Westerners.

In the early hours of the morning of the first day of the Tibetan New Year, 3 March 1984—soon after we'd moved into the house in Streatham—we received a phone call from California that our beloved Lama Yeshe had died. Lama had been unwell for some time, and from the day I met him, I knew he had heart trouble, but the reality of his passing away was still a shock. Robina and I flew to the US for his cremation at Vajrapani Institute, his first American centre, and when we returned to London, put together a commemorative issue of the new FPMT magazine, of which only one issue had been published so far.

Lama had often spoken of having a magazine to glue his many far-flung centres, to promote, as he put it, a 'family feeling' among his international students. In 1983, we had published the first issue of the new FPMT magazine, calling it *Wisdom*. Sadly, the second issue, the tribute to Lama Yeshe, would be the last, but about ten years later, it would reincarnate as *Mandala*, with Robina as its editor.

One of the first general-circulation Tibetan Buddhist magazines in the West was the *Shambhala Sun* founded by Trungpa Rinpoche, whose students had also started Shambhala Publications. It began in newspaper format in 1978 as the *Vajradhatu Sun*, changed its name in 1992 and went into magazine format in 1993. Under the editorship of Melvin McLeod, its circulation has climbed from just under 2,000 in 1991 to about 60,000 today. Published every two months, it is the most widely read Buddhist magazine of all.

Tricycle, which started in 1991 and has since grown rapidly, is not a Tibetan Buddhist magazine, but often features teachings from Tibetan Buddhism and interviews with Tibetan Buddhist teachers. Published quarterly, it is not aligned with any particular Buddhist tradition, although its founding editor, Helen Tworkov, is a Zen practitioner. It is beautifully produced and its circulation is roughly the same as that of the *Sun*.

The Lama Yeshe memorial issue of *Wisdom* was a wonderful effort and a tribute to the skill and dedication of Robina, but with Wisdom Publications getting busier with books and mail-order distribution, we just couldn't keep it going.

After Lama Yeshe's passing away, Lama Zopa Rinpoche took over as spiritual director of the FPMT, and the organization continued to blossom and has benefited tens of thousands of people all over the world. With this growth, the need to sustain the network became ever more pressing, and eventually Robina, who had left Wisdom in 1987, was asked to start another FPMT magazine. It was called *Mandala*, and became a great success within the FPMT, fulfilling Lama Yeshe's original vision of something that would create a feeling of oneness and cohesion throughout his widespread organization. At first, it was published every other month, but when Nancy Patton took over from Robina as editor at the beginning of 2001, it went quarterly. With a circulation of 5,500 when Nancy took over, the figures are a healthier 12,000 now and *Mandala* can truly be considered a great success.

In the mid-1980s, I took stock of Wisdom's situation. We were a non-profit, charitable organization unlike Shambhala and Snow Lion, both of which were privately owned, but, more significantly, they were in America and we weren't. The US market was the biggest in the world, especially for Dharma books, and we couldn't access it with any great degree of success from England.

So in 1987, we established a distribution office in Newburyport, just north of Boston. A British businessman, who owned a large office building there, offered us free space, his marketing expertise and $50,000 a year for five years, provided we incorporated Wisdom in America and had a functioning board of directors. I readily agreed and later that year we transferred all our American business to Newburyport. With the expectation of a donation of $1,000 a week and greatly increased sales, that year we published seventeen titles, more books than we ever had before and, in the process, ran up quite a big bill with our Singapore printer.

Unfortunately, the dream didn't last too long. Within months, our friend's business encountered many obstacles and he finished up having neither time nor money to give us and gradually asked back for the space we were using. Thus, all the income from American sales had to be spent locally and we stopped receiving funds in London. I was still finding it hard to get donations and had to borrow large amounts of money just to keep going.

Despite the hurdles that kept cropping up in our path, we kept on publishing beautiful books to growing acclaim, if not income. A couple of our books won prestigious prizes, such as the Thomas Cook Award for the best travel book of the year (Stephen Batchelor's *Tibet Guide*) and the inaugural Christmas Humphreys Award established by the Buddhist Society (Ayya Khema's *Being Nobody, Going Nowhere*). We also started publishing an art calendar that has been acclaimed as the most beautiful one of its kind in the world, the *Tibetan Art Calendar*, and initiated some major projects, including *Deities of Tibetan Buddhism* (which took fifteen years to complete!), *Liberation in the Palm of Your Hand, The Nyingma School of Tibetan Buddhism* and the wonderful 'Teaching of the Buddha' series, including, eventually, the *Long, Middle Length* and *Connected Discourses of the Buddha*.

As Wisdom's finances had begun to look increasingly dismal, its board asked Lama Zopa Rinpoche whether it would make sense to move the entire company to the American office. With Rinpoche's approval, the company was transferred to its new office across the Atlantic. Boston-based Tim McNeill, who I'd invited into the board in 1987, was to take over from me as director. I was to assume the post of editorial director.

Thus, in May 1989, Wisdom moved from London to Boston, and my life underwent another great change. For the first time since I'd gotten involved in Dharma, I wasn't running the operation at the establishment where I was working, and for the first time in almost twenty years, I was actually getting a salary. But I had liked being in charge and having greater control over my life. Now, here I was, all set to become an employee.

Compared to the halcyon days of 1974, my life suddenly seemed to have become very ordinary. I'd already lost my ordination in 1986 when, as the Lama had predicted, London got the better of me and, with Lama Zopa Rinpoche's reluctant permission, I disrobed. Although we were doing wonderful Dharma work, it was the life of a regular office goer. In retrospect, I often think things would have been so different if only my mind had been stronger, but that was not to be. When I became a monk, I envisaged leading a life of study, meditation and teaching—I wanted to be just like my Lamas and help people in the way they did. Clearly, that was not going to be possible any longer.

So, I accepted my fate and looked at the bright side. I had never really wanted to run a business, which is what Wisdom was, and had always been interested in working directly on the teachings in order to make them available to others. This was my chance to get back to doing what I really wanted.

Unfortunately, even with relocation and the new management, Wisdom's financial position did not improve much since the debt inherited from London was too great. Finally, in 1991, we wrote to the many people who'd lent us money over the years to see if they would convert their loans into donations. Thankfully, most did, which took an incredible load off our shoulders. After that, my new designation became director of development, which is American for fund-raiser. Over the next four years, again due to the kindness of many people, I managed to raise about $1 million, which really kept the company afloat and enabled us to push ahead with our mission of spreading the Dharma for the sake of all sentient beings.

Everything was going reasonably well except for one thing—we were not publishing many of our founders' teachings. In the twenty years of Wisdom's existence, we had managed to publish only six books by Lama Yeshe and Lama Zopa Rinpoche.

In 1996, Lama Zopa Rinpoche suggested that we remove his own and Lama Yeshe's teachings from the Wisdom archives and established the Lama Yeshe Wisdom Archive, to focus more attention on this essential work. It was not that Rinpoche ever thought it important to make his own teachings available; he was thinking more of preserving and making available those of Lama Yeshe. But there were many of Rinpoche's students who wished equally fervently to preserve the precious words of their guru. I and my wife, Wendy Cook—who was also working at Wisdom, running the marketing and publicity departments—went on to establish the Archive as an independent FPMT entity.

That project began six years ago and is yet to be concluded. As usual, no funds came with my new assignment, so getting the money became the priority once again. We decided that the best way to create awareness of the archive and the treasures it contained was to publish free books of teachings; we hoped that these books would inspire people to support us. Sponsoring the publication of free books is a well-established practice in the East, but relatively rare in the West. But I will have to say that we have been quite successful so far, having published about fourteen books for free distribution. We've also put together one book for publication by Wisdom, called *Ultimate Healing*, by none other than the illustrious Lama Zopa Rinpoche, several others are on the way.

It is wonderful how interest in Buddhism has grown over the past three decades; wonderful to see the volumes of Dharma books being published and sold; astonishing to see a book by His Holiness the Dalai Lama spend more than a year on the *New York Times* best-seller list and find his books in airport bookstores all over the world.

At first glance, a Buddhist looking at all this might feel optimistic, but I will not celebrate so soon. History shows that Buddhism has surged before only to decline, and while the next few years look good, what we see today won't last.

Although, personally, I believe that only Buddhism, purely practised, can offer true peace and happiness to the world, it's not going to happen. The world is getting worse, not better. Society is far too deluded and immature for Buddhism to gain wide acceptance. The planet is grossly overpopulated, and there are too few resources and far too many powerful and dangerous weapons in the hands of ignorant, angry people. The main problem, of course, is that we believe that happiness comes from external phenomena; we don't understand karma and how peace, happiness and satisfaction are created by the mind.

I got interested in books right at the beginning; they've kept me going, and I hope they'll be there at the end. I would like to continue editing and publishing Dharma books for the benefit of all sentient beings until the day I die. It sure beats being a boxer's second.

❖

Batchelor, Stephen, *The Tibet Guide*, London: Wisdom Publications, 1987.

Brown, Edward Espe, *The Tassajara Bread Book*, Boston: Shambhala Publications, 1970.

Dipankara Shrijnana, *Atisha's Lamp for the Path to Enlightenment*. Commentary by Geshe Sonam Rinchen; translated and edited by Ruth Sonam, Ithaca: Snow Lion Publications, 1997.

—. *Illuminating the Path*, Commentary on Atisha's *Lamp for the Path to Enlightenment* by His Holiness the Dalai Lama. Translated by Geshe Thupten Jinpa and edited by Rebecca McClen Novick and Nicholas Ribush, Long Beach: Thubten Dhargyey Ling Publications, 2002.

Dudjom Rinpoche, *The Nyingma School of Tibetan Buddhism*. Translated by Gyurme Dorje and Matthew Kapstein, Boston: Wisdom Publications, 1991.

Gyatso, Tenzin, His Holiness the Dalai Lama, *Kindness, Clarity and Insight*, Ithaca: Snow Lion Publications, 1984.

Hopkins, Jeffrey, *Meditation on Emptiness*, London: Wisdom Publications, 1983.

Humphreys, Christmas, *Buddhism*, London: Pelican, 1951.

Khema, Ayya, *Being Nobody, Going Nowhere*, London: Wisdom Publications, 1987.

Pabongka Rinpoche, *Liberation in the Palm of Your Hand*. Translated by Michael Richards, Boston: Wisdom Publications, 1991.

Rabten, Geshe, and Geshe Ngawang Dhargyey, *Advice from a Spiritual Friend*. Translated and edited by Brian Beresford, New Delhi: Publications for Wisdom Culture, 1977. (Boston: Wisdom Publications, 2001.)

Russell, Bertrand, *Why I Am Not a Christian, and Other Essays*, (Current edition) New York: Simon & Schuster, 1977.

Shakyamuni Buddha, *The Long Discourses of the Buddha*. Translated by Maurice Walshe, London: Wisdom Publications, 1987.

—. *The Middle Length Discourses of the Buddha*, Translated by Bhikkhu Nyanamoli and Bhikkhu Bodhi, Boston: Wisdom Publications, 1995.

—. *The Connected Discourses of the Buddha*, Translated by Bhikkhu Bodhi, Boston: Wisdom Publications, 2000.

Sparham, Gareth, *The Tibetan Dhammapada*, Translated by Gareth Sparham, New Delhi: Mahayana Publications, 1983. (London, Wisdom Publications, 1986.)

Willson, Martin and Martin Brauen, *Deities of Tibetan Buddhism*, Boston: Wisdom Publications, 2000.

Yeshe, Lama Thubten, *Introduction to Tantra*, Edited by Jonathan Landaw, London: Wisdom Publications, 1987.

—. *The Tantric Path of Purification*, Edited by Nicholas Ribush, Boston: Wisdom Publications, 1994.

Yeshe, Lama Thubten, and Lama Thubten Zopa Rinpoche, *Wisdom-Energy*, Edited by Jonathan Landaw and Alexander Berzin. Kathmandu: Publications for Wisdom Culture, and Honolulu: Conch Press, 1976. (Boston: Wisdom Publications, 2000.)

—et al. *Teachings at Tushita*, Edited by Glenn Mullin and Nicholas Ribush, New Delhi: Mahayana Publications, 1981.

Zopa Rinpoche, Lama Thubten, *The Wish-Fulfilling Golden Sun of the Mahayana Practice*, Kathmandu: Kopan Monastery, 1972. (Can be seen at www.LamaYeshe.com.)

—. *Ultimate Healing*, Edited by Ailsa Cameron, Boston: Wisdom Publications, 2001.

Buddhist Magazines

Mandala. PO Box 888, Taos, NM 87571, USA. www.mandalamagazine.org.

Shambhala Sun. 1585 Barrington St., Halifax, NS, Canada, B3J 1Z8. www.shambhalasun.com.

Tricycle. 92 Vandam St., New York, NY 10013, USA. www.tricycle.com.

Web Sites

www.LamaYeshe.com. Teachings by great lamas and links to many other Buddhist sites.

www.lamrim.com. Internet radio site with many audio teachings.

16

Buddhist Oikoumene
Lokesh Chandra

As a historical phenomenon, Buddhism is one of the most grandiose edifices of the human spirit. It has been the dynamic equilibrium of Asia, living in a centripetal world of implication, creating incredible heights. It has been the glory and silence of inexplicable and obscure pages of time, and still it is supremely alive and deeply touches the hearts of men to our day. Like a musical instrument, it vibrates to the hidden impulses that govern the breath of the universe. It is the awareness of a life beyond forms and ideas, wherein the individual subconscious merges into the object of its thought, into the Ineffable.

In the course of 2,500 years, it has exercised an abiding influence on the minds and horizons of India, Indo-Greek principalities that arose in the wake of the conquests of Alexander the Great, Central Asian kingdoms, the Middle Kingdom of China, Korea the Land of Morning Calm, Japan the Country of the Rising Sun, Vietnam, Tibetan Region, Mongolia, Siberia, Sri Lanka, Burma, Thailand, Laos, Kampuchea and Indonesia. Some of the most noble works of man are the contribution of Buddhism. The universal implications of Buddhism are vast qualitatively, as well as in terms of quantum: embracing every form of human activity, tracing esoteric and philosophical developments, political and social history, ordinary life and proto-technological discoveries. It has been a mighty propulsive force in the onward march of ideas and a profound movement touching the hearts of men with *karuna* or compassion, leading to peace eternal.

The intrinsic strength of Buddhism lay in its lofty moral sense, the universality of its message, the serenity of its tenor, its scorn for excesses, its golden mean, and above all the personality of Lord Shakyamuni, so serene, so strong, so fascinating, and so human. The pain of life became the poem of Primal Buddhism. It sought a dispassionate analysis of the causes of suffering and a scientific search for their remedy. Away from ritual, the human personality and its will for virtue were elevated to a supreme place. The gods became poetical figures, possessing the majestic impersonality of principles that govern the universe.

As happens when a spiritual movement is alive, Buddhism diversified. Variations arose due to interpretations. The inexorable trend of geospiritual forces contributed to transformations. The Buddha Shakyamuni was transformed from Master into Lord. Solar myths, fire cults and immemorial fantasies transmuted him into an idealized figure. The Enlightened One became the Enlightening One, the Radiator of Light. From Buddha, the interest shifted to the abstraction of Buddhahood. From an individual, he became a symbol, the science of Buddhahood. Nirvana was transformed into paradise, and karma became modifiable by prayer. Elaborate patterns emerged. Buddhism was face to face with the Absolute, the Ultimate, the First, the Eternal, the Everlasting and the All-pervading which now was the adamantine purity of the Adi-Buddha.

With metaphysical daring, this Eternal *par excellence,* definable by negatives alone, became the bejewelled sambhoga-kaya, passionately embracing his transcendant consort or prajna. Extreme serenity was identified with extreme passion, the crystal light with the fire of love, the intangible with all the intoxication of the senses. Sensuality and symbolism, metaphysical filigree of jewels, caresses and cerebrality, earth and sky were celebrated in proportion and serenity, in portraiture and cryptograms. Hymns incarnated into miniatures and scrolls, and into statues to carry eternal depths to the eyes of the faithful of the earth.

The invasion of Alexander in the fourth century BC was prompted, *inter alia,* by the vast quantum of golden tablets on which Zoroastrian scriptures were preserved under the Achaemenians. A sumptuous copy of the Scriptures on gold was deposited in the 'Stronghold of Records' at Persepolis, and another set inscribed on golden tablets was preserved in the treasury of the fire-temple at Samarkand. Both these archetype copies vanished in the invasion of Alexander in 330 BC when he put to fire the palace at Persepolis and when he razed Samarkand to the ground. The Iranian-speaking lands henceforth stood culturally denuded. Buddhism filled the vacuum. These Udicya regions in the northwest of India became alive in the transmission of Buddhism to Central Asia.

The foundations of Khotan had been laid by the son and ministers of Emperor Ashoka in the third century BC, as we are informed by two Chinese and by two Tibetan sources. Buddhism, Sanskrit and Indian scripts were in vogue in Khotan. A new Buddhist *oikoumene* was in the offing. Buddhist monasteries, with hundreds of monks, arose on our NW frontiers and across Central Asian routes that led to the greening of these desert areas. Mighty literary movements were generated. The Parthians, and not Indians, were the earliest translators of Buddhist texts into Chinese. The very first translator was the Parthian prince An Shih-kao 安世高, Sukhavati-vyuha into Chinese. The Iranian world-view had a profound influence on the development of Buddhism, while Buddhism enriched Iranian-speaking peoples by giving them scripts for trade and administration and a spiritual culture to win the hearts of China.

In 138 BC, Chang Ch'ien, the envoy of the Chinese Emperor, took back musical instruments and MahaTukhara melodies from Kucha to the Chinese capital, Ch'ang-an. The son-in-law of the Emperor Wu-ti wrote twenty-eight new tunes based on this melody which were played as military music. Along with Buddhism, the Tokharians of Central Asia introduced milk to China. The Chinese ideograph *lo* 酪, pronounced *lak* in ancient times, which meant various kinds of fermented milk products, was a loan from Indo-European (Latin *lactic*). The peach and pear reached India in the reign of Kaniska and were known as *cinani* and *cina-rajaputrika*. Paper had been manufactured out of silk in Han times, but with the introduction of Buddhism, cotton also became a component of paper, as is evident from the old lexicon entitled *Ku-chin tzu-ku* where the silk radical 糸 of the character *chih* 紙 for silk is replaced by 帋 with the cotton radical 巾, after the invention by Ts'ai Lun. Cotton cultivation had been introduced from Kashmir and East Bengal to China in the second century BC.

With Buddhism, sugar came to China. Sugar is termed *shi-mi* 石蜜 'stone honey' in the Sui Annals (ch. 87 f.7b), which renders the Sanskrit *sarkara*, from *sarkara* 'granules, stonelets'. In AD 285, Kambuja included sugarcane in its tribute to China. In AD 647, Emperor Tai-tsung sent a mission to Magadha to study the secrets of boiling sugar. This method was adopted by the sugarcane growers of Yang-chou (T'ang Annals, ch. 100 f. 21). The official history of the Sui dynasty, completed in AD 610, contains a catalogue of Sanskrit works on astronomy, mathematics, calendrical methods and pharmaceutics under the generic caption of P'o-lo-mên or Brahmin Books.

The earliest specimen of printing from China is a printed sheet with the figure of the six-armed goddess, Pratisara, in the centre and with Sanskrit mantras in the ornamental Ranjana script, written concentrically around the figure. It is dated AD 757. The world's oldest printed book, dated 11 May 868, is a Buddhist work on transcendental wisdom entitled Vajracchedika, now in the British Museum. Printing flourished as an integral part of Buddhist requirements of large number of sutras and mantras for mass distribution by bereaved descendants so that their deceased parents may acquire due merit. The book in Buddhism was a written medium of spans of inner space. Sutras sanctified the state: for instance, the *Jên-wang-ching* 仁王經 or Karunika-raja-sutra brought protection, peace and prosperity to the country.

The collective sought its continuity in the enduring flow of the Dharma of the Tathagata. Buddhist monasteries fortified the trade caravans on the Silk Route and it ensured the flow of art and thought, as well as gave rise to a Buddhist *oikoumene*. Buddhist Central Asia and East Asia were linked in their Buddhist faith. When the Chinese refused aid to the prince of Tashkent in 751, the battle of the Talas river was lost. It proved to be one of the decisive battles of world history. This region, which had been a stronghold of Buddhism from its earliest times, succumbed to Islam.

The contact of China with India declined and thereby the receptivity of China was replaced by xenophobia. In 828, Emperor Wen-tsung had an image of Avalokitesvara set up in each of the 44,600 monasteries of the empire. In 1950, about a million Buddhist shrines, stupas, temples and monasteries had sanctified the sprawling spaces of China. A Chinese poem speaks of the new moon, the flowing clouds, the drizzling rains and the blooming white lotus in one breath. The White Lotus refers to Buddhism, which is inextricably interwoven with the woods, lakes, mountains and hearts of China.

Korea, a peninsula jutting out from the north-east corner of the Asian continent, is one of the three major cultural entities of East Asia, significantly affected by continental influence of Buddhism. Yet, in its peculiar environment, it has created an art with characteristics uniquely Korean. In 384, the monk Mallananda (Korea Marananta) brought Buddhism to Paekche, together with scholars, painters, sculptors and architects. Following T'ang models, the Silla capital, Kyongju, had Buddhist temples throughout the city, countless Buddhist images were cast, and political and social systems were influenced by Avatarhsaka thought. The famous Silla pilgrim, Hyech'o, visited India and wrote an informative account of his travels to India. The Great Silla was replaced by the Koryo in 935. Buddhism was the national religion under Koryo. To secure the assistance of Shakyamuni in times of stress, the Tripitaka was carved on 80,000 woodblocks over two hundred years, beginning in the reign of King Munjong (1047-82).

The printing blocks were destroyed by fire during the Mongol invasion. They were carved anew and completed by 1251. These blocks are still preserved at the Haein-sa monastery and are a national treasure of Korea's cultural history. The famed celadon wares of Koryo were intimately connected with Dhyana Buddhism. In the beautiful deep of the blue porcelain were reflected the ideal planes of Dhyana. In 1443, the Hangeul script was developed in Korea on the pattern of the Sanskrit alphabet.

The Pulguk-sa is the oldest surviving Buddhist monastery of Korea, founded around AD 535. It means: *put* 'Buddha', *guk* 'land', *sa* 'monastery': a monastery that springs from the deeps of Buddhism, to celebrate the new dynamic and vital order that was to determine the whole tonality of Korean life.

In the middle of the eighth century, it was rebuilt and enlarged by King Kyongdok. The same master architect built the rock chapel of Sokkur-am a mile away, on the crest of Mt. Toham-san. It enshrines the best Korean sculptures of all times. They are reminiscent of the sculptural glories of T'ang China, and yet are unique in their ethereal quality. Superb examples of warm naturalism, they sprout from the passion of everything that the eyes embraced, celebrating its essence in the eternity of stones:

There is a tradition that the sculptor who carved these bas-reliefs was in love with the King's daughter and used her as the model for the images of Avalokitesvara in order to immortalize her beauty.

The piety of the patron and the love of the sculptor sinks into the silent rapture of these sculptures. Over the centuries Buddhism was the creativity and supportive philosophy of all facets of life in Korea.

The vast Japanese world is referred to as *karyu-kai,* that is, 'the world of flowers and willows'. From an empirium of sensitive and sinuous ideograms, it has come to be the *Troisième Grand* in one century.

The *wakon yosai* 'Japanese Spirit and Western technology' is the space where jet-age modernity is an intimate companion to her ancient frontiers of myth, proverb and folksong. Much of what moves modern Japanese to leap forward is due to their roots that carry vital fluids from Dharma, from the craft of busshi or sculptors of statues in conjunction with the cold abstract researches in the stream of an international style. The monastic gardens of Kyoto are spaces disciplined with elegant serenity, into families of rectangles and squares: from their depths, new spring steps out. The stones set in a carpet of moss, await the bare feet of a goddess. The Land of the Rising Sun combines action and art in a new paradigm of 'Sun and Steel'.

In sixth century Japan, Buddhism made a stormy entry on a scene where virulent civil war between the Soga and Monobe clans in AD 587 ended in the victory of Soga who espoused Buddhism. A religion of peace and moral grandeur, it contributed to far-reaching political, social and spiritual advances. It was the Korean kingdom of Paekche whence Japan received her Dharma and along with it her first scribes, painters and calligraphers, an event deemed momentous enough to be recorded in the *Nihon Shoki* in the years AD 463, 544, 588, etc.

Astrologers, landscape architects, painters, bridge-builders and bhiksus arrived. Japan emerged from the limbo of her prehistory under Prince Shotoku (AD 574-621) who drew up her first Constitution in Seventeen Articles wherein the Triratna (Buddha, Dharma and Sangha) were a fundamental factor. The new order was consecrated by the Usmsavijaya-dharani, whose Sanskrit manuscript is preserved at the Horyu-ji monastery.

In AD 806, Kobo Daishi returned to Japan with the new way of Shingon or Mantra-yana, wherein every individual was a potential Buddha. This led to the universalization of education. The personal contacts of Kobo Daishi with the great Kashmirian Prajnatara during his sojourn in China, were to produce a profound effect on the cultural evolution of Japan. After his return, Kobo Daishi started spreading education to the common man. Till then, education had been restricted to the privileged classes, and only children of families above the fifth rank could attend academies and universities. Kobo Daishi opened the Shugei Shuci-in 'Institution of General Arts and Wisdom' for children of all classes. The courses were both secular and sacred. To democratize and advance literacy, Kobo Daishi invented the syllabary of Fifty Sounds *(goju-on)*, starting *a i u e o, ka kl ku ke ko* and so on. Its basis was the Sanskrit alphabet. He further wove the entire alphabet into a poem termed *Iroha*. This *Iroha* poem— wherein the complete alphabet of fifty letters was included and each letter occurred only once—was a literary marvel. It speaks of the gleaming colours that blow away, the deep mountains of ephemeral life, shallow dreams, and the crossing over them all— one of the greatest poems in the Japanese language, it was inspired by the Sanskrit work *Mahaparinirvana-sutra*. Every Japanese child learns it in the kindergarten. The Japanese State was protected by Shingon. In A.D. 823, Kobo Daishi established the monastery of Kyo-o-Gokoku-ji, 'Temple of the Protection of the Land through the Noble Dharma', at Kyoto.

Kobo Daishi's major work, *Hizo-hoyaku*, begins with an invocation to the Sanskrit alphabet as the dharma-mandala:

I take refuge in That One
Who is the Adamantine Life of all beings,
Transcendental, Immaculate, Causeless, and Infinite.

> [*Mahavairocana*]

In the Silent One
Ka the Evolving, *Ca* the Involving, *Ta* the Majestic
Ya the Suchness, *Pa* the ultimate Truth, and
Ya the absolute Vehicle on which all beings are carried
forth.

> [*Dharma-mandala*]

Herein the Sanskrit alphabet is expressed by:

ka-varga	*ka*rya	evolving
ca-varga	*cy*uti	involving
ta-varga	*ta*nka	majestic
ta-varga	*ta*thata	Suchness
pa-varga	*pa*ramartha-satya	the Ultimate Truth
ya to ha	*ya*na	the Vehicle

Buddhism encompassed the living skills and arts of Japan. Gagaku, the Buddhist music of the T'ang court, has survived up to modern times and is the supreme expression of Japanese music. Assimilation has been a vigorous philosophy in Japan in the *honji-suijaku* 本地垂迹 theory. Hereby, indigenous Japanese gods became manifestations of Buddhas and bodhisattvas. It became the foundation on which the convergence of the Japanese Spirit and Western technology has worked wonders.

Buddhism has conditioned to the minutest detail the life and thought of Tibet in spite of its forbiddingly high mountains, untamed rivers, deep gorges, immense waterless deserts and icy winds. The Tibetan script, grammar, vocabulary, literary style, paintings, medicine, astronomy, folksongs—all bear the deep impress of Buddhism. Entire literature, whether translated from Sanskrit or the flame of intellectual life, arose and evolved, centred around Buddhism. For all knowledge is centred in the *nan-rig* or exploration of the Inner Deeps. The warm reality of Tibetan life pulsates in the vibrant levels of her Buddhist culture.

Buddhism reached Mongolia in the sixth century, when two Buddhist teachers, Sakya-vamsa and Narendrayasas, went and worked there. Ever since, Buddhism has been the subtle invasion of the spirit, setting the heart and soul of the Mongols on fire. It replaced to a degree nomadic life by a sedentary civilization. It brought peace to the Mongols and a high degree of civilization which was the envy of Russian deportees in the seventeenth and eighteenth centuries. This can be seen in the open air ethnographic museums in Siberia where the residences of the Buryats stand far ahead of the Russian homes.

The 334 huge volumes of the Buddhist canon at the Library of the Academy of Sciences are loved by the Mongolian people as 'pearls of our literature'. You may hear the Mongolian Professor Rinchen relate with pride, 'If you happen to stop in any yurt, the first one falling on your way in the vast steppes, where the night may overtake you, before the fire of a hearth, you will hear from the mouth of an old shepherd the philosophical poem *Bodhicaryavatara*, composed by the famous Indian poet and thinker, *Santideva,* well known to Europeans through the beautiful translation by Finot and translated into the Mongolian language already in the thirteenth century. You will not be surprised if the old shepherd sitting thoughtfully on the hillock near the grazing herds, having come to know you to be a philologist, will enter into animated conversation with you regarding the Sanskrit grammar of Panini which was translated into the Mongolian language already in the seventeenth century, the level of which was achieved by European linguists only during the last century.'

Genoese merchants secured Mongol slaves from traders wholesaling in the Black Sea ports (Lazari, *Del traffico e delle condizione deglishiavi in Venezia net tempe di mezzo,* 1862, 1.470). Thousands of these Tartar slaves worked in every major Italian city, which reached its climax in the middle of the fifteenth century. These Buddhist slaves used hot-air turbines for turning their prayer-cylinders. This gave rise to screw propeller of ships, and steam-jet blowers in the shape of birds, dateable to 1579.

The Museum of Revolution at Ulanbator has preserved a conch. More than sixty years ago, a young Mongol, Sukhebator, blew a conch to summon his countrymen to the Revolution whereby came into being the second Socialist state of the world and the first of Asia, lying in the very heart of the Asian continent. The national flag of Mongolia is Soyombo with a golden five-pointed star, topped by an emblem of the semilune, circle and soaring sonance: the *candra, bindu* and *nada* of *pranava.* Let us not forget that Goraksh was the first Mongolian cosmonaut to go into *sansar.*

Space is *sansar* in modern Mongolian. Buddhism is the invariable presence in Mongolia.

The most magnificent cultural presence of Indonesia is the historic cosmogram of Borobudur, the grey silence of endless stone reliefs, enshrining the vision of a king in an ecstasy of form. Conceived and given shape by a poet, thinker and architect, named Gunadharma, it holds the heart in rapture. The Indonesian word for independence is *merdeka,* derived from the Buddhist term *maharddhika.* The Constitution of Indonesia is called *Pancasila,* evidently from Buddhist terminology. The national motto *Bhinneka tunggal ika* 'unity in diversity' is derived from the Buddhist poem, *Sutasoma Kakawin,* in the classical Kawi language.

In Kampuchea, into the spacious majesty of Angkor Vat, monument follows on monument, ruins edge upon ruins, the walls of vegetation screen and hide and curtain, masonry masses mingle into the fantastic flowering of the jungle. By moonlight, these buildings take on an appearance of solid majesty which is awe-inspiring. In the twilight gloom of these jungles, a naga slithers over the sensuous limbs of an apsara, petrified in a seductive pose of her dance in honor of a Devaraja of lost Angkor. The shrines seem to have been transported by divine magic straight from the Land of Sakyamuni.

Buddhism is a panorama that unfolds the perennial flow of culture and civilization in Sri Lanka, Burma, Thailand and Laos. It has shed glamour on man's existence in these lands as elsewhere. In the words of the poet Tagore, Buddhism is the eternal seeking:

To bathe in the living stream that flows in thy heart,
Whose water descends from the snowy height of a sacred time,
On which arose, from the deep of my country's being,
The sun of Love and Righteousness.

Man is fast approaching the threshold of a newer world as Professor Y.D. Prokoshkin and his group discover 'antimatter', using the world's biggest synchroton at Serpukhov. The Committee for Inventions and Discoveries under the USSR Council of Ministers has entered this outstanding discovery in the State Register. The pranks and paradoxes, blows and bumps of Economic Man face aching flashes and devastating shocks. Man cannot burn in the fire he has kindled by allowing himself to forget who he is. While history passes on in its carriage, Man has to proclaim that he is the rim and the axis. A painter once said, 'Give me a branch to sit on and I will sing like a bird.' Buddhism may be that branch; its message that song.

17

Some Thoughts on the Future of Buddhism

Lama Zopa Rinpoche

In order to hazard a guess at the future of Buddhism in the world, we need to look at how it has survived and spread since our precious founder, Guru Shakyamuni Buddha, first turned the wheel of Dharma 2,500 years ago.

Guru Shakyamuni Buddha revealed the path to enlightenment so that all sentient beings would be happy and free from suffering. Having experienced the bliss of liberation and enlightenment, he realized that all beings had the seed of enlightenment within their minds and could attain that ultimate goal by following the same path that he had. Therefore, starting with the four noble truths, he began to impart teachings according to the various levels of mind of those who came to him for instruction.

Under his guidance, his disciples began to practice, and many were able to gain the same realizations that he had, proving that others could attain the enlightenment he had attained. As his students became teachers, their disciples gained realizations of the path, showing that Guru Shakyamuni Buddha's teachings were indeed transmissible, thus beginning the oral tradition that survives to this day.

For 1,500 years, Buddhism flourished in India and spread from there in all directions, to South-East Asia, Sri Lanka, China, Japan and Korea, countries to the West, Nepal and Tibet.

Around 650 AD, the king of Tibet, Songtsen Gampo, married Buddhist women from Nepal and China and under their influence, began to introduce Buddhism to Tibet. One hundred years later, the king Trisong Detsen, invited the great Indian monk-scholar Shantarakshita and the tantric yogi, Padmasambhava, to establish Buddhism in Tibet. Shantarakshita, the 'Great Abbot Bodhisattva,' introduced the monastic tradition to Tibet, ordained the first five Tibetan monks, and inspired the construction of Tibet's first monastery, Samye. Padmasambhava, 'Guru Rinpoche,' pacified hindrances to the establishment of Buddhism and introduced the practice of Vajrayana to Tibet.

Over the next century, the practice of Buddhism spread gradually throughout Tibet, until the anti-Buddhist king, Langdarma, ascended the throne and began a violent campaign to destroy Buddhism in Tibet. Within a few years, the Dharma had all but disappeared from Central Tibet, but survived to a certain extent far to the east and west.

Thus fragmented, the practice of Dharma began to degenerate, and many corrupt practices and ideas were introduced to Tibet. Despairing at the situation, the king of Guge, in Western Tibet, invited the renowned Indian pandit, Atisha, to Tibet, to reintroduce the pure practice of Dharma.

I can't talk much about Atisha's life here, but a detailed description is given in Pabongka Rinpoche's book, *Liberation in the Palm of Your Hand*. Here we see how, like Guru Shakyamuni Buddha, Atisha was born into a royal family but abandoned his inheritance in favour of Dharma practice. He studied with many teachers and realized the central importance of the loving, compassionate bodhicitta in the practice of Dharma. In order to further his study and practice of bodhicitta, Atisha undertook a long and dangerous sea voyage to Indonesia, to meet Serlingpa, the pre-eminent teacher of bodhicitta of the time.

When he went to Tibet in 1042, Atisha carried with him the two crucial Dharma lineages of method and wisdom, and when we talk even now about the survival of Buddhism in the world, we have to talk in terms of these two lineages.

The wisdom lineage passed from Guru Shakyamuni Buddha to Manjushri and then down on through great masters such as Nagarjuna and Chandrakirti to Atisha. The method lineage passed from the Buddha to Maitreya and then down on through Asanga, Vasubandhu, Haribhadra, Lama Serlingpa, and to Atisha. Thus, combined in the mind of the great Atisha, the two lineages of method and wisdom arrived in Tibet.

In Tibet, Lama Atisha wrote a very short text entitled, *A Lamp for the Path to Enlightenment*, which for the first time presented all the teachings of the Buddha in an organized, step-like path, making it *very* easy for the individual practitioner to get an overview of the entire path and to understand what practice might be relevant to her or him. The benefits of Atisha's coming to Tibet are infinite, beyond measure, but even if the only thing he'd done was to write this text, that would have made it worthwhile.

Atisha's work was the original *lam-rim* (steps of the path) text, and over the subsequent centuries, many lamas from all Tibetan traditions wrote commentaries on Atisha's *Lamp* and the lam-rim genre is one of the hallmarks of Tibetan Buddhism. Perhaps the most famous of all lam-rim commentaries is Lama Tsong Khapa's *lam-rim Chen-mo*—the *Great Treatise on the Steps of the Path to Enlightenment*. Lama Tsong Khapa was a great yogi and scholar who wrote many texts on all aspects of sutra and tantra, including several lam-rim commentaries of varying length, but his *Great Treatise* is a work of unparalleled genius.

Lama Tsong Khapa also founded the Gelug tradition, one of the four great schools of Tibetan Buddhism. He and his disciples founded some of the greatest monasteries in Tibet, including the three near Lhasa—Ganden, Drepung, Sera—and Tashilhunpo, Kumbum and Labrang, in other parts of the country which were founded by his various disciples and were like small towns, housing tens of thousands of monks.

In the Gelug monasteries, the monks followed a rigorous

schedule of memorization, study, debate and practice. Often they would forgo sleep in order to debate all night. One of my teachers, Geshe Rabten, has written in detail about life in the monasteries, *Life of a Tibetan Monk,* and his book is worth reading to find out what an intensive schedule the monks followed.

By some estimates, more than 20 per cent of Tibetan men were monks. This is an important issue to note when thinking about the future of Buddhism, because the viability of the Dharma in a certain country or place is determined by whether or not the lineage of the monastic ordination exists there. These days, there seems to be a tendency, especially in the West, to downplay the importance of the ordination of monks and nuns in the survival of Buddhism. Suffice it to say that wherever one cannot be ordained, Buddhism is dead.

Many Tibetan practitioners, however, were not monks but laypeople, and some of them led amazing lives high in the snow mountains of Tibet. Perhaps the most famous of all is Tibet's great yogi, Milarepa, who reached enlightenment under the guidance of his guru, Marpa, the Translator.

In his early years, Milarepa studied black magic, and at the insistence of his mother, in order to avenge the harm done to his family after his father had passed away, he caused a building to collapse, trapping and killing many of his mother's enemies. Later on, realizing the terrible mistake he had made, he sought out a Dharma teacher, and eventually found Marpa. However, instead of receiving teachings from his guru, Milarepa received rough treatment. Marpa never missed an opportunity to publicly humiliate Milarepa, kicking him out of any teaching sessions that he might manage to sneak into, and forced him to do unbelievably backbreaking work, building and tearing down a stone tower.

Marpa taught Milarepa how to build a nine-storey tower out of rocks, and when, after a great deal of effort carting the rocks from the remote areas where he found them to the building site, Milarepa finally finished and proudly showed Marpa his handiwork, the guru shouted angrily, 'Who told you to build this tower? Put every rock back exactly where you found it.' When Milarepa had done this, Marpa then angrily demanded to know why he had taken down the tower he'd been told to build. This happened three or four times. Each time, Milarepa humbly accepted his guru's criticism and, with unshakable faith and devotion, did exactly as he was told.

Eventually, Marpa sealed Milarepa into a cave and told him to meditate on impermanence and death and other important Dharma subjects until he had realized these topics. In this way, having essentially abandoned sleep, Milarepa's wisdom grew. After a few years, he had a dream that he should return home, which he did, to find his mother dead and the family home in ruins. Milarepa then fled to the snow mountains, where he meditated in icy caves, wearing nothing but a simple cotton cloth. There he realized the nature of mind and attained enlightenment. He had spent so much time sitting in meditation that his buttocks were thick with calluses.

Why am I telling this story? It's simply to show how hard one has to practice in order to make serious spiritual progress. In Tibet, there were many practitioners like Milarepa, which is why Buddhism flourished in Tibet. If it is to survive, let alone flourish, in the world today, this is the type of practice that must be done for the as yet unbroken lineages to continue.

When we talk about the propagation of Buddhism, we have to remember that there are two types of teaching—the words and the realizations. Of these, it is the latter that makes the difference. It is easy for the words to continue for centuries—all we need is a few good libraries. But without the living experience of the meaning of words that comes through purification, creation of merit and effective meditation, the words are dry and tasteless and cannot be a vehicle for Buddhism to continue into the distant future. For this to happen, we need serious meditators spending years, if not their entire lives, in retreat under the supervision of experienced masters. Is this happening today?

Jan Willis's book, *Enlightened Beings,* narrates the inspiring biographies of six prominent tantric meditators from the Gelug School of Tibetan Buddhism, including that of the great Gyalwa Ensapa. Reading his story, we can understand the kind of practice required to ensure the survival of the lineage of the teachings. From an early age, he took teachings from many great masters; studied the vast treatises of sutra and tantra; became a monk; and undertook prolonged retreats in isolated places. As a result, he attained enlightenment in his lifetime. And he was not the only one. Countless other practitioners in Tibet followed similar courses of action and gained realization. How common is this in the world today? Even in Tibet, it no longer happens.

All this, then, is the answer to the future of Buddhism on Earth. Even though there may be an upsurge of interest in Tibetan Buddhism over the past decades, mainly due to China's brutal occupation of Tibet and the resulting exile of His Holiness the Dalai Lama and more than one hundred thousand other Tibetans, which has brought Tibetan Buddhism to the limelight, my impression is that it is almost totally devoid of the depth that characterized the Buddhism of Tibet and other Asian countries in the early centuries. Therefore, it may not last that long.

The future of Buddhism notwithstanding, what is the reason for this heightened interest in Buddhism, especially in the West? One would have to say, people turn to Buddhism because they want to be happy. Why Buddhism? Because they find through experience that ordinary methods, such as family, friends, money, material possessions, work, art and so forth are not inherently satisfying.

The great secret, if you want to call it that, is that happiness, which we all want, and suffering, which none of us wants, come primarily from the mind, and if Buddhism is about anything, it's about the mind. As Lama Yeshe said,

When we study Buddhism, we are studying ourselves, the nature of our own minds. Instead of focusing on some supreme being, Buddhism emphasizes more practical matters, such as how to lead our lives, how to integrate our minds and how to keep our everyday lives peaceful and healthy. In other words, Buddhism always accentuates experiential knowledge-wisdom rather than some dogmatic view. In fact, we don't even consider Buddhism to be a religion in the usual sense of the term. From the lamas' point of view, Buddhist teachings are more in the realm of philosophy, science or psychology.

He also pointed out that,

In Buddhism, we're not that interested in talking about the Buddha himself. Nor was he. Lord Buddha wasn't interested in people believing in him, so to this day Buddhism has never encouraged its followers simply to believe in the Buddha. We have always been more interested in understanding human psychology, the nature of the mind. Thus, Buddhist practitioners always *try* to understand their own mental attitudes, concepts, perceptions and consciousness. Those are the things that really matter.

In other words, Buddhism is not about blind faith, scriptural reference or blaming others. It's about mind as the principal source of happiness and suffering, personal responsibility, and compassion for all sentient beings.

When Guru Shakyamuni Buddha taught the four noble truths—the truths of suffering, its cause, its cessation and the path—he made it clear that anybody can totally eradicate suffering, and countless practitioners since then have accomplished this great feat. These days, many people understand just from hearing or reading teachings that Buddhism offers a better path to happiness that anything they've yet tried, so they start to put the teachings into practice. As they gain experience, they find it works the way it's supposed to, so they have confidence to proceed further along the path.

I think it's wonderful that people are prepared to try something radically different when they discover that everything they're doing doesn't lead to satisfaction and, recognizing that there might be something else that will bring them the happiness they seek, open the door to their own, inner wisdom. This is, of course, the door to the ultimate happiness and cessation of suffering that Guru Shakyamuni Buddha explained when he spoke about the cessation of suffering; the door to the practice of Dharma; the door out of the prison of wrong conceptions.

What is Dharma? In general, it means holding, or protecting, like the fence or rail that stops people from falling over a cliff. However, Dharma is an inner method that requires the practice of meditation. And since we have thousands of different problems in our mind, there are thousands of meditation techniques for solving them. One method cannot solve all problems. We study Dharma in order to understand which meditation technique should be applied to solve which problem.

The modern world also has inner methods for helping people solve problems—psychiatry, psychology and so forth, but even if people spend their entire lives applying these, they can never solve all their problems. Only the Dharma can do that. There is not a single method missing from the Dharma that cannot solve the problems of sentient beings.

Therefore, Dharma is a complete method for protecting ourselves from problems, their cause and making our lives meaningful. When we know how to practise Dharma, we can protect ourselves from suffering. That is Dharma which is not a limited method like simply going to a temple or church. Dharma is something that we can practise day in and day out, no matter what else we are doing in our everyday life—working, eating, talking to people, sleeping and so forth—something that constantly guides us away from our delusions, the cause of suffering.

However, even though it is easy to practise Dharma, to transform all our actions into Dharma, to escape from suffering and create the cause of ultimate happiness, we have to know how. If we don't, then Dharma is very difficult to practise. And again, happiness and suffering do not arise mainly from external factors but from the mind. We may not be able to see this upon hearing about it for the first time, but it is simply a matter of being aware. Although we experience suffering all the time, we're not aware of how or why we're experiencing it. We always think happiness and suffering arise from external factors, which is opposite to our own experience; they come mainly from the mind.

For example, say, a person has enough material possessions— a place to live, enough food, clothing and so forth—but with attachment, the person starts thinking, 'This is not enough; I want better; I want more,' making his mind worried, unhappy and dissatisfied. If, then, he changes his mind and decides, 'Actually, this is enough. I'm content with what I have,' that determination can be enough to counteract the previous unhappiness, dissatisfaction, suffering of attachment and bring peace into his mind. At the very moment he makes the decision, happiness enters his mind; that is Dharma happiness, and shows how Dharma can bring happiness the moment we start to practise.

Anger can be stopped in the same way, by recalling, for example, the previous kindness of the person who has upset you. If we do this effectively, our mind relaxes and the anger subsides. This again is Dharma happiness, and protecting ourselves from the consequences of anger in this way is practising Dharma.

Thus, suffering comes from the mind and can be stopped by the mind; happiness can arise simply from a change of mind. Other problems in life can also be stopped like this, by changing the mind, not the object. If, for example, we're abroad and are suffering because we miss the food that we're used to, instead of obsessing over what we're missing, we think of those who are starving in various parts of the world. We can feel lucky that we have anything at all to eat, and in this way overcome the suffering from missing the food we like. Similarly, whenever we experience any kind of suffering, all we need to do is think about those whose problems are far worse and our own suffering can simply fade away. Again, this shows how happiness arises from the mind.

However, it is not enough to just focus on solving the problems and suffering of this life, because after death, the mind continues, and we need to ensure the happiness of our future lives as well.

We can also appreciate how happiness does not come from external phenomena by stepping back and observing the way in which our world has developed. However, despite all the development, people's problems have not stopped and peace has not been attained. The only effect of all this has been to make people more busy and less peaceful, especially over the past century.

At the very beginning, human beings were relaxed and not fixated on external development and machinery like we are today. However, rather than decreasing, problems in the world are increasing, getting worse. The world is becoming a more dangerous place. That means that there's something missing in the method that people have been using.

What's missing? It's a method that decreases problems, that brings peace to the mind. That's the method that's missing. The means that increases peace and happiness in the mind; the inner method that has to be developed within the mind. Why is it missing? Because of ignorance, not knowing or recognizing the method. People cling strongly to the wrong conception that only external development can bring happiness. That's what has been keeping us constantly mired in problems, preventing our minds from becoming more and more peaceful.

Also, the person who has everything, every material thing, whatever he wants, is still not satisfied, still wants better and more, still gets bored with what he has. Things to which he was attached become objects of aversion, things he liked now bring discontent. All these things, these problems and sufferings arise from the mind.

We can see how things are by looking at kings and beggars. If happiness depended on material conditions alone, a beggar who didn't have enough food for even a day should have more problems and difficulties than those who have everything. Such people's minds should be much more peaceful and happy than those of beggars; more satisfied. If it were up to external conditions alone, the richer you were, the more satisfied you should be.

However, when we look into it, even if one is the most famous or wealthiest person in the world, one still has so many troubles, so much to worry about, and fear of losing one's power, reputation or possessions. He is very worried that he will not get more; worried that others will become richer than him and gain control over him; worried that his guards will be unable to protect him and his family, possessions and power. He can't relax at night; can't get a comfortable sleep. People are always criticizing and complaining about him. When the whole country doesn't like you, it's very difficult to relax. It doesn't matter how rich you are, how beautiful, how wonderful the food you eat and the clothes you wear, that your feet never touch the ground. When your mind is filled with worry, you can't enjoy what you have; you can't even taste the food you eat.

The beggar, on the other hand, doesn't have any responsibilities, has no wealth, no material possessions. Others don't criticize him. As long as he gets something to eat, he's satisfied. He can sleep with a comfortable mind. Of course, it may not always work like this, but this example, too, makes it clear that happiness and suffering come from the mind, not from external circumstances.

While Buddhism appeals today to the well-educated seekers for its rational approach to psychology and the nature of the mind, it also attracts for the clear structure of the path of Tibetan Buddhism which serves as a kind of road map to enlightenment. Looking at the outline of the entire path, a practitioner can see clearly the whole range of practices that must be undertaken and accomplished to reach the final goal of all sentient beings' enlightenment.

The path taught by Guru Shakyamuni Buddha and presented by the great Atisha in his *Lamp for the Path* is a complete way that allows any sentient being to attain the full enlightenment that the Buddha attained. It's a Mahayana teaching that was clearly expounded by the great propagators, Nagarjuna and Asanga, a profound teaching whose essence was explained by the great Atisha and Lama Tsong Khapa. It contains the essential points of the 84,000 teachings of Guru Shakyamuni Buddha, with nothing missing, and is set up in such a way that any individual can follow it gradually to enlightenment.

The root of the path is devotion to the guru; without a guru, there's no way to progress efficiently along the spiritual path or to attain enlightenment. Once we've found the right guru, we need to persuade ourselves to extract the essence from our perfect human rebirth, the human life that affords us every opportunity to practice Dharma in the best possible way. Once we have decided to make good use of our life, we have to train our mind in the paths of the three types of being—those of least, middling and greatest capability.

The lower scope path teaches us to focus more on the happiness of future lives than that of this one, and to train ourselves to do this, we meditate on impermanence and death and on the suffering of the three lower realms of existence—the hell, hungry ghost and animal realms. Then, having become persuaded that future lives are more important than this one, we need to practise the methods for benefiting our future lives—we go for refuge to the Three Jewels and dedicate ourselves to following karma by avoiding actions that lead to suffering and engaging in those that bring happiness.

The intermediate scope path leads to complete liberation from cyclic existence. We meditate on the sufferings of samsara in general and of each realm in particular, and in practising the three higher trainings of morality, concentration and wisdom.

The highest scope path explains the benefits of bodhicitta, how to generate it, and how to engage in the deeds of a bodhisattva. This is the Mahayana path, which leads to enlightenment, but success in attaining this goal depends on the two lower levels.

Bodhicitta, the principal cause of enlightenment, can be developed through the seven-point cause-and-effect technique, the technique of exchanging self for others or a combination of the two, which was developed by Lama Tsong Khapa. Whichever technique we use, its foundation is the equilibrium meditation, in which we equalize in our view all sentient beings by abandoning discrimination of friend, enemy and stranger.

The six causes are seeing all sentient beings as mother, remembering the mother's kindness, the thought of repaying her kindness, love, compassion and the special intention, where we take responsibility for the enlightenment of all sentient beings. The effect that these causes lead up to is the development of bodhicitta. The meditation on exchanging self for other has four sections: reflecting on the disadvantages of cherishing oneself and the advantages of cherishing others, actual exchange of self for others and the technique of giving and taking (*tong-len*).

While bodhicitta is the main cause of enlightenment, it has to be developed along with two other principal aspects of the path to enlightenment, renunciation and the right view of emptiness. The well-educated seekers of today appreciate the clear, scientific approach that the lam-rim path offers. They are not asked to accept anything they don't understand and, having gained a clear intellectual understanding of the path, are happy to put it into practice. Once they do so, they achieve the results predicted, which gives them the confidence they need to proceed further and undertake more advanced practices. I think this is one reason why Buddhism has become so popular today.

Details about the Contributors

Tenzin Gyatso, His Holiness the Fourteenth Dalai Lama of Tibet, is the spiritual and temporal leader of the Tibetan people. He was born on 6 July 1935 in Takser, a small village in north-eastern Tibet. At the age of two, he was recognized as the reincarnation of the thirteenth Dalai Lama. In accordance with the Buddhist tradition, he was brought to Lhasa, and enthroned in 1940. At the age of fifteen, he was called upon to assume full responsibility as Head of State and Government. His efforts to bring about a peaceful solution to the Sino-Tibetan problem were thwarted, and following the suppression of the Tibetan national uprising on 10 March 1959, His Holiness escaped to India where he was given political asylum. In exile, he has successfully led his people in the field of education, rehabilitation and preservation of the ancient and unique Tibetan culture. He is recognized as an advocate of world peace and inter-religious understanding. His Holiness has written several books. He has received many international awards including the Nobel Peace Prize in 1989.

Donna Brown holds First Class Honours and Masters degrees in Economics and has worked for the Canadian government in economic development for more than fifteen years. She has been active in the charitable sector in Canada and in India, serving on several Boards of Directors, and working as a financial manager, administrator of a school for disadvantaged children, teacher, event organizer, retreat centre coordinator and fund-raiser.

Kabir Saxena was born in Delhi in 1956 to an English mother and an Indian father. He was educated in London and at Oxford where he studied Modern History. He became a Buddhist in 1977 and since 1981 has been working for various centres in England, Nepal and India for the Foundation for the Preservation of the Mahayana Tradition, under the guidance of Lama Zopa Rinpoche. He ordained as a monk in January 2002 and is currently working in Bodhgaya, Bihar, for the Maitreya Project Universal Education School.

Robina Courtin has been a Tibetan Buddhist nun since 1978. For ten years, she was the editorial director of the Buddhist publishing house, Wisdom Publications, in London, and since 1987 has taught Buddhist philosophy and meditation around the world. She has been based in the US since 1994, and for six years was the editor of *Mandala*, the international Buddhist magazine of the Foundation for the Preservation of the Mahayana Tradition (FPMT). She is now director of FPMT's Liberation Prison Project, which takes care of the spiritual needs of thousands of people in prison in the US, Australia, and other countries.

An award-winning film, *Chasing Buddha*, made by her nephew, Amiel Courtin-Wilson, documents her life and includes her work at Kentucky State Prison with death-row inmates. She is one of the subjects of Vicki Mackenzie's *Why Buddhism?* and Christina Lundberg's film about Buddhist women teachers, *On the Road Home*. She began studying martial arts in Alice Springs in 1974 in her quest for a spiritual path, continuing her training in New York and Melbourne. In 1976, she attended a Tibetan Buddhist course in Queensland given by Lama Thubten Yeshe and Lama Zopa Rinpoche of the FPMT. She went to Kathmandu eighteen months later to become ordained.

Suresh Jindal has been a student of Buddhism for five years. He has a degree in Electronics Engineering from the University of California at Los Angeles and has worked for five years in the aero-space industry in the US. On returning home to India, he became a film producer. Among the many award-winning films he produced was Satyajit Ray's *Shatranj ke Khilari*. He was also the Associate Producer of Richard Attenborough's *Gandhi*. He has written many articles on cinema and Buddhism for Indian newspapers and magazines. He has been the Vice-President of the Indian Motion Pictures Producers Association and was awarded the coveted *Chevalier des Arts et Lettres* by the Government of France.

Karma Lekshe Tsomo is an Assistant Professor of Theology and Religious Studies at the University of San Diego. She studied Buddhism in Dharamsala for fifteen years and completed her doctorate in Comparative Philosophy at the University of Hawaii with research on death and identity in China and Tibet. Her books include *Buddhist Women and Social Justice: Ideals, Challenges, and Achievements*; *Innovative Buddhist Women: Swimming Against the Stream*; *Buddhist Women Across Cultures: Realizations*; *Sisters in Solitude: Two Traditions of Monastic Ethics for Women*; *Buddhism Through American Women's Eyes*; *Sakyadhita: Daughters of the Buddha*; and *Living and Dying in Buddhist Cultures* (with David W. Chappell). She is president of Sakyadhita: International Association of Buddhist Women, and director of Jamyang Foundation, an initiative to provide educational opportunities for women in developing countries, especially in the Indian Himalayas and Bangladesh.

Dharmakirti, a disciple of His Holiness the Fourteenth Dalai Lama, was born in a Sikh family. He studied Biochemistry in college, and later worked as an advertising executive and computer programmer. After encountering the Prasangika Madhyamika system of Arya Nagarjuna, he left home when he was twenty-seven, and became a disciple of His Holiness the Dalai Lama. During the six years he spent at the feet of his guru in Dharamsala, he received initiation and further instructions in the practice of Mahayana Buddhist Highest Secret Mantra, into the lineage of Lama Tsongkhapa. He now lives in retreat in the Kullu valley, and occasionally teaches. He is also the author of *Introduction to Tantrayana*.

Lama Thubten Yeshe was born in Tibet in 1935. When he was six, he entered the Sera Monastic University at Lhasa where he studied until 1959, when the Chinese invasion of Tibet forced him into exile in India. In 1967, with his chief disciple, Lama Zopa Rinpoche, he went to Nepal where he established Kopan monastery. In 1974, the Lamas began making annual teaching tours to the West, and as a result, a worldwide network of Buddhist teachings and meditation centres—the Foundation for the Preservation of the Mahayana Tradition—began to develop. At the age of forty-nine, Lama Yeshe passed away. His books include *Wisdom Energy, Introduction to Tantra, The Tantric Path of Purification* and *The Bliss of Inner Fire*.

Bhikshuni Thubten Chodron was ordained as a Buddhist nun in 1977. She studied and practised Tibetan Buddhism under the guidance of His Holiness the Dalai Lama, Tsenzhap Serkong Rinpoche, Zopa Rinpoche and other Tibetan masters in India and Nepal. She was resident teacher at Amitabha Buddhist Centre in Singapore for two years, resident teacher at Dharma Friendship Foundation in Seattle for ten years, and has taught Buddhist philosophy, psychology and meditation internationally. Ven. Chodron is active in interfaith dialogue, was co-organizer for the 1996 training programme of Western Buddhist nuns in Bodhgaya,

India, and attended three meetings of Western Buddhist teachers with His Holiness the Dalai Lama. She is now involved in founding Sravasti Abbey, a Buddhist monastery, in the US. Her books include *Open Heart, Clear Mind; Buddhism for Beginners; Working with Anger; Taming the Monkey Mind; Blossoms of the Dharma: Living as a Buddhist Nun*; and *Transforming the Heart: The Buddhist Way to Joy and Courage* (with Geshe Jampa Tegchok). For more information, please see www.thubtenchodron.org and www.sravastiabbey.org

Vivek Kumar, Assistant Professor at the Centre for the Study of Social Systems, Jawaharlal Nehru University (JNU), New Delhi, was born in a Dalit family at Lucknow in Uttar Pradesh, India. He completed his Ph.D from JNU. Prior to this, Kumar was a lecturer in the Unit for Sociology of Education, Mumbai, and also a correspondent with the *Pioneer*. He has contributed more than a dozen articles in a number of reputed journals and is the author of two books, *Dalit Leadership in India* and *Dalit Assertion in Uttar Pradesh*. His major areas of specialization are Social Stratification and Social Movements.

Peter Kedge, Director and CEO Maitreya Project International, Director FPMT Inc, holds a First Class degree in mechanical engineering. His career began as a design engineer with Rolls Royce Aero Engine Division, UK. He moved to Asia in 1971 and in 1980 founded East Asia's leading logistics consultancy in Hong Kong. He was involved in major engineering projects throughout Asia while owning and managing the business for eighteen years. He divested his business interests in order to devote his time to the Maitreya Project, which he has been heading since May 1997. Peter has been a student of Lama Zopa Rinpoche since 1972 and has played a leading role in many of FPMT's Buddhist projects around the world during the last thirty years. During the 1970s, Peter was a monk and travelled together with

Lama Thubten Yeshe and Lama Zopa Rinpoche as their attendant.

Adriana Ferranti graduated from the School of Modern Languages for Translators and Interpreters at the University of Trieste, Italy, in 1964 and attended a college year (1962-63) in the US as a Fulbright scholar. In 1979, she met the Tibetan Buddhist Master, the Ven. Lama Thubten Zopa Rinpoche, and in 1982, spent one year in India where she studied at major leprosy research centres at Karigiri, Tamil Nadu, and at Wardha, Maharashtra. From 1984 to 1986, she served at a major FPMT Buddhist centre in Italy, first as an assistant director, and then as a director. At the end of 1986, she moved to South Asia and in 1987 initiated the MAITRI Leprosy Prevention, Treatment & Rehabilitation Centre, which carries out other integrated programmes.

KTS Sarao did his Masters in History with First Class First in 1979, M.Phil in Chinese Studies in 1981 and a Ph.D in Buddhism in 1984, all from Delhi University. He won the prestigious Commonwealth Scholarship to Cambridge University in 1985, and did his second Ph.D on Buddhist Literature and Archaeology in 1988. He joined the Department of Buddhist Studies, Delhi University, and has been teaching there since as a Professor of Buddhist Studies. He was the Head of the Department of Buddhist Studies from 1993-96 and 1999-02. He has been a Visiting Professor to different universities in France, Singapore, Canada, US, and Taiwan. At present, he is a Visiting Professor of Pali at the Fagu-Shan University in Taiwan. He has published eight books and over fifty research papers in various journals of repute.

Lama Doboom Tulku was recognized as the incarnation of the previous Doboom Tulku at the age of three by Ven. Lama Phurchog Jamgon Rinpoche. His formal education was initiated when he was seven and comprised reading and memorizing Buddhist scriptures at the Dhargye monastery. When he was twelve, he went to Lhasa to enter the Drepung monastery but had to flee to India during the uprising of 1959. In 1969, he joined the Institute of Higher Studies at Sarnath and studied Buddhist philosophy for three years and received Geshe-Acharya degree in 1972. In 1977, he joined the Private Office of H.H. the Dalai Lama as Secretary and since 1981 has been Director of Tibet House, New Delhi.

Nicholas Ribush first encountered Buddhism at Kopan monastery in 1972. Since then he has been a student of Lamas Yeshe and Zopa Rinpoche and a full-time worker for the FPMT. He was a monk from 1974 to 1986. He established FPMT archiving and publishing activities at Kopan in 1973 and, with Lama Yeshe, founded Wisdom Publications in 1975. He has edited and published many teachings by Lama Yeshe and Lama Zopa Rinpoche and has been involved in various FPMT activities.

Lokesh Chandra is a scholar of Tibetan, Mongolian and Sino-Japanese Buddhism. He has to his credit over 400 works and texts. He has been a vice-president of the Indian Council for Cultural Relations, and chairman of the Indian Council of Historical Research. Currently, he is working on a Dictionary of Buddhist Iconography in twenty volumes.

Lama Zopa Rinpoche was born in Thami, Nepal, in 1946. When he was three, he was recognized as the reincarnation of the Lawudo Lama. When ten, he went to Tibet and meditated at Domo Geshe Rinpoche's monastery, until the Chinese occupation of Tibet in 1959 forced him to forsake Tibet for the safety of Bhutan. Rinpoche then went to the Tibetan refugee camp at Buxa Duar, West Bengal, where he met Lama Yeshe, who became his closest teacher. Over the next few years, the lamas built the Kopan and Lawudo monasteries in Nepal. In 1974, with Lama Yeshe, Rinpoche began travelling around the world to teach and establish centres of Dharma. When Lama Yeshe passed away in 1984, Rinpoche took over as spiritual head of the FPMT. Rinpoche's published teachings include *Wisdom Energy* (with Lama Yeshe), *Transforming Problems*, *The Door to Satisfaction* and a number of transcripts and booklets.

❖